REVELATION

The Last Book in the Bible

REVELATION

The Last Book in the Bible

LUTHER POELLOT

NORTHWESTERN PUBLISHING HOUSE
MILWAUKEE, WISCONSIN • 1976

Concordia Publishing House, Saint Louis 18, Missouri
Concordia Publishing House Ltd., London, W.C. 1
Library of Congress Catalog Card No. 61-18228

Copyright 1962 by Concordia Publishing House

Reprinted 1976 by
Northwestern Publishing House, Milwaukee, Wisconsin
with permission of the original publishers

Manufactured in the United States of America

Lo, heaven's doors lift up, revealing
How Thy judgments earthward move;
Scrolls unfolded, trumpets pealing,
Wine-cups from the wrath above;
Yet o'er all a soft voice stealing,
"Little children, trust and love."

JOHN KEBLE

PREFACE

On a Sunday morning in the spring of 1952 the Bible class of a small congregation cast a ballot to choose a course of study. Four of the 20 votes were for the Book of Revelation. The others were scattered over such a variety of topics that it was resolved to follow the lead of the four. Through devious circumstances a copy of the notes prepared for the discussions reached the hands of some who encouraged a larger venture. This book is the result.

The New Testament of the *New English Bible* was published after the manuscript of this book was nearly complete. — In textual criticism there is room for difference of opinion and for new evidence; the judgments expressed in this book reflect the position of the author at the time of writing.

The undersigned is grateful to all who helped make this book possible. Above all, thanks be to our God and Savior, without whom we can do nothing, whose Word in the last book in the Bible is the subject of this study, and to whose glory it is dedicated.

LUTHER POELLOT

CONTENTS

1. The overruling providence of God

2. The trials of the church

3. Warnings against sin

4. Encouragements to faithfulness

5. Satan and his agents and followers in their opposition to the Lord and His church

6. God's judgment on Satan and his agents and followers

7. God's loving and watchful care over His own here in time, and the final triumph of the kingdom of God in the reward of grace and glory which He gives the faithful hereafter in eternity

The major visions are: Page

Besides the standard abbreviations for the books of the Bible, the following are among the abbreviations used in this volume:

A. D.   — Anno Domini; after Christ

ASV   — American Standard Version

B. C.   — Before Christ

Cf.   — Compare

ch.   — chapter

CTM   — *Concordia Theological Monthly*

e. g.   — for example

EGT   — Expositor's Greek Testament

etc.   — and so forth

esp.   — especially

ff.   — and following

KJV   — King James Version

LXX   — Septuagint

Lit.   — literally

loc. cit.— in the place cited

MSS   — Manuscripts

n.   — note

n. d.   — no date

NEB   — New English Bible

p., pp.   — page, pages

resp.   — respectively

RSV   — Revised Standard Version

supra   — above

v., vv.   — verse, verses

INTRODUCTION

Name Open your Bible at the beginning of the last book in the New Testament. In the KJV it is called the Revelation of Saint John the Divine. Other translations give it a similar name. There are many revelation*s* in the Book of Revelatio*n*. The book takes its name from its first verse: "The *Revelation* of Jesus Christ, which God gave unto Him, to show unto His servants things which must shortly come to pass; and He sent and signified it by His angel unto His servant *John*." Sometimes the book is called the Apocalypse, which means about the same as "Revelation." "Apocalypse" comes from the Greek; "Revelation" comes from the Latin.

Author and Writer The Author of the Book of Revelation is God, and the writer is John (Rev. 1:1). We take this John to be the disciple and the writer of the Fourth Gospel and the three epistles of John. He outlived the other writers of the New Testament. According to Eusebius, he was exiled A.D. 95 by Domitian. It is said that he was permitted to return to Ephesus A.D. 96 after the death of Domitian. According to Jerome, he was hardly able to walk in his old age. He was carried with difficulty to the meetings of the faithful, where, too weak to speak at length, he simply said: "Little children, love one another!"

To Whom?   In Rev. 1:4 John addressed "the seven churches
            which are in Asia." They were to read Rev. 4—22
also; the beginning of Rev. 4, "After this," attaches it to Rev.
1—3. But the Book of Revelation was not written for these
churches alone. Its words of warning, instruction, comfort, and
strengthening have a timeless ring.

Why?   John wrote to the seven churches at the impulse of the
        Holy Spirit. It was also natural for him to write to them
if there is any truth in the tradition that Ephesus, with its surrounding territory that included the other six churches, was the
scene of his chief activity after he left Palestine about A. D. 67.

Where?   The island of Patmos is near the southern end of the
          Aegean Sea, about 60 miles southwest of ancient
Ephesus. To this small, barren, rocky island, about 15 miles in
circumference, John was banished (Rev. 1:9). It was there that
he saw the visions and wrote them in the Book of Revelation.
(Rev. 1:9-11; 10:4; 21:5)

When?   We regard the Book of Revelation as the book of the
         Bible written last, probably A. D. 95 or 96. There is
no compelling reason to believe that the Gospel and the epistles
of John were written later. The Book of Revelation is traditionally
assigned to the end of the Bible as God's last revealed Word to
man.

Purpose   The purpose of the Book of Revelation is indicated by
           the fact that it is a prophetic book and by the nature
and scope of its prophecy. It points to the time when all opposition against the Lord and His church shall end at the final coming
of Christ and when the kingdom of God shall come into its own
in complete and everlasting glory. It is a book which God gave
His people to help them through the temptations, trials, and
afflictions which they experience on earth. It expands on the mes-

sage which Paul and Barnabas had brought to other Christians in Asia Minor (cf. Acts 14:22), and it is to serve for warning, instruction, comfort, encouragement and strengthening in the faith.

Place in the   "It was the church's conviction that the Apoca-
Early Church   lypse was apostolic in origin. . . . It is clear that apostolicity was the organizing principle of the New Testament of the Old Catholic Church, in which the Apocalypse had a very secure place among 'the apostles.'. . . The Apocalypse was included in the apostolic instrument of John. . . . It was to the apostles that the Spirit was to call to mind the things concerning the Lord and that the Lord had entrusted the knowledge of the mysteries of the Kingdom. The Apocalypse was naturally grouped with these writings, which had a permanent significance for the life of the church and not with the only transiently significant oracles of the early Christian prophets." [1]

In the Bible   The Book of Revelation is part of the Bible, though apparently at first, and for a time, some did not regard it as such. Only after it had successfully passed through a severe trial under the eyes of a vigilant church was it given a recognized and permanent place in the canon of Scripture by a decree of the Council of Carthage, A. D. 397. But this did not make it the Word of God; it was God's Word ever since He gave it to John. In 1522 Martin Luther wrote of it: "My spirit cannot adjust itself to the book." But the book was in his Bible, and in 1545 he fully accepted it. [2]

Interpretation   We certainly ought to learn as much as we can from the Book of Revelation. Among its most difficult passages are those which use figures of speech, mysterious

[1] N. B. Stonehouse, *The Apocalypse in the Ancient Church* (Grand Rapids, Mich., 1930), pp. 152 ff. (quoted in *CTM,* VIII [Feb. 1937], 133, 134).

[2] R. C. H. Lenski, *Interpretation of St. John's Revelation* (Columbus, Ohio, 1951), pp. 13, 14.

symbolism, colors, numbers, etc. Some of these are explained (e. g., in Rev. 1:20). But in most cases the Book of Revelation does not interpret itself; we must look to other books of the Bible for help. And even after we have searched the Scriptures, some passages remain in the Book of Revelation for which we can only suggest an explanation. Some questions are unanswered by our fault, others because we do not now need to know the answers.

Rev. 1:1-3: Title Page

Rev. 1:1-3 may be called the title page of the book. These verses contain the title of the book, a few things about the Author and the writer, and an inscription. They may have been written after the rest of the book. (Cf. Rev. 22:6,7)

Title   "Apocalypse" is the first word (in the original) and the title of the book. It means revelation, an unveiling, a revealing. It refers to things which man by himself could never know and which only God could make known to him.[1] Since John was aged (Jerome says that he lived to be 100), the revelation which he received on Patmos may be regarded as a fulfillment, beyond Pentecost, of the prophecy: "Your old men shall dream dreams." (Joel 2:28; Acts 2:17)

Author   The heading "The Revelation of St. John the Divine" links the title with the writer. But the title page links the title closely and directly with the Author: "The revelation of Jesus Christ, which God gave unto Him." [2] Jesus Christ, true and omniscient God, is also true man. God gave Him this revelation

---

[1] Dan. 7; Hos. 12:10; 2 Cor. 12:1-7.

[2] Rev. 1:1. Cf. 2 Tim. 3:16: "All Scripture is given by inspiration of God." Theodore Engelder, in his *Scripture Cannot Be Broken* (St. Louis, 1944), p. 262, points out that "Scripture" in 1 Tim. 5:18 refers to both the Old and the New Testament.

according to His human nature.[3] Here "God" does not mean the
Holy Trinity, but God the Father, as in 2 Cor. 13:14. God the
Holy Spirit is also, indirectly, in evidence in Rev. 1:1. By divine,
verbal inspiration He moved John to write and put into his mind
the very thoughts he expressed and the very words he wrote.
(Cf. Rev. 1:4; 2:1, 7, etc.)

Subtitle   The Book of Revelation is to show the servants of
           Jesus Christ (John, Rev. 1:1; others, 2 Cor. 5:15; cf.
Acts 9:6; Matt. 13:11a) "what must soon take place" (Rev. 1:1
RSV). God being what He is, the devil being what he is, and
human beings being what they are, certain things are bound to
happen.[4] They will happen "shortly" (Rev. 1:1 KJV), that is,
soon. But we are not told how soon (Acts 1:7). The fulfillment
of the prophecies in the Book of Revelation began "soon" in the
common sense of the word.

That His servants might know, He (Christ, Rev. 1:1; cf. Rev.
22:16) sent and signified these things by His angel to John.
"The thing sent was rather the message than the angel."[5] The
angel was chosen from among many for this mission. (Cf. Ps.
103:20, 21)

Writer   John accepted and carried out the commission to write
          the Book of Revelation. Like Paul, he did not handle the
Word of God deceitfully, but was a faithful witness to it (2 Cor.
4:2; Rev. 1:9). Rev. 1:2 refers specifically to the Word of God
in the Book of Revelation, which contains the "things that he
saw."[6]

[3] "Die Gott der Vater Christo, nach seiner erhöheten Menschheit, gegeben
hat. Rev. 5:5-9; John 12:49; 16:15." *Hirschberger Bibel,* with foreword by L.
Fuerbringer (Constance, Carl Hirsch Verlag, 1926 reprint), p. 495.

[4] Cf. the notes on "must" in Rev. 20:3. Also see Rev. 22:6.

[5] Albert Barnes, *Notes Explanatory and Practical* (New York, 1854), on
Rev. 1:1.

[6] KJV. Rev. 1:2 RSV: John "bore witness to the Word of God and to the
testimony of Jesus Christ, even to all that he saw." The last phrase, "even to all
that he saw," summarizes the first two, "the Word of God" and "the testimony of

Inscription   The Book of Revelation has this beatitude, the first
of seven, inscribed on its title page: "Blessed is he
that readeth, and they that hear the words of this prophecy and
keep those things which are written therein, for the time is at
hand" (Rev. 1:3. Cf. Rev. 14:13; 16:15; 19:9; 20:6; 22:7, 14).
Revelation is the only book in the Bible singled out in this way.
As those who use it properly see the things come to pass that are
written in it, they need not cringe in mortal fear and terror and
say to the mountains, "Fall on us," and to the hills, "Cover us"
(Luke 23:30; Rev. 6:16; Hos. 10:8). When these things begin
to come to pass, they can look up and lift up their heads, knowing
that their redemption draws near. (Luke 21:28)

"The time is at hand" (Rev. 1:3). Instead of losing precious
time in speculation as to when the end of the world will come,
it is better for everyone to remember that the end of his earthly
life will come in a comparatively short time and to say with the
psalmist, "O Lord . . . my times are in Thy hand." (Ps. 31:14, 15)

Rev. 1:4-7: The Writer's Preface

The Book of Revelation was written as a letter. Its preface,
or introduction, is in the form often used at that time at the beginning of letters. The writer states his name and says to whom
he is writing; he continues with a greeting, followed by a doxology (Gal. 1:1-5), and ends with a brief summary of the entire
book.

The mention of John's name at the beginning of v. 4 establishes a direct and close connection with vv. 1, 2. His name is not
in his other books in the Bible. But here it is twice in four verses,[7]
lending this book from its outset the weight of his reputation as
an apostle.

Jesus Christ," and these two refer back to God and Jesus Christ in v. 1. "The
testimony of Jesus Christ" is the testimony which Jesus Christ bore, specifically in
the revelation which He gave John on Patmos. "The Word of God" and "the
testimony of Jesus Christ" are identical here.

[7]Also Rev. 1:9; 21:2 KJV; 22:8.

Greeting   John addresses himself "to the seven churches which
              are in Asia" (Rev. 1:4), that is, proconsular Asia, the
western part of Asia Minor. The seven churches were in the following cities in that part of the peninsula: Ephesus, Smyrna,
Pergamos, Thyatira, Sardis, Philadelphia, and Laodicea. These
seven were singled out for John by the Lord.[8]

"Grace...   Divine grace is undeserved kindness, the free, un-
and peace!" merited favor of God (Eph. 2:8, 9; cf. also Rev.
               22:21). The peace of which John speaks here is
peace between God and man. It is the peace of heart, mind, and
conscience which flows from the assurance of the forgiveness of
sins (John 14:27; Rom. 5:1; 1 Cor. 1:3; Phil. 4:7; 2 Peter 1:2).
Grace and peace come from the Triune God. (Rev. 1:4, 5)

Father   He "which is, and which was, and which is to come"
            (Rev. 1:4; 1:8; 4:8) is the Eternal One, without begin-
ning and without end (Ps. 90:2). He who is eternal is also unchangeable (Ps. 102:27; Mal. 3:6). How fitting that this is established at the very outset in this book, which deals at length with
the raging of Satan against the Lord and His church! (Deut.
33:27)

Holy Spirit   "The seven Spirits which are before His throne"
                 (Rev. 1:4; 4:5). We take this as a reference to
the one Holy Spirit,[9] the Third Person in the Holy Trinity, true
God with the Father and the Son. This Spirit speaks to the

---

   [8] Rev. 1:11. Other churches in Asia Minor were at Hierapolis and Colossae
(Wm. Arndt, in *Concordia Pulpit*, XVI [St. Louis: CPH, 1945], 587), Miletus,
Magnesia, and Tralles (Jamieson, Fausset and Brown, *Commentary* [Grand Rapids,
1935], on Rev. 1:11). Cf. the references to Troas in Acts 16:8; 2 Cor. 2:12;
2 Tim. 4:13.

   [9] Cf. the use of the Hebrew plural form for "wisdom" in Prov. 9:1. — Com-
pare Zech. 3:9 and 4:6, 10 with Rev. 5:6. — See Is. 11:2, which is associated with
Zech. 12:10 in the Lutheran rite of confirmation. — Cf. P. E. Kretzmann, "Der
Spiritus Septiformis," in the CTM, III (April 1932), 245—251.

churches.[10] "The seven Spirits" are "of God." (Rev. 3:1; 4:5; 5:6)

"The seven Spirits" are "before His throne" (Rev. 1:4), but not according to the concept of physical space.[11] The "throne" is not a literal chair or seat, and there is no space "before" it. Space, like time,[12] is part of creation, not part of the infinite abode of God. Here God accommodates Himself to human language to picture Himself as a ruler and His Holy Spirit as one who not only is with Him in the intimate fellowship of the Holy Trinity but also is sent out from Him. Some hold that the number seven symbolizes God's dealing with man, being the sum of three, for the Trinity, and four, for the world. (Rev. 7:1; 20:8)

Son   "Jesus Christ" (Rev. 1:5), usually mentioned second in listing the three Persons of the Trinity, here is mentioned last.[13] The order makes no essential difference. The three Persons of the Trinity are equally God. Here Jesus Christ is spoken of, with the Father and the Holy Spirit, as the Source of grace and peace, which come only from God.

The human nature of Christ is also referred to here (Rev. 1:1). He is "Jesus" (Rev. 1:5), that is, Jesus of Nazareth (Matt. 21:11; John 19:19, etc.). He had to be true man in order to make God's grace and peace available to us by His suffering and death. (Heb. 9:22)

He is, moreover, the "Christ" (Rev. 1:5), the Anointed One, the Messiah, of whom the Old Testament prophets spoke.[14] He

10 Rev. 2:7, 11, 17, 29; 3:6, 13, 22.

11 Just as little as Christ in heaven is sitting at one side, to the right, of God the Father. Mark 16:19, etc. See the notes on Rev. 4:1, 2.

12 See the notes on Rev. 1:6 and 4:2.

13 In 2 Cor. 13:14 He is mentioned first.

14 Compare Is. 61:1, 2 with Luke 4:16-21; Dan. 9:24-26; John 1:41; 4:25, 26; Ps. 45:7.

was anointed with the Holy Ghost (Acts 10:38) to be our Prophet,[15] Priest,[16] and King.[17]

Jesus Christ is further described in a threefold way:

1. "The faithful Witness" (Rev. 1:5). "Witness" here refers to a person without reference to the occasion of his testimony. Christ is always "the faithful Witness." We can believe and trust His Word in the Book of Revelation and everywhere else in the Bible just as confidently as those who heard Him speak.[18]

2. "The First-Begotten of the dead" (Rev. 1:5). He is the first who rose from the dead never to die again. By His resurrection He overcame death for us.[19]

3. "The Prince of the kings of the earth" (Rev. 1:5). "Prince" here means ruler. "The kings of the earth" are the high and mighty among men and the powers for which they stand. Many of them are wicked (Ps. 2:2, 3; Rev. 17:2). The church had been, and would again be, persecuted and oppressed by them. John suffered at the hands of one. But all are under the overruling, almighty hand of Christ in His kingdom of power. He rules the world in the interest of the church. (Eph. 1:22)

Doxology   The doxology to the exalted Christ has a threefold address:

1. "Unto Him that loved us" (Rev. 1:5). He loved us before the beginning of the world.[20] He loved us while we were still sinners (Rom. 5:8), loveless and unlovely unbelievers. He loved His own unto the end (John 13:1). He still loves us. His is the love of God, everlasting and personal.[21] Through Him who loves

---

15 Cf. Deut. 18:15; 1 Kings 19:16.

16 Cf. Ex. 28:41; Heb. 7:26, 27.

17 Cf. 1 Kings 19:15, 16; Matt. 28:18; John 1:41, 49; 18:36, 37; 2 Tim. 4: 18; Rev. 17:14; 19:16.

18 John 14:6; Heb. 13:8; Rev. 3:14.

19 1 Cor. 15:20-23; John 11:25, 26; 14:19; Col. 1:18; Rom. 6:9.

20 Compare John 17:24 with 15:9.

21 Jer. 31:3; Gal. 2:20; Is. 43:1-7.

us we are "more than conquerors" (Rom. 8:37), having the victory of our faith, which overcomes the world, assured forever.[22]

2. "Unto Him that . . . washed [23] us from our sins in [or by] His own blood" (Rev. 1:5). We were bound, like slaves, by the chains of sin, from which there was no release until Christ struck these shackles off.[24] He was the sinless Son of God, who gave Himself into death in our place. His blood makes us forever free.

3. "Unto Him that . . . made us kings and priests unto God and His Father." [25] The "kingdom" is Christ's kingdom of grace and glory. It is a spiritual kingdom, not of this world.[26] Its members have royal power and dignity. By faith they possess all that Christ, their one great King, has. They rule with Him. They concur in all that He does. They do with Him all that He does. They own the universe, the world, and all things in the world (1 Cor. 3:21, 22). "What the Second Psalm says only of Christ, Christ Himself in Rev. 2:26, 27 ascribes to all that are His: 'He that overcometh and keepeth My works unto the end, to him will I give power over the nations; and he shall rule them with a rod of iron; as the vessels of a potter shall they be broken to shivers; even as I received of My Father.' It is true, of course, that the reign of the believers over the world will become manifest only on Judgment Day. But even now, before Judgment Day, this reigning of believers is a fact, though to all appearances they are the oppressed, the dying, the slain." "In short, the Christians are the wealthiest and mightiest group in the world. Heaven's sluices of grace and blessing have opened for them through their faith in Christ. The

22 1 John 5:4; John 5:24; Rom. 8:35-39.

23 Or "set us free," which seems to be the better reading, depending on one letter in a Greek word: *lusanti* means "set free," while *lousanti* means "washed."

24 Rom. 6:16-23; Matt. 16:19; 18:18; John 8:31-36.

25 Rev. 1:5, 6. Rather, "has made us a kingdom, priests unto His God and Father." Also see Ex. 19:6; Is. 61:6; 1 Peter 2:9; Rev. 5:10; 17:14; 19:16; 20:4-6.

26 John 17:14-16; 18:36; Luke 17:21.

believers have everything, the unbelievers nothing." [27] Christians alone are the children and heirs of the kingdom.

We are also priests. Our sacrifices are to be the sacrifices of repentance, prayer, and praise in a life of service and thanksgiving.[28] This spiritual priesthood of believers is not an "optional extra." It is a built-in, essential feature of true Christianity. He who made us priests, "His God and Father" (Rev. 1:6), is our God and Father.[29]

"To Him be glory[30] and dominion[31] forever and ever. Amen" (Rev. 1:6; cf. 5:13, 14). So this ringing doxology reaches its climax and close. "The adoration of Christ which vibrates in this doxology is one of the most impressive features of the book."[32] We have no adequate positive words for the opposite of time, or for a "world without end" (Is. 45:17). Our mind is so closely bound with time that the wisest philosopher can speak of timelessness only in repetitious or negative terms. Even Einstein could find no completely satisfying definition of time before his "fourth dimension" caught up with him. Let us be content, until time shall be no more, to use the words "forever and ever,"[33] which the Holy Spirit of God condescended to use, adding like an exclamation point the "Amen" of the confident assurance of faith!

Summary of the Book   Rev. 1:7 is a brief but powerful summary of the main theme of the Book of Revelation: the final coming of Christ at the end of the world.

"Behold" occurs at least 27 times in the Book of Revelation.

---

[27] Francis Pieper, *Christian Dogmatics*, III, trans. Walter W. F. Albrecht (St. Louis, 1953), 523 and 415. Cf. Matt. 13:38; 25:34; the notes on Rev. 3:21.

[28] Ps. 51:17; 141:2; Rom. 12:1; 1 Cor. 10:31; Heb. 13:16; 1 Peter 2:5.

[29] Rev. 21:3; John 20:17; 2 Cor. 6:16; Matt. 27:46.

[30] That is, praise, or honor.

[31] That is, power, might, strength, or force in action.

[32] James Moffatt, in the *Expositor's Greek Testament*, V, 339.

[33] Lit., "unto the ages of the ages."

It adds liveliness to the style of writing and points up what follows as being especially important, worthy of close attention and thoughtful consideration. "He [34] cometh with clouds." [35] Christ was the "Coming One" of Old Testament prophecy (Mal. 3:2). The present tense is used here in the prophetic sense, emphasizing the certainty of Christ's coming. The clouds are evidence of His magnificent majesty, power, and supremacy.

"Every eye shall see Him" (Rev. 1:7). Not only will His coming be personal and visible, but He will also actually be seen by all. No one will be able to shut his eyes against Him. "That Christ will not appear successively to nation after nation, but to all at once, is not only stated in Matt. 24:27, 30 and Luke 17:24 . . . but is also implied in His appearance to all living on earth 'as a thief in the night' (1 Thess. 5:2), 'in such an hour as ye think not' (Matt. 24:44), so that, for example, Europe will not be able to flash word of His coming to America." [36]

"Every eye" includes those who have died before that day. [37] "They also which pierced Him" (Rev. 1:7) shall see Him. Here is a flashback to the moment, many years earlier, when John had stood at the foot of the cross and had seen a soldier pierce the side of Jesus with a spear. One part of the prophecy in Zech. 12:10 was fulfilled that day (John 19:34-37). Another part will be fulfilled on the Last Day, when those who brought about the crucifixion and death of Christ will see Him again, together with all others who pierced Him with their sins. (Ps. 22:16)

Finally, "all kindreds [or tribes] of the earth shall wail because of Him" (Rev. 1:7). They are the unbelievers, making up the large majority of mankind (Matt. 7:13, 14). Their wailing is not evidence of last-minute repentance, but is the weeping

---

[34] That is, Jesus Christ (Rev. 1:5).

[35] Rev. 1:7; Matt. 24:30; 26:64; Mark 13:26; 14:62; Luke 21:27; Acts 1: 9-11; 1 Thess. 4:16, 17; Rev. 14:14; Dan. 7:13.

[36] Pieper, III, 516, n. 30.

[37] Matt. 25:32; John 5:28, 29; Rev. 20:12, 13; Job 19:25-27.

and mourning of hopeless bitterness, grief, and sorrow.[38] The
time of grace is over. That is the first and overwhelming thought
which strikes the unbelievers in that moment. It finds expression
in their howl of helpless terror and despair in view of what they
have done to Christ and because of what He now does to them.
They cannot escape. Their verdict is sealed with a solemn "Even
so" [39] and "Amen." [40] There will be no "second chance" or split-
second, last-moment opportunity for repentance on Judgment
Day.

Rev. 1:8: The Author Describes Himself

In religious symbolism, the letter *A,* or alpha, the first letter
of the Greek alphabet, is combined with another letter not as well
known, Ω, or omega, the last letter of the Greek alphabet. Together those letters symbolize the beginning and the end. In the
Book of Revelation this combination is used as a name.[41]

This name is not explained in Rev. 1:8.[42] Elsewhere, however, "the Beginning and the Ending" and "the First and the
Last" are added (Rev. 21:6; 22:13). Some have taken "Alpha"
and "Omega" as a reference to the entire alphabet, suggesting that
Christ here calls Himself God's only Revelation to men in written form. Others speaks of "Genesis, the Alpha of the Old Testament, and Revelation, the Omega of the New Testament," the
two books meeting together in Christ: "the last book presenting
to us man and God reconciled in Paradise, as the first book presented man at the beginning innocent and in God's favor in
Paradise. Accomplishing finally what I begin." [43] Others find
here a reference to God's eternity and deity.

[38] As in Matt. 24:30 and Zech. 12:10.

[39] Rev. 1:7. Translation of a Greek word of confirmation.

[40] Rev. 1:7. *Amen* is a Hebrew word also used in Greek and other languages.
Its literal meaning is "truly," "verily."

[41] Rev. 1:8; 21:6; 22:13; a few MSS of Rev. 1:11.

[42] "The Beginning and the Ending" (KJV) is not in the best MSS of this
verse.

[43] Jamieson, Fausset, and Brown, on Rev. 1:8.

We understand the name "Alpha and Omega" in the light of Is. 44:6: "I am the First, and I am the Last, and *beside Me there is no God.*" It is "the Lord God," [44] the *only true God.* He will not give His glory to another, neither His praise to graven images (Is. 42:8). All other explanations of the name "Alpha and Omega" must flow out of this. For example: Only the true God could be "the *Author* and *Finisher* of our faith" (Heb. 12:2); only of the true God can it be truthfully said, "He which hath begun a good work in you will perform it until the Day of Jesus Christ" (Phil. 1:6). Only the Lord God is eternal: "which is, and which was, and which is to come." [45]

God here also calls Himself the Almighty (Rev. 1:8). This name of God is used in the New Testament almost exclusively in the Book of Revelation.[46] He who speaks here has all power and rules over all things. He is therefore able to keep all the promises of divine grace and love, mercy, forgiveness, providence, and salvation which He makes to those who are His, and He is able to overthrow in everlasting confusion, destruction, and damnation those who are not His, as it is written in the Book of Revelation.

Rev. 1:9-20: John's Commission to Write

John wrote by specific authority of Christ. This is restated (Rev. 1:1) in the record of his commission to write (Rev. 1:9-20), which may be divided as follows:

Rev. 1:9, 10	The place, day, and manner of receiving the commission to write
11	What John heard first
12-16	What John saw when he turned to see who was speaking to him

[44] The best reading in Rev. 1:8.

[45] Repeated from Rev. 1:4 for emphasis. Also see Heb. 9:14; 13:8.

[46] Rev. 1:8; 4:8; 11:17; 15:3; 16:7, 14; 19:6 "omnipotent"; 19:15; 21:22. It occurs elsewhere in the New Testament only in 2 Cor. 6:18 in connection with a reference to the Old Testament. In the LXX the name "Almighty" is often used for the word "Sabaoth," e. g., Amos 5:27; Jer. 5:14.

17 a   John's reaction

17 b-20 The commission repeated, expanded, and
         concluded

*Rev. 1:9, 10: The Place, Day, and Manner of Receiving the
Commission to Write.* John mentions his name again,[47] identify-
ing himself clearly and unmistakably to the seven churches. He
had a very warm spot in his heart for them, being their "brother"
(Rev. 1:9) by common faith in the blood of Jesus Christ. He
was also their "companion in tribulation," [48] and reminds them
that beyond the cross of trial lies the crown of "the Kingdom."
They were already in the kingdom of grace (Rev. 1:6), with
"patience" [49] awaiting their "crown of life" (Rev. 2:10) in the
kingdom of glory. Aged John himself had not long to wait.

Tribulation had brought John in exile to "the isle that is
called Patmos." [50] He was banished "for the Word of God and
for the testimony of Jesus Christ" (Rev. 1:9). In his preaching
and teaching he had been faithful to his God and Savior. Now
he had to suffer for it. But he was strengthened, encouraged,
and upheld by the knowledge that he was an heir of the Kingdom.
Perhaps he remembered the words of Jesus: "Blessed are they
which are persecuted for righteousness' sake, for theirs is the kingdom of heaven." (Matt. 5:10)

John sanctified the Lord God in his heart (1 Peter 3:14, 15).
On bleak Patmos he kept a record of the passing days so that he
could identify "the Lord's Day" (Rev. 1:10). This is the first
time this expression occurs in the ancient Christian literature
which has come down to us.[51] It is commonly understood that

[47] Rev. 1:9, cf. vv. 1, 4. On the combination "I John" cf. Rev. 22:8; Gal. 5:2;
Dan. 7:15; etc.

[48] Rev. 1:9; see 1 Peter 5:9; 2 Tim. 3:12.

[49] Rev. 1:9. See Rom. 5:3; Rev. 2:2, 19; 13:10; 14:12. Chrysostom called
patience the queen of virtues.

[50] Rev. 1:9. See the introductory chapter.

[51] John 20:19-29; Acts 20:7; 1 Cor. 16:2.

John was speaking of the first day of the week. He does not explain the expression, indicating that it was in general use among the seven churches and that they would immediately know what it meant.

On the Lord's Day of which John spoke he was "in the spirit," [52] that is, in a frame of heart and mind favorable to receiving a message from God. Perhaps he was all wrapped up, as we might say, in meditation and devotion, contemplating the mysteries of the resurrection of Christ, which the church commemorated every Lord's Day. He was fully conscious, but his senses, especially of sight and hearing, were completely given over to those things which God conveyed to him. So vivid was it all that his entire body responded, as when he turned (Rev. 1:12), fell as dead at the feet of Him whom he saw (1:17), engaged in an exchange of remarks (7:13, 14), followed directions (10:8, 9), etc. He was neither hypnotized nor in a self-induced trance. [53] God simply chose to use a very special way of communicating with him.

While John was "in spirit" on that day he heard behind him a "great," or loud, voice. Its sound was "as of a trumpet" (Rev. 1:10), but it spoke words which he could understand. The natural tone of a trumpet is one of golden clarity, with a penetrating and noble, even defiant quality; it can also be exceedingly expressive, soft, rich, and moving. Its principal duty is to furnish sonority and brilliance. Accordingly, the loud voice which John heard was also clear and distinct, so that he was not mistaken in any way about it and what it said, though this revelation came as a complete surprise and at first involved only his sense of hearing, since the voice was behind him.

Rev. 1:11: What John Heard First. The words "What thou

[52] Rev. 1:10. See Rev. 4:2; 17:3; 21:10. Lit., "in spirit," without the definite article and with no compelling reason to use a capital "S."

[53] Acts 10:10 uses a different word — lit., "ecstasy."

seest, write in a book," etc.,[54] enabled John to prepare himself for the vision which was to follow. They alerted him to pay special and close attention. Not as though his record depended entirely on his memory, but from the very outset his attention was captured, so that what he wrote by divine verbal inspiration was also the clear-cut record of his own perception.

John's attention was even more firmly riveted by the next words: "Send it unto the seven churches"[55] specified by location: (1) "Ephesus," where John had spent most of the last 30 years. He must have known practically every member of the church there. (2) "Smyrna," with its model congregation, one of the only two to escape all censure in the letters which John was to write. (3) "Pergamos," where faithful Antipas had suffered as a martyr (Rev. 2:13). (4) "Thyatira," the home of Lydia, who had helped to open all Europe to the Gospel by opening the doors of her house to Paul at Philippi (Acts 16:14-40). (5) "Sardis" — how the church there needed spiritual strengthening! How its faithful few needed encouragement! (6) "Philadelphia," with its model congregation, like the one at Smyrna. And (7) "Laodicea," rich in this world's goods, but poor in spiritual riches. How well John knew them all! Quite naturally he turned (Rev. 1:12) to see the voice, that is, who it was that was speaking to him.

Rev. 1:12-16: What John Saw When He Turned to See Who Was Speaking to Him. When John turned, he saw "seven golden candlesticks,"[56] representing the seven churches (Rev. 1:20). Gold is valuable and beautiful, a symbol of God's high regard for the church.

"The churches of the Lord are lampstands as bearers of His light which is to benefit their entire surrounding and ultimately

[54] Rev. 1:11. The oldest MSS omit "I am Alpha and Omega, the First and the Last; and."

[55] Rev. 1:11. The words "which are in Asia" are not in the best MSS here, but only in Rev. 1:4.

[56] Or "lampstands," "candelabra" (Rev. 1:12).

the whole world. They are not themselves the light, just as little as a lampstand by itself is able to shine, but their light is that of Christ's Spirit, who works by means of Word and Sacrament and not only illumines them but also makes them instruments for illuminating others." [57]

Rev. 1:13-16 is the counterpart of Dan. 10:5, 6. The "son of man" in the vision is "the Son of God" (Rev. 2:18). He was "in the midst of the seven candlesticks" (1:13), which were in a group (2:1). This is a reminder of Christ's constant presence with His people on earth. (Matt. 18:20; 28:20)

In the vision He was "like unto the Son of man," [58] and was "clothed with a garment down to the foot" (Rev. 1:13), perhaps similar to the garment extending to the ankles which was worn by priests.[59] He was "girt about the paps with a golden girdle," [60] a mark of dignity and well suited to calm, majestic movement.[61] The Jewish high priest's girdle was partly gold (Ex. 28:8; 39:5), with all his holy garments designed "for glory and for beauty" (Ex. 28:2, 40). The similarity between this and the prophecy of the Messiah in Is. 4:2 [62] is scarcely a coincidence, especially in view of the fact that the Old Testament priesthood was in many ways a type of Christ. In addition, there are the candlesticks, further associating the Man with the functions of the Old Testament

[57] Kemmler, quoted in Lenski, p. 63. Also see Matt. 5:14; Ps. 119:105.

[58] Rev. 1:13 KJV. Here the piety of Wm. Tyndale (1525) and others exceeded their accuracy. Literally translated, the words read: "a son of man." There is no definite article, and there is no need to spell "son" with a capital "S." Martin Luther correctly translated: *"eines* Menschen Sohn gleich." The One whom John saw resembled a man. See Ezek. 1:26. That is all that John tells us at this point. We must look to the rest of the passage, and to the light which other Scripture passages provide, to learn that He who resembled a man in this vision was indeed *the Son* of man, as Jesus Christ often called Himself, Matt. 8:20, etc.

[59] Cf. Ex. 25:7 in the LXX. Also see Is. 6:1.

[60] Rev. 1:13. "Paps," breast.

[61] Cf. Josephus, *Antiquities,* III, 7, 2, cited in Jamieson, Fausset, and Brown, on Rev. 1:13. Also see Rev. 15:6.

[62] "In that day shall the Branch of the Lord be beautiful and glorious"; lit., "beauty and glory."

priests in the temple, not as confirming their service but as fulfilling their type.

The Son of man's "head and His hairs were white like wool, as white as snow" (Rev. 1:14). White is a symbol of holiness (Is. 1:18). The "Ancient of days" (Dan. 7:9) also had white hair, which may be taken as a symbol of His infinite age, or eternity. His eyes "were as a flame of fire." [63] Fiery eyes are commonly associated with zeal, penetration, power and authority, and the intent to overcome or destroy.[64] God's omniscience is implied indirectly through the penetrating quality of the eyes.

From the head of the Son of man the description shifts to His feet, which were "like unto fine brass, as if they burned in a furnace," [65] that is, shining brightly, like metal under intense heat.[66] God is not an idol, with feet of clay (Dan. 2:31-45). He shall stand forever and tread all His enemies underfoot; they shall be burned by the fire of His wrath and consumed by His anger and hot displeasure. (Mal. 4:1-3)

His voice was "as the sound of many waters" (Rev. 1:15 b), surging, restless, rising and falling, overwhelming, and irresistible in persistence and power.[67]

"And He had in His right hand seven stars" (Rev. 1:16), symbolizing the "angels" (Rev. 1:20; Dan. 12:3), or pastors, of the seven churches. God's right hand is a symbol of His divine power and majesty. How John must have taken comfort in this part of the vision, feeling encouraged by it in his commission to write, rather than give up in his old age in despair at the prospect of continued exile! He had been an "angel" at one of those churches not long before.

Let God's enemies beware! "Out of His mouth went a sharp

63 Rev. 1:14; see Rev. 2:18; 19:12.

64 Heb. 12:29; 2 Thess. 1:8; Deut. 4:24.

65 Rev. 1:15; cf. 14:2; 19:6.

66 Rev. 2:18; 10:1; Ezek. 1:7; Dan. 10:6.

67 Ezek. 43:2; 1:24; Rev. 14:2; 19:6; Dan. 10:6.

two-edged sword" (Rev. 1:16): "the sword of the Spirit, which
is the Word of God." [68] Here John saw the sword moving to
action, and in Rev. 19:15, 21 it effectively accomplishes its purpose, striking and slaying the nations. This sword of the Word
is a devastating thing for the unbelievers,[69] but a warm comfort
for the children of God.[70]

"His countenance [71] was as the sun shineth in his strength"
(Rev. 1:16), as bright and brilliant as the clearest and strongest
noonday sun. Not only His face but also His entire person radi-
ated a light and splendor which even the eyes of St. John the
Divine, holy man and inspired as he was, could not steadfastly
behold or endure.

Rev. 1:17 a: John's Reaction. Under the impact of this vision,
John fell to the ground at the feet of Him whom he saw and lay
there "as dead" (Rev. 1:17), completely overwhelmed.[72] Men
whose eyes have seen the King, the Lord of hosts (Is. 6:5), have
every reason to humble themselves before Him and await His
word and pleasure.

*Rev. 1:17 b-20: The Commission Repeated, Expanded, Con-
cluded.* The Lord does not let His humble servants continue to lie
in the dust. Having received their homage, He bids them be up
and doing. "He laid His right hand upon" John (Rev. 1:17),
touching him (Dan. 8:18; 10:10). John was "as dead" (Rev.
1:17), motionless, but not unconscious. He felt the Lord's hand
and knew what touched him. His eyes were open and observant,
and he heard the most precious, comforting, and encouraging
words which God ever spoke to man: "Fear not!" [73] As long as
fear holds men in its grip they are all their lifetime subject to

[68] Eph. 6:17; Heb. 4:12.
[69] John 12:48; Ps. 34:16; 1 Peter 3:12.
[70] John 10:27-29; 15:3-7; 16:33.
[71] Or whole "appearance," as in John 7:24.
[72] Ezek. 1:26-28; Matt. 17:1-6; Acts 9:3, 4; 26:13, 14.
[73] Rev. 1:17; Gen. 15:1; Luke 2:10; etc.

bondage and slavery (Heb. 2:15). Sinful man is filled with fear in the presence of God. Unless and until God bids fear to cease, there is no hope, but only doubt and despair. Not for even one unnecessary moment does God leave man without hope and assurance.

"I am the First and the Last" (Rev. 1:17), the eternal God.[74] Because John was well acquainted with the Old Testament, we may assume that these words told him clearly who it was that spoke to him.[75]

"I am He that liveth and was dead, and behold, I am alive forevermore." [76] This is the second mark by which John was to recognize Him. The Old Testament prophecies of the Messiah had been fulfilled in Jesus of Nazareth, with whom John had lived and whom he had seen die on the cross. On Easter morning John had outrun Peter to the open, empty grave (John 20:1-10). He had seen the Savior alive after His resurrection, had witnessed His ascension, had heard His parting words, "Lo, I am with you alway, even unto the end of the world" (Matt. 28:20), and must often have thought about them. "I am alive forevermore" and "with you alway" — also on Patmos. The limitations of space could not contain Him, and death could not hold Him either for time or for eternity (Rom. 6:9; 1 Cor. 15:20; Col. 1:18; Rev. 1:5; 4:9). There is a remarkable parallel in thought here with 1 John 1:1-3, where John heaps expressions to emphasize his own personal contacts with the living Christ as the "eternal Life."

"I have the keys of death and of hell." [77] "Death" is the separation between body and soul. The word translated "hell" in the KJV of this verse is literally *Hades* and may here be taken to denote the beyond as the dwelling place of the souls of those who

[74] Rev. 1:8; 2:8; 21:6; 22:13.

[75] Cf. the references to Isaiah in John 12:37-41; also see Is. 41:4; 44:6; 48:12.

[76] Rev. 1:18. The "Amen" in Rev. 1:18 KJV is not in the best MSS. It is omitted by Luther and by modern translators.

[77] Rev. 1:18, with the words in the original order.

have died, until the resurrection of the body; this dwelling place
has two sections: one is Paradise (Luke 23:43; 2 Cor. 12:4; Rev.
2:7), or heaven, and the other is *Gehenna*, as the Greek text
calls it,[78] the place of infinite and eternal suffering which we
commonly call hell.[79] In the Book of Revelation Hades is always
associated with death (Rev. 1:18; 6:8; 20:13, 14). The phrase
"the keys of death and of Hades" may have reminded John of the
words which Christ spoke to Peter, referring to "the keys of the
kingdom of heaven" (Matt. 16:19). The keys to the doors of
death and the hereafter are in the controlling hand of God.
(2 Tim. 1:12; 4:18; John 14:19)

"Write, therefore" (Rev. 1:19, literally). With these words
John's commission to write is repeated (1:11), and its authority
is based on the great truths of Rev. 1:17, 18. It is also expanded
to include all the visions he saw in this connection: "The things
which thou hast seen (Rev. 1:10-18), and the things which are,[80]
and the things which shall be hereafter." [81]

It seems best to begin a new sentence with Rev. 1:20, which
explains part of the vision: "As for the mystery of the seven stars
which thou sawest in My right hand and the seven golden lampstands — the seven stars are the angels of the seven churches, and
the seven lampstands are the seven churches." This is one of the
clearest examples of the Bible interpreting itself. There could
have been no question or doubt in the mind of John and of his
readers as to what was meant.

For us, however, who are removed from them both in time
and in language (Greek) a question has arisen regarding the
meaning of the word *angel* in this verse and in Rev. 2 and 3.

[78] Matt. 5:22, 29, 30; 10:28; 18:9; 23:15, 33; Mark 9:43, 45, 47; Luke 12:5;
James 3:6.

[79] This follows the interpretation of the word *Hades* in William Arndt, *The
Gospel According to St. Luke* (St. Louis, 1956), pp. 312, 365.

[80] Rev. 1:19, 20 and present conditions on earth, in heaven, and in hell as
they enter into Rev. 2—22.

[81] Rev. 1:19. Future conditions and events pictured in Rev. 2—22.

We hold that it does not refer to the world of spirits but that it means "messenger" and refers to the pastors of the churches.[82] "It is practically inconceivable that John should be commissioned to write to, or act as the messenger to, such a superterrestrial being as an angel, instructing him what to do in connection with each of these churches." [83] Elsewhere in the Bible we read of God sending angels as messengers to men, but never of God using men to send a message to angels.

[82] Cf. "Haggai, the Lord's messenger" (Hag. 1:13). Here the word for "messenger" in the LXX, the Greek translation of the Old Testament, is the same word that John uses in Rev. 1:20. Similarly, in Mal. 2:7, the priest, as a teacher of the people, is called the messenger [Greek: angel] of the Lord of hosts. John the Baptist is called the messenger [Greek: angel] of God (Mal. 3:1; Mark 1:2). So the Bible permits us to regard the "angels" of the seven churches as the messengers, or pastors, whom the Lord gave them as preachers and teachers of the Word. (Eph. 4:11)

[83] C. H. Little, *Explanation of the Book of Revelation* (St. Louis, 1950), p. 16.

CHAPTER

2

The entire Book of Revelation was written for the seven churches mentioned in Rev. 1—3 (Rev. 22:16). But in Rev. 2 and 3 there are seven individualized messages, one for each of the seven churches addressed through their "angel," or pastor.[1] These churches may have been chosen because of their prominence and representative standing.[2]

The seven letters have a number of things in common. All follow one general pattern. In each, Christ, the Author, identifies or describes Himself in a way suited to the church and its message. Each message emphasizes the fact that Christ knows the conditions which prevail in the church. Praise and promise or reproof and warning are extended according to these conditions. Each conclusion includes an admonition to be and remain faithful and a promise to those who are faithful until death. The order of the thoughts in the conclusion, however, is not the same in all letters.

The letters also take into account the differences between the churches, which are so great and so varied that in them can be traced the various situations and conditions which arise in churches

---

1 The fact that the congregations, and not only the pastors, were addressed is indicated by the words "the rest of you in Thyatira" (Rev. 2:24). Also note the plurals (Rev. 2:10, 23-25).

2 Wm. Arndt, loc. cit. (ch. 1, n. 8, supra). He inclines to the thought that *seven* is a sacred number, with a "representative significance" here "standing for all the churches of Christendom."

of all times everywhere. This makes Rev. 2 and 3 profitable,
timely, and practical for us. (Rev. 2:7 a; etc.)

Rev. 2:1-7: Letter to the Church in Ephesus

Ephesus   Take a bus out of Izmir,[3] on the western coast of Turkey
in Asia, and after about an hour's ride of some 35 miles
southeast, plus a little walk, you reach the ruins of ancient
Ephesus. "Today it is 'a miserable village called Ayasalook.' "[4]
It was a large and well-known city in its day, quite magnificent as
the first metropolis of Asia Minor. Famous for its cultural achieve-
ments, it was located in the mild, fertile, and densely populated
province of Lydia, about 150 miles directly east across the Aegean
Sea from Athens and about 35 miles north of Miletus. Situated
at the mouth of the river Cayster, at the junction of several natural
trade routes, it was assured of growth. Its temple of Diana (Acts
19:21-41), with its great altar carved by Praxiteles, the most
gifted Athenian sculptor of the fourth century B. C., was one of
the Seven Wonders of the ancient world. The city derived revenue
from the sale of "Ephesian Letters," regarded as talismans and
worn as amulets for a safe journey, health for the sick, a child for
the childless, victory in sports, and success in general. There
were more Jews in Ephesus than in any other heathen city except
Alexandria. But with the spreading of the Gospel the city became
third in importance among the early centers of Christianity, out-
ranked only by Jerusalem and Antioch.

Church at   The word *church* as used in the Book of Revelation
Ephesus   (Rev. 1—3; 22:16) means a body of Christians,
a congregation. The church at Ephesus was founded
by Paul,[5] who spent about three years there,[6] suffering many and

[3] The modern name of Smyrna (Rev. 2:8).

[4] *Concordia Bible with Notes* (St. Louis: 1946), p. 1462.

[5] Acts 18:19-21; 19; 20:17-38; 1 Cor. 15:32; 16:8, 9.

[6] Acts 20:31. As we take it, Paul's stay in Ephesus lasted from some time in
A. D. 52 to the beginning of May A. D. 55. Cf. Wm. Arndt, *The Life of St. Paul*

great hardships, but finally seeing the Lord crown his efforts with success. His Epistle to the Ephesians, probably written from Rome about A. D. 62, sheds some light on conditions in the church at Ephesus at that time.

According to tradition, John came to Ephesus during the Jewish War, A. D. 66—70. Perhaps all seven churches mentioned in Rev. 1—3 enjoyed some of his personal care. Eusebius says that John lived at Ephesus.[7] Some think that Mary, the mother of Jesus, also lived there. A large double church called St. Mary's was later built on the north side of the city. The Third General Council met there A. D. 431 and decided that Mary lived, died, and was buried in Ephesus,[8] and here Mary was proclaimed to be *Theotokos*.[9] "Christian pilgrims to Ephesus today spend much time among the ruins of the Church of St. John and in the tiny chapel believed by many to stand over the site of the house of the Virgin Mary. We know that Jesus, from the cross, entrusted His mother to the care of St. John [John 19:26, 27]. There is a local tradition that the beloved apostle brought her to Ephesus to escape the persecution of Christians in Jerusalem. . . ."[10]

The church at Ephesus had been served also by Timothy[11] and Apollos (Acts 18:24-26). Aquila and Priscilla had instructed Apollos there (Acts 18:26), and Tychicus carried messages to Ephesus for Paul (Eph. 6:21; 2 Tim. 4:12). Some of

(St. Louis, 1944), pp. 74—80. According to Wm. Dallmann, *Paul* (St. Louis, 1929), p. 173, the apostle arrived at Ephesus in the fall of A. D. 53. John D. Davis, *A Dictionary of the Bible* (Philadelphia, 1936): "Paul, probably in A. D. 54, began his third journey."

7 *Ecclesiastical History* (Philadelphia, 1834), III, 1.

8 W. M. Thomson, *The Land and the Book* (New York, 1880—82), I, 430 and 431.

9 Wm. Dallmann, *John* (St. Louis: 1932), pp. 90, 106. — The title *Theotokos*, that is, bearer, or bringer-forth, of God (often inaccurately translated "Mother of God"), confirmed by the Council of Chalcedon A. D. 451, was not so much intended to honor Mary as rather to express the fact that Jesus Christ, born of Mary, is true God, over against the heresy of Nestorius.

10 *National Geographic Magazine* (Dec. 1956), pp. 743—747.

11 1 Tim. 1:3. Timothy is said to have been the first bishop of the church at Ephesus. Cf. the note at the end of 2 Tim.

these may have welcomed John when he came. Having the benefit of the services of such men, the church at Ephesus grew and flourished under the inspired leadership of the last remaining apostle of the Lord. In many respects this church is an example for us. But it also had its weaknesses. When Paul sent from Miletus to Ephesus and called the elders of the church, he warned them that "grievous wolves" would "enter in among" them, "not sparing the flock" and that false prophets would arise in their midst (Acts 20:17-30). This prophecy had been fulfilled. (Rev. 2:4,5)

Address   Such was the church to which John was directed to write the first of the seven letters. In the address of this letter the Lord reminds the church, its pastor and members, that He is present with them, with all that this implies.[12]

A much stronger word is used here than in Rev. 1:16 in speaking of the relationship between the Lord and the seven stars, which are the "angels" (or pastors) of the churches. Rev. 1:16 says that He "had" them in His right hand. Rev. 2:1 says that He "holds" them in His right hand.[13] Similarly, in Rev. 1:13 the Lord is simply described as "in the midst" of the seven candlesticks (candelabra), whereas Rev. 2:1 expands and amplifies this to "walking in the midst," which advances the thought and enlarges the picture by adding a form of majestic motion.

Verbal   "Write!" [14] is equivalent to "Take a letter," except
Inspiration   that God, in choosing His words, fully took into con-

[12] Rev. 2:1. See Gen. 16:13; Ps. 139:7-12; Jer. 23:23,24; Matt. 28:20. The words run exactly parallel to Rev. 1:16a, 13a, and 20, with only one or two exceptions.

[13] The word used in Rev. 2:1 is translated in other passages of the KJV as follows: "lay hold on; lay hold upon; lay hands on; take; take by; obtain; hold fast; hold by; keep; retain." The thought is exactly the same as in John 10:28,29: "They shall never perish, *neither shall any man pluck them out of My hand. My Father, which gave them Me, is greater than all, and no man is able to pluck them out of My Father's hand.*"

[14] Rev. 2:1. Cf. Rev. 2:7, 8, 11, 12, 17, 18; 3:1, 6, 7, 13, 14, 22; 2 Peter 1:21; 1 Cor. 2:13; 2 Sam. 23:1, 2.

sideration the vocabulary and style of the writer. "St. John did not protest against serving as an amanuensis in a somewhat literal sense." [15] "The Lord Jesus is the Author, and John has wielded the pen." [16]

Message to Ephesus   The omnipresent Lord (Rev. 2:1) is om-
Rev. 2:2-6   niscient (John 21:17; Heb. 4:13).
                                "I know thy works" (Rev. 2:2) is a general statement included in most, if not all, of the seven letters. It refers to all that the members of the church did, both good and bad, and was a reminder that the Lord was in a position to deal with them according to their works. (Rev. 2:23)

Next, the Lord speaks of that which was commendable among them, giving the words "I know" the warmth of approval and encouragement.[17] The "labor" (Rev. 2:2) of the church includes toil and trouble to the point of weariness. The pastor is included in the commendation. His was probably a large congregation, and he worked hard at his task.[18] The members of his church readily and willingly labored side by side with him (Neh. 4:6b; 1 Cor. 15:58) setting an example worthy of imitation by every church.

The Lord also took note of their "patience" (Rev. 2:2) and commended them for it. No doubt they had profited by the example of John, their "companion in . . . patience." (Rev. 1:9)

The church at Ephesus was faced with the problem posed by those who professed Christianity but did not practice it. A good church member is one who is good *for that which God requires.* It is not enough to have your name on the membership list and to be a "good" member in the negative, passive sense of "do no evil." Also required is the positive doing of that which is right and good. Soldiers who are remiss in their duties as soldiers are

15 Engelder, p. 315.

16 J. A. Bengel, *Gnomon of the New Testament,* as quoted in Hanns Lilje, *The Last Book of the Bible* (Philadelphia, 1957), p. 39.

17 Ps. 1:6; 2 Tim. 2:19; Nah. 1:7; John 10:14.

18 Rev. 2:3; Heb. 6:10; 2 Cor. 6:5; 1 Cor. 15:10.

in that respect not good, but "evil," though in other ways they may be model citizens. Church members who are remiss in the things which make good church members are "evil" in that respect, though they may be good in other ways (James 4:17). The church at Ephesus is commended because it could not "bear" (Rev. 2:2) them. Patience and church discipline (Matt. 18: 15-18) can go hand in hand. (2 Tim. 2:24; Eph. 4:15)

When men arose claiming to be apostles, the church at Ephesus tested them.[19] The Bereans had tested Paul's preaching with God's Word (Acts 17:11). This standard reveals as liars those who falsely claim to be apostles.[20] Tertullian tells of a presbyter in Asia who forged an epistle, the Acts of Paul and Thekla, was caught, and was removed from office.[21]

[19] Rev. 2:2; see 1 John 4:1. — Chemnitz, *Examen* (Leipzig, 1915), p. 23B: "When the rest of the apostles had died, and John was in exile on Patmos, Ebion and Cerinthus sorely perturbed the churches by stirring up strife concerning the divinity of Christ, His earthly kingdom, Levitical observances, etc. But hear, I beg, how, and by what pretense and pretext they did this. Eusebius, Book 3, ch. 28, quotes Caius, that Cerinthus wanted to bring his monstrous teachings into the church under the pretext of revelations, as though received from a great apostle. And he adds that he was an enemy of the Scriptures of God. Therefore, since up till then it was fresh in the memory of the church that the apostles had delivered certain other things concerning the works and discourses of the Savior, besides those which were extant in writing in the accounts of the three evangelists, Cerinthus and the rest used this as a false pretext and set forth their corrupt doctrines — which they could not prove by the apostolic writings that were extant then — under this pretense that the apostles had taught such things orally; and they contended that those things which were written were to be best to match those fabricated traditions. John referrs to these issues, Rev. 2, when he says: 'Thou hast tested those who boast themselves to be apostles, but are not.' Likewise, 'Jezebel, who calls herself a prophetess, etc.' So they boasted of both revelations and traditions to which they wanted to attribute apostolic authority. And as John says in the epistle to Thyatira, they called those doctrines of theirs 'the depths,' that is, not such common doctrines of the apostles as were known to all in the church also from writings, but profound, recondite, and abstruse mysteries, which the apostles did not deliver to just anybody among the common people, but privately to their friends by word of mouth, from hand to hand, as mysteries to be venerated in silence. However, John calls them depths, not of the apostles but of Satan." Cf. Rev. 2:20, 24.

[20] Is. 8:20; Matt. 24:24; 2 Cor. 11:13-15; 2 Peter 2:1; 2 John 10, 11.

[21] "On Baptism," ch. 17. Cited in M. F. Sadler, *The Revelation of St. John the Divine* (London, 1906), p. 19.

"Patience" is mentioned again in Rev. 2:3,[22] this time in connection with bearing up for the sake of Christ's name in the face of opposition and persecution (2 Tim. 2:24, 25). Emperor worship was widely enforced in Asia Minor. Christians were not exempt. When they refused to comply, they were charged with treason, atheism, and superstition. Some were punished by confiscation of property, others, like John, by exile, others by death. We are told, for example, that Timothy spent his last days under stress at Ephesus, where he was bishop and "zealously governed the Church until A. D. 97. At this period, as the pagans were about to celebrate a feast called Catagogion, Timothy, meeting the procession, severely reproved them for their ridiculous idolatry, which so exasperated the people that they fell upon him with their clubs and beat him in so dreadful a manner that he expired of the bruises two days after." [23]

The times tried men's souls and required great Christian patience. There were many things to bear (Matt. 10:22). "I know," said Jesus, and continued in effect: "You have done well under the circumstances. You have not grown weary" (Rev. 2:3). The Ephesian Christians were well along on the way toward reaping without fainting.[24]

But not all was well with them. John probably remembered the words of Jesus "The love of many shall wax cold," [25] and now it was happening in his own beloved church in Ephesus. Though it must have grieved him to write, "You have left your first love"

22 In Rev. 2:3 Erasmus of Rotterdam added a few words to the Greek New Testament, in an attempt to complete his Greek text by retranslation from the Latin. Because the Greek text which he established was used by Luther and also by the translators of the KJV, the words which Erasmus added were carried over into those translations. The RSV conveys the thought of the original as follows: "I know you are enduring patiently and bearing up for My name's sake and you have not grown weary."

23 John Foxe, *Book of Martyrs* (Philadelphia and Chicago, c. 1926), p. 7.

24 Gal. 6:9; Heb. 12:3, 5, 12, 15.

25 Matt. 24:12; Rev. 2:2-4 runs remarkably parallel to Matt. 4, 9-12.

(Rev. 2:4), the truth needed to be stated, in love (Eph. 4:15), to prevent matters from becoming worse. Love toward God and man (1 John 4:7-21) was not entirely dead, but was growing cold. (1 Tim. 5:12; Jer. 2:1-13)

John the Divine writes almost as if he were John the Baptist.[26] "Repent" appeals to the heart. "Remember" appeals to the mind. "Do" lays claim to the entire body and all of life, which is to be a constant, ceaseless repentance: not only sorrow over sin but also a return to love in action as the evidence of faith. Where this is lacking, worse follows.[27] Ancient Ephesus and its church are no more. The silting up of the Cayster River led to the decay of the city and its removal to a site nearly two miles away, where it has now sunk to an insignificant village. A modern traveler found only three Christians there, and they scarcely familiar with St. Paul and St. John. Ephesus is the head of the church in Asia in name only. The "bishop of Ephesus" does not reside there, but in another city. Modern churches can be wiped out by silting up with the mud of sluggishness, indifference, and layer on layer of things which are foreign to the spirit and life of Christianity (Matt. 13:3-7). Not every so-called Christian church is actually a "lampstand" in the sight of God. (Matt. 25:41-46; 7:21-23)

To end the letter on a positive note, the attitude of the church toward false teachers is mentioned again, with special reference to the "Nicolaitanes" (Rev. 2:6), a sect in Ephesus and Pergamos (2:15) whose doctrine and life were contrary to the Christian religion and hated by God and his people (Ps. 139:21, 22). Mystery shrouds their origin and name, but this we know, that their deeds were evil and that the faithful at Ephesus were opposed to them from the bottom of their heart. Jesus commends the church for this and adds that in this respect they were a people after His own heart.

---

[26] Compare Rev. 2:5 with Matt. 3:2, 8.

[27] Rev. 2:5b; but "quickly" is not in the best MSS. Also see John 5:14; 2 Peter 2:20-22.

Conclusion   Not John but God, specifically the "Spirit" (Rev.
2:7a), composed this letter. In God's Word we
have God's words, to which man should listen attentively and
obediently.[28]

In one tremendous sweep the closing promise of this letter
(Rev. 2:7b) swings the hearts and thoughts of the faithful up
into heaven, their eternal home. "He that overcometh" is a victor,
a conqueror. We are not told here what he overcomes, but in the
light of the preceding and following context it is clear that all
enemies of his soul are defeated. The best commentary is in Rom.
8:31-39 with its shout of triumph: "We are more than conquerors through Him that loved us!" This victory is timeless.
It is ours in this life and in that which is to come. The rewards
of this victory are a gift of the Lord's boundless grace.[29] He will
give him who overcomes "to eat of the tree of life," that is, of its
blessed fruit. (Matt. 10:22b)

Paradise regained! Man did not eat of the tree of life in the
original Paradise, the Garden of Eden (Gen. 2:9—3:24). Death
had entered the world by sin (Rom. 5:12). But in heaven, the
Paradise which is to come, the saints eat of the tree of life,[30] drink
of the water of life (Rev. 21:6; 22:1, 17), and never die (Rev.
21:4). The devil, who by the tree of the knowledge of good and
evil once overcame, likewise by a tree, the tree of the cross, was
overcome, through Christ, our Lord.

The "Paradise of God" (Rev. 2:7b) is heaven. "Paradise"
means a beautiful park or garden. Luther began his delightful
letter about heaven to his four-year-old son Hans: "I know
a lovely, pleasant garden where many children are." The Septuagint calls the Garden of Eden paradise (Gen. 2:8; 3:1). But in

[28] Rev. 2:7a; also see Matt. 11:15; 13:9, 43; Mark 4:23; 7:16; Rev. 2:11,
17, 29; 3:6, 13, 22; 13:9. Also see the notes on verbal inspiration in connection
with Rev. 1:1; 2:1.

[29] Rom. 3:28; Eph. 2:8, 9; Rev. 2:10; etc.

[30] Rev. 22:2, 14, 19. The word for "tree" in these passages is used in reference to the cross in Acts 5:30; 10:39; 13:29; 1 Peter 2:24; and in Gal. 3:13,
quoting Deut. 21:23, where the same word is used in the LXX.

our English Bible the word is used only of heaven,[31] where, in the presence of God, there is fullness of joy and at His right hand pleasures forevermore. (Ps. 16:11)

Rev. 2:8-11: Letter to the Church in Smyrna

Smyrna   Stand on the deck of a ship approaching Izmir, in Turkey in Asia, and as you move up an arm of the Aegean Sea which runs far inland, the abrupt height of Pagos, "the Hill," provides a very prominent part of the backdrop of the scene, rising boldly into view in the distance. You draw closer, and the buildings of the city seem to rise out of the water in the foreground, clustered in a hollow at the foot of the hills. Farther back they climb the hillside toward the summit. This is Smyrna, as it was called in the days of John. Now it is a city of 250,000, full of brightness, life, and activity. Then it was the "first of Asia in beauty and size," according to its coins. It was well over 1,000 years old. Ideally situated for commerce, on natural trade routes, it had been reborn and rebuilt after devastation by war several hundred years before Christ. It is about 35 miles north and a little west of old Ephesus. On August 18, 1952, it was chosen to be the "southeastern headquarters of the North Atlantic Treaty Organization land forces." Today "new houses, hotels, and office buildings line the quay." [32]

Church   Christianity may have come to Smyrna from Ephesus
at Smyrna   while Paul was preaching there (Acts 19:10), or it
             may have been brought there by Paul himself. The church at Smyrna was one of the two churches which escaped censure in the seven letters of Rev. 2 and 3.[33] Polycarp, one of the Apostolic Fathers and a disciple of John, may have been its bishop when Revelation was written. Whatever difficulties it had

[31] Luke 23:43; 2 Cor. 12:4; Rev. 2:7.

[32] National Geographic Magazine (Dec. 1956), p. 743. — 1953 Annual of the Americana (New York and Chicago, 1953), p. 513.

[33] The church at Philadelphia was the other (Rev. 3:7-13).

to deal with at this time came upon it at the hands of enemies from without. Today about half of the city population is considered Christian.

Address   "The First and the Last, which was dead and is alive," [34]
          literally, "became alive," is the only, eternal, and everliving Savior, Jesus Christ. He died that we might live and lived that we might never die.[35]

Message to Smyrna   "I know thy tribulation." [36] Perhaps no one
Rev. 2:9, 10   had as yet suffered martyrdom in Smyrna.
                      But there was unmistakable opposition to the Christian faith, persecution, affliction, and distress. The church should not think that God doesn't know what is happening.

He also knows the poverty — and riches — of the church.[37] The paradox is not hard to explain. Christianity had not yet come into its own so far as the world was concerned. It was not fashionable to be a Christian. Most of the members of the church were drawn from the lower classes of society, without standing, influence, prestige, or wealth. The property and goods of some were confiscated when they refused to worship the emperor. These factors combined to make the church literally poor in this world's goods (1 Cor. 1:26-29). Probably it was not easy for its members to find profitable, gainful employment.

The church at Smyrna was rich, as we take it, in God and His blessings of the forgiveness of sins through faith in a loving, ever present Savior, peace of heart, mind, and conscience, and all of the other gifts and fruits of the Spirit.[38] Meanwhile, however,

34 Rev. 2:8; also see Rev. 1:5, 8, 17, 18; 22:13.

35 1 Cor. 15:54-57; John 14:19; also see Is. 44:6; 48:12; Rev. 21:6.

36 Rev. 2:9. The words "works and" are generally omitted from modern translations as perhaps not being part of the original.

37 The church at Smyrna has been called the poor rich church, whereas the church at Laodicea was termed the rich poor church (Rev. 3:14-22).

38 Matt. 6:19, 20; 2 Cor. 5:1; 6:10; 8:9; Gal. 5:22, 23; Heb. 13:14; James 2:5.

there was the opposition of the Jews to the Gospel of Christ.[39] Paul and others had suffered much at their hands. The good name of the Christians was made the object of attack at Smyrna.

Quite justly the Jews, whose tongues broke their own Law, come under judgment and condemnation. They are liars (Rev. 2:9; 3:9). They say they are Jews, but so far as the higher meaning of the name is concerned, as referring to God's own people in a spiritual way, they are not Jews (Rom. 2:17-29; 9; 11) but a "synagog of Satan" (Rev. 2:9). The word "church" is never used in the Bible with a bad connotation. But the word "synagog" lends itself as a symbol of Jewish religious opposition to the church and of boasting in the Law, which was read in the synagogs. The Jews, as followers of Satan, whose name means "adversary, opponent" (Job 1:6 ff.), rejected the Gospel of Christ and made life difficult for the Christians.

Satan and his followers often operate under the guise of religion (Matt. 4:6; 2 Cor. 11:13-15), deceiving the hearts of the simple (Rom. 16:18). He is the archenemy of God and of man and does all he can to destroy the works of God.[40] But those who put their trust in the Lord [41] have nothing to fear in the things which they shall suffer. (Rev. 2:10)

Forewarned is forearmed. The faithful were to know not only that these things would happen among them, but they were also to be very clear in their own hearts and minds as to the cause and source of these severe trials, namely, the devil.[42]

"Devil" means slanderer,[43] or false accuser.[44] In speaking of him the Bible always uses the word transliterated "devil" in the singular; perhaps for this reason some spell the word with a cap-

---

[39] Rev. 2:9b. "Blasphemy," slander.

[40] Luke 13:16; Acts 5:3; Luke 22:3, 31.

[41] Ps. 4:5; 1 Peter 5:9; James 4:7.

[42] Rev. 2:10; also see Matt. 14:3; John 16:2; Acts 12:1 ff.; 16:19-24; 2 Tim. 3:12; 1 Peter 4:12.

[43] 1 Tim. 3:11. The same Greek word is used for both and for "false accuser."

[44] 2 Tim. 3:3; Titus 2:3; Job 1:9-11; Zech. 3:1.

ital "D." [45] In Rev. 12:9, 10 we are told not only that the devil
was cast out of heaven but also: "the accuser of our brethren is
cast down, which accused them before our God day and night."
That is cause for rejoicing in heaven (Rev. 12:10-12a) and
among the people of God on earth (Rom. 8:31-39). Here on
earth, however, the children of God continue to suffer slander,
evil speaking, false accusations, and even imprisonment, and worse,
at the instigation of the devil.[46] But they should know that the
purpose of these afflictions is that they are to be "tried," [47] that
is, tested, proved and improved, and so strengthened in their saving faith. At such a prospect the question, often unspoken, wells
up instinctively in the heart: "How long, O Lord, how long?"
The church at Smyrna had an answer: "Ye shall have tribulation
10 days" (Rev. 2:10), that is, it would be limited and comparatively short.

Polycarp, bishop of Smyrna and a disciple of John, suffered
martyrdom by burning at the stake in the stadium at Smyrna after
the middle of the second century after Christ. His death might be
included in the "ten days' tribulation."

As God is faithful and will not suffer His promises to fail, but
will keep His covenant and mercy, even so He says to each of
His own: "Be thou faithful unto death, and I will give thee
a crown of life." [48] Because of its sheer loveliness, beauty, and
power, this is perhaps the most favorite of all confirmation
memory verses. Many have gone out of this earthly vale of tears
to their eternal home in heaven, meeting and greeting death with
these words in their heart.

[45] The passages in which the KJV has the plural "devils," e. g., Rev. 9:20;
16:14; 18:2, have a different Greek word, which is transliterated "demons" and
which we take as referring to other fallen angels.

[46] Matt. 10:16-26; 1 Peter 3:16; 5:8; Rev. 2:10.

[47] Cf. Luke 22:31 ff.; John 21:15-19; Acts 12:3 ff.; 14:22; 1 Peter 5:9, 10;
James 1:2, 3, 12.

[48] Rev. 2:10; also see Matt. 10:16-39; 1 Cor. 10:13.

"A crown of life" is theirs. Literally, *"the* crown of *the* life," the only crown that matters, the only life that endures! Among the Greeks the winners in the athletic games were crowned with a wreath as an emblem of victory.[49] But the wreaths which crowned their brows have long ago faded and decayed. They are dust and ashes, like those who once proudly wore them. Faithful loyalty to the Lord, however, through suffering, and to the very point of death, leads to an inheritance and a crown incorruptible, undefiled, and that does not fade away, reserved in heaven for those who are kept by the power of God through faith for salvation ready to be revealed in the last time.[50] The crown is not earned by any effort or striving, but is a pure gift of God's grace and favor.[51] First the cross, then the crown. One religious symbol shows a cross thrust through a crown, usually a kingly crown, or diadem, to indicate that those who receive it from the hand of Christ also reign with Him.

Conclusion   "He that hath an ear, let him hear what the Spirit
Rev. 2:11   saith unto the churches. He that overcometh (Rev.
        2:7) shall not be hurt of the second death," that is, he shall not be injured by it, shall suffer no violence from it. The "second death" is everlasting damnation (Rev. 20:14; 21:8); it shall never claim anyone who is "faithful unto death" (Rev. 2:10) and leaves this world with the Christian, saving faith in his heart. The word "death" is used here of an experience rather than a state or condition. The first death, accordingly, is not the

---

[49] 1 Cor. 9:24, 25; Phil. 3:14; 2 Tim. 2:5; 4:7, 8; James 1:12; 1 Peter 5:4.

[50] 1 Peter 1:4, 5. Cf. Phil. 4:1, where Paul calls the Christians at Philippi his "crown." "He is thinking of the 'day of Christ.' His loyal Christian converts will then be his garland of victory, the clear proof that he had not run in vain" (H. A. A. Kennedy, in the EGT, III, 464, on Phil. 4:1). Also see 1 Thess. 2:19, 20; Phil. 2:15, 16; Prov. 12:4; 14:24; 16:31; 17:6; Sirach (Ecclesiasticus) 6:32: "Thou shalt put her on as a robe of glory, and thou shalt set her upon thee as a crown of joy." With some of these thoughts in mind, Eliza E. Hewitt wrote the popular religious song "I Am Thinking Today of That Beautiful Land" (also known as "Will There Be Any Stars in My Crown?").

[51] Rom. 3:28; 6:23; Eph. 2:8, 9.

REVELATION 2:12-17 39

natural state, or condition, of man (Eph. 2:1), but is temporal death, the separation of the soul from the body. Nor shall this hurt him who overcomes.[52]

Rev. 2:12-17: Letter to the Church in Pergamos

A courier running north out of Ephesus to make a clockwise circuit of the cities mentioned in Rev. 1—3 would come to them in the order in which they are mentioned: Ephesus . . . Smyrna . . . Pergamos[53]. . . .

Pergamos Pergamos was a royal city, "with its immense acropolis [1,000 ft. high] on a rock rising out of the plain like a mountain, self-centered in its impregnable strength, looking out over the distant sea [15 to 20 miles west] and over the land right away to the hills besides far-off Smyrna [about 50 miles south]."[54] Its population today is about 14,000. Also in ancient times it was a city of some size and importance. Like Ephesus, it challenged Smyrna's claim of "First in Asia," and it gives one the very definite impression of permanence, strength, and sure authority. Situated on the north bank of the navigable river Caicus, it was a city of kings as early as 241 B.C., and later it was the residence of a Roman proconsul. It also became known for its library.[55] The Roman scholar and author Varro says that Eumenes II[56] of Pergamos restored the use of parchment for writing when the king of Egypt forbade the export of papyrus from Egypt. It is probable that parchment was the common material for copies of the Old Testament. At Pergamos the animal skin used

[52] Rom. 8:38; 1 Cor. 15:51-57; Phil. 1:23; 2 Tim. 4:8; Matt. 9:24a; John 11:11; Rev. 20:6.

[53] Also called Pergamus and Pergamum, and in modern times, Bergama.

[54] W. M. Ramsay, *Letters to the Seven Churches of Asia* (London, 1904), pp. 43, 44.

[55] Said to have contained 200,000 "books." See the notes on Rev. 5:1.

[56] See the notes on Rev. 3:7.

in parchment was prepared in a special way to make it smooth and more suitable for writing.[57] The word "parchment" is usually taken to mean literally "of, or pertaining to, or belonging to Pergamos." Emperor worship was well established in the city, which boasted the first provincial temple of this religion, built on the acropolis about 29 B. C. Near this temple was another, erected to Athena, and an immense altar dedicated to Zeus.[58] Not far outside the city there was a shrine for the worship of Aesculapius, regarded as the god of medicine.

Pergamos was quite a city. But much of its ancient glory had departed by the time of St. John the Divine. Mark Antony (died 30 B. C.), infatuated by Cleopatra, had caused the famous library, which did not belong to him, to be removed to Alexandria, Egypt, as a gift to "the man-trap of the Nile." In 6 B. C. the residence of the Roman proconsul was moved to Ephesus. But even so the influence and authority of Pergamos had not yet come to an end when John wrote Rev. 2:12-17.

Church at Pergamos   The church at Pergamos is referred to only twice in the Bible (Rev. 1:11; 2:12-17). All that we know about it is in seven verses. We do not know when it was founded, or by whom, or whether it was large or small.

Address   Pergamos was the official capital of the Province, the
Rev. 2:12   seat of authority in the ancient kingdom and in the Roman administration. But the one who speaks in Rev. 2:12-17 has *absolute* authority and is invested with the power of life and death (Rom. 13:4). Let his enemies beware, and let those who have offended him not delay repentance, lest the sword fall on them quickly in punishment (Rev. 2:12, 16; cf. 1:16).

[57] A. T. Robertson, *An Introduction to the Textual Criticism of the New Testament* (Nashville, 1925), p. 43.

[58] Reckoned by some among the Seven Wonders of the ancient world.

The sword, sharp and "two-edged" — literally, "two-mouthed" — to devour fiercely,[59] is the Word of God.[60]

Message to Pergamos   Life in Pergamos was not favorable to
Rev. 2:13-16   Christianity. Satan's "seat" [61] was there.
It will not do to think here only of "the power or influence that withstands the Church and all who belong to it," or "the official authority and power which stands in opposition to the Church." [62] The Bible speaks of a personal being, not simply a power or influence, when it uses the name "Satan" (Rev. 2:9; Job 1:6 ff.). Pergamos was a center at which he had succeeded in co-ordinating a number of factors against the church: the Roman state religion of emperor worship, with its temptation to deny the Christian faith by lighting a bit of incense on a pagan altar, and often death for those who refused; the temple of Zeus and his occasional love affairs with mortal women; the cult of Athena, the gray-eyed warrior-maid goddess; and the shrine of Aesculapius, with its reputation for "dream cures," [63] and a serpent, the Christian symbol for Satan (Gen. 3), as its distinguishing emblem. There were temptations to violate the apostolic decree of Acts 15:29 (Rev. 2:14, 15) and to believe false doctrine. It was a place where the devil was active with a vengeance through various agencies which lent themselves to his use and purpose. A person will do well to measure and judge environments with Christian standards and to count well the cost of liv-

[59] Deut. 32:42; 2 Sam. 2:26; 11:25; Is. 49:2; and esp. Prov. 30:14 for similar graphic imagery.

[60] Heb. 4:12; Eph. 6:17; Hos. 6:5; John 12:48.

[61] Rev. 2:13. Literally, "throne." Jack Finegan, in *Light from the Ancient Past* (Princeton, 1959), p. 345, suggests that "Satan's throne" was probably "either the Altar of Zeus or the Temple of Rome and Augustus." — The words "thy works, and" are not in the best MSS.

[62] Ramsay, p. 293.

[63] "Patients would spend nights in the temple, in so-called incubations, and many would leave their crutches in token of their healing." H. M. Zorn, in *Concordia Pulpit* (St. Louis, 1945), XVI, 604.

ing in neighborhoods which present particular hazards to Christian faith and life.

But though the church at Pergamos was subjected to severe trials and temptations, it did not yield to all pressures. The Lord had praise for it (Rev. 2:13b). Its members bore both the name of Christ and the reproach (1 Peter 4:14) well. They did not deny being Christians, with all that this implied. To hold fast the name of Christ means to hold fast the faithful Word of God (Titus 1:9). One who does that, does not deny the faith, but continues in the Word of Christ as a faithful and true disciple (John 8:31, 32), with saving faith in his Lord.

The church at Pergamos was faithful even in times of persecution unto death. "Where Satan dwells" Christian martyrdom is to be expected. One martyr is mentioned by name: "Antipas... My faithful martyr" (Rev. 2:13). According to a legend, he was bishop of the church at Pergamos and was burned alive in a heated metal image of a bull during the days of Domitian. His greatest reward is indicated by the word "My." As he was Christ's in life and in death, so is he also now in heaven to all eternity. (Is. 43:1-3)

But not everything was right with the church at Pergamos. There were a few things which the Lord had against it (Rev. 2:14, 15). Among them was this, that some of its members held [64] the doctrine of Balaam. (Rev. 2:14)

Balaam (Num. 22—24; 31:8; Joshua 13:22) was a soothsayer, or diviner, son of Beor, and a resident of Pethor, on the Euphrates River, in Aram, in the hill country of the East. Balak, a king of Moab and an enemy of Israel, asked Balaam to curse Israel. Instead, Balaam repeatedly blessed Israel. But finally he counseled Balak to lead the Israelites "to eat things sacrificed unto idols" and to have "the daughters of Moab" seduce them "to commit fornication" and "whoredom" (Num. 25:1, 2; Ex. 34:14, 15).

---

[64] A play on words. The word "hold" is the same as in Rev. 2:13: "Thou holdest fast My name." In Rev. 2:14 there are also some who "hold fast," but something entirely different — the doctrine of Balaam.

This "stumbling block" [65] was cast also before the Christians at Pergamos, who were tempted to eat the food of the idol feasts and to take part in the rituals of the pagan temples. Some of these rituals involved sex orgies with the temple prostitutes — a temptation which in some cases served just as effectively as fire and flame and the stake to lead a man to fall from the faith (Ps. 106: 28-39). The Lord's rebuke was brief but sharp and to the point. Idolatry and fornication are an abomination in His sight.

"So hast thou also them that hold the doctrine of the Nicolaitanes." [66] The church at Ephesus was commended for its stand against them (Rev. 2:6). But the church at Pergamos tolerated some of their followers in its midst. Apparently church discipline was not practiced in Pergamos as it should have been.

"Repent, therefore," [67] says God, calling for a thoroughgoing change of heart in these matters. To show that this is not an empty, idle call, He adds a twofold threat. The first threat applies to the church and its pastor for not moving to action against the manifest offenders in their midst. Where church discipline (Matt. 18:15-18) is neglected the church involved falls under God's wrath and condemnation. "I will come unto *thee* quickly" (Rev. 2:16, cf. v. 5). Repentance ought never to be postponed. The second threat: "I will fight against *them* with the sword of My mouth" (Rev. 2:16). There is no effective defense when that sword goes to war.[68]

Conclusion   The promise [69] to this church is individualized and
Rev. 2:17   personalized, as in the other letters. Everyone must
                  believe, and so "overcome," for himself; no one can

---

[65] Rev. 2:14. The word literally means the movable stick, or trigger, or tongue, of a trap or snare. If you "stumble" against it, or trip it, the trap snaps shut, and you are caught, perhaps killed. The specific reference here is to the trap which had been set for the Christians in the idol worship at Pergamos.

[66] Rev. 2:15. The words "which thing I hate" are not in the best MSS.

[67] Rev. 2:16, lit. See Matt. 3:2; Mark 1:15; Acts 3:19; Rev. 2:5.

[68] Rev. 1:16; 2:12; 6:8; 19:15, 21; John 12:48; Is. 11:4; 2 Thess. 2:8.

[69] For comment on the first part of Rev. 2:17 see the notes on Rev. 2:7.

be saved by another's faith. Only "to him that overcometh," says
God, "will I give to eat of the hidden manna," in contrast to the
"things sacrificed unto idols," which others were eating (Rev.
2:14). "Manna" recalls the experience of the Children of Israel
in the wilderness (Ex. 16). It is, so to say, the bread of heaven,
"angels' food" (Ps. 78:24, 25). The expression "hidden manna"
occurs nowhere else in the Bible. The promise expressed here
refers to heaven. We cannot now know the full riches of the
blessings which are in store for those who are kept by the power
of God through faith unto salvation; these riches are "hidden"
from us now and will be revealed only in the last time.[70] This is
therefore not a reference to the Lord's Supper but a promise which
is fulfilled after this life by the Lord, who will give the faithful
a place at His heavenly table, where they shall eat of the eternal
manna and drink of the river of His pleasure forevermore.[71]

We cannot say with certainty what the meaning and interpretation of the "white stone" is (Rev. 2:17). White is a symbol of
holiness (Rev. 1:14). The symbolism here may be based on a custom of wearing white stones as amulets for safety. In, or on, the
stone will be "a new name written" (Rev. 2:17). It is quite useless to speculate what name will be on any given stone, because
we are told that no one knows it except he who receives it.[72]

Rev. 2:18-29: Letter to the Church in Thyatira

Thyatira   Acts 16 tells how Paul was directed in a vision to go
to Macedonia. At Philippi, the first important city
he visited in Europe, he found welcome Christian hospitality at
the home of "a certain woman named Lydia, a seller of purple,
of the city of Thyatira." [73] Her home city was known for its

[70] 1 Peter 1:4, 5; 1 Cor. 2:9; 1 John 3:2.

[71] Matt. 8:11; Rev. 2:7; John 6:31-35, 48-58.

[72] Mysterious passages, such as Rev. 2:17b, are often misunderstood and mis-
applied. See, e. g., Duncan's Masonic Ritual and Monitor (Chicago, 1947), pp. 171
and 172; Albert G. Mackey, Encyclopedia of Freemasonry (Philadelphia, 1917),
p. 1004, under "White," and p. 1005, under "White Stone."

[73] Acts 16:14. Modern name, Akhisar. Present population, about 18,000.

purple dyes or dyed goods, its trade guilds, and its workers in bronze.[74] It was not large, but it was in an important place, in the region of Lydia, near the boundary of Mysia, about 40 miles southeast of Pergamos, on a Roman road from Pergamos to Sardis. This road was strategic in war and in peace.

Church at   We do not know when the church at Thyatira was
Thyatira   founded, or by whom; Lydia of Thyatira may very
              well have helped the cause along. Nor do we know how large the church was. Though the city was the smallest of the seven mentioned in Rev. 1—3, the longest of the seven letters was sent there. This letter, the most difficult of the seven for us to understand, confronts us with several problems regarding its correct wording and meaning.

Address   "These things saith the Son of God,[75] who hath His
Rev. 2:18   eyes like unto a flame of fire." [76] The false prophetess
              Jezebel (Rev. 2:20-23) would not be able to endure the penetrating, consuming look of those holy eyes, flaming hotly with the fire of righteous indignation. She would not be able to stand, but would fall and be crushed under His feet, which "are like fine brass." [77]

Message to Thyatira   "I know thy works,[78] and charity" (1 Cor.
Rev. 2:19-25   13), that is, Christian love toward God
                        and man, one of the fruits of the Spirit
(Gal. 5:22). It had grown cold in the church at Ephesus (Rev. 2:4), but was still warm in Thyatira.

[74] See the last words in Rev. 2:18.

[75] This expression prepares us for Rev. 2:27, where Jesus refers to His Father, citing Ps. 2:7 ff.: "Thou art My Son."

[76] See the notes on Rev. 1:14.

[77] Or burnished bronze. See the notes on Rev. 1:15, where the words "as if they burned in a furnace" are added.

[78] See the notes on Rev. 2:2.

"Faith" [79] here is not simply some kind of belief, but it is complete trust in Christ alone for salvation, and faithfulness in serving Him. "Service" is everything by which we serve God and man. It is not the service which a servant, slave, or employee renders his master in return for a consideration (Eph. 6:5-8), but it is the service which flows out of Christian love as its source and motive. It is the same word from which the words "deacon" and "deaconess" are derived. It includes the "daily ministration" to the needy (Acts 6:1); Martha was "cumbered about much serving";[80] the Christians at Antioch helped the Christians in Jerusalem in a time of drought by sending "relief";[81] Mary performed a God-pleasing service at Bethany when she anointed Jesus, doing what she could. (Mark 14:8)

The last part [82] of Rev. 2:19 reads literally: "and thy last works to be more than [exceed] the first." The Christians at Thyatira were growing in sanctification, doing more good works than they did when they first became children of God.

The first part of Rev. 2:20 reads literally: "But (Rev. 2:4, 14) I have this [83] against you, that . . ." The Lord minces no words in stating the issue. A woman was deceiving and seducing the church and its members, leading them astray into misbelief and other great shame and vice, and the church was tolerating her instead of moving to proper and necessary action to meet the situation.

The woman was called Jezebel. Perhaps this was her real name. Perhaps it is a symbolic name,[84] used because she was similar to that wicked, idolatrous queen Jezebel, the wife of King Ahab of Israel.[85]· What that Jezebel was for Israel, this other

---

79 This word precedes "service" in the best MSS.

80 Or "service" (Luke 10:40).

81 Lit., service (Acts 11:29).

82 On "patience," or "patient endurance, steadfastness," see the notes on Rev. 1:9 and 2:2, 3.

83 The words "a few things" are not in the best MSS.

84 Like "Babylon" in Rev. 16:19—18:24.

85 1 Kings 16:31; 21:25; 2 Kings 9:7, 22, 30 ff.

woman was for the church at Thyatira: a notorious, manifest, and
impenitent sinner, permitted to continue in her evil works and
ways and pernicious influence without reproof or rebuke. God
did not call her. She was a self-styled prophetess, one of those
of whom the Lord had said: "I have not sent these prophets, yet
they ran; I have not spoken to them, yet they prophesied." (Jer.
23:21; cf. Rev. 2:2, 24)

The language in the last part of Rev. 2:20 is very vivid, literally, "You tolerate the woman Jezebel — and she teaches and
seduces My servants . . . !" Religion and sexual vice were connected in her, as they often are in heathen religions. Her temptation also included eating food sacrificed to idols. In these matters
the church at Thyatira was similar to the church in Pergamos.
(Rev. 2:13, 14)

The Lord is a God of patience (Rom. 15:5). He was patient
also with Jezebel of Thyatira. He "gave her space [time] to
repent of her fornication." [86] But she would not repent. She
despised the riches of God's goodness and forbearance and long-
suffering (Rom. 2:4). Therefore the church at Thyatira should
not have permitted her to continue in its membership. She was
one of a kind with those mentioned and described in Rev. 9:20, 21.

God's judgment on such is inevitable and inescapable (Rev.
2:22, 23): "Behold," He says, pointing up and emphasizing that
which follows. "I will cast her into a bed." "Her bed of sensu-
ality will be turned into a bed of sickness." [87] She made her bed;
now she will have a bed to lie in, with a vengeance: an example
of sin and its punishment in this life.

The threat extends and hangs also over her followers. It is
true that she seduced them, but it is also true that they yielded
to her temptations. Therefore they cannot shift the entire blame
on her (Gen. 3:12-19). Sin is and remains an individual, personal
thing (Ezek. 18:4, 20). In the "tribulation" of Rev. 2:22 this is
to be brought home, through affliction, to each and every in-

[86] Rev. 2:21. Cf. 2 Peter 3:9; 1 Tim. 2:4; Is. 55:6, 7.
[87] Little, p. 29.

dividual who is involved. God speaks a language which they can understand. He gives them a final opportunity for repentance.

The one ray of hope in this passage shines through the words "except they repent of her deeds." [88] Since one person cannot repent for another, we may take this as referring to the type of sinful works commonly associated with Jezebel of Thyatira. As sin is a personal, individual thing, so must repentance be personal and individual. Everyone must repent of his own sins. But there is no reason to believe that Jezebel or her followers repented. Rather the picture grows darker as it expands to include Jezebel's "children," that is, those who follow in her footsteps. (Ex. 20:5 b)

"Kill with death" [89] is not redundant, but is highly expressive (1) of God's fierce anger, divine wrath, and hot displeasure, and (2) of His firm, unalterable, and irrevocable decision and determination.

One result of God's judgment on Jezebel of Thyatira and her followers and children is that all the churches will know that He is the one who "searcheth the reins and hearts" (Rev. 2:23). "Reins" are literally the kidneys, or loins, which in olden times were regarded as being the seat of the inmost thoughts, feelings, and purposes of the soul. In the Old Testament the "reins" were also often associated with the heart, as here (Ps. 7:9; Jer. 11:20; 17:10). The implication is that though sin may be committed with a perfect "front" which deceives the eye of man, God's knowledge and judgment strike deep into the roots of sin, which lie hidden within (1 Sam. 16:7; Rev. 1:14; 2:18). The Lord's course of action in dealing with unrepentant sinners is such as to put a plain object lesson before "all the churches," that is, those of Rev. 1—3 and, in a larger sense, all others.

The Lord continues: "I will give unto every one of you according to your works" (Rev. 2:23). This is addressed to the evildoers.[90] "The wages of sin is death." (Rom. 6:23)

---

88 Rev. 2:22 according to the best MSS; "their deeds," KJV.

89 Rev. 2:23. For a similar expression, "die the death," see Matt. 15:4.

90 The others are addressed in Rev. 2:24 ff. Also see 2 Cor. 5:10; 11:14, 15.

From the unrepentant sinners the Lord turns to the faithful: "But I say unto the rest of you in Thyatira," [91] "as many as have not this doctrine," that is, the teaching set forth by Jezebel, "and which have not known the depths of Satan, as they speak." [92] The last of these words raise some questions. What are these "depths," or deep things, of Satan, according to those who endeavor to plumb them? "If, in good faith, you ask them a question," writes Tertullian about the Gnostics, "they answer, with stern look and contracted brow, that 'it is deep.'" And Irenaeus says: "They say that they have come to the depths of the depth." [93]

The Spirit searches the deep things of God (1 Cor. 2:10). But man, having a knowledge of that which was good, was led by Satan to eat of the tree of knowledge of evil also (Gen. 3:5). As a counterpart of the deep things of God there were "the deep things of Satan" to invite investigation on the part of man. Jezebel and her followers were determined to investigate them thoroughly. Accordingly, they indulged in the lust of the flesh, the lust of the eyes, and the pride of life (1 John 2:16), while at the same time they clothed and shrouded their licentiousness and idolatry in mystery.

The faithful had enough to bear in the requirements of God's Law: "Thou shalt have no other gods before Me. . . . Thou shalt not commit adultery" (Ex. 20:3, 14). It was hard enough to live the life of true and faithful followers of the Lord in the environment of Thyatira, with all its attractive temptations to sin. The Lord would lay no other burden on them. (Rev. 2:24 b)

"But that which ye have already, hold fast till I come" (Rev. 2:25). They were not to lose ground in charity, service, faith, patience, and an increase in good works (2:19) but continue in them steadfast and faithful until the Lord would come (3:11;

[91] Rev. 2:24 according to the best MSS.

[92] Rev. 2:24. The RSV translates: "What some call the deep things of Satan." — Cf. Rev. 2:2, 20.

[93] Quoted in *Concordia Pulpit*, XVI (St. Louis, 1945), 612.

Matt. 10:22). He does not say when He will come.[94] We are to
be prepared at all times to meet our God. (Amos 4:12; 2 Peter
3:11-14)

Rev. 2:26-28 contains a precious promise for the faithful.
"He that overcometh" [95] is described also as he that "keepeth My
works unto the end." "Keep My works" means do them. "My
works" are those which the Lord requires and which "are wrought
in God." [96] Faith and works are to go hand in hand, side by
side, together through life. As faith is to continue "unto death"
(Rev. 2:10), so are works to continue "unto the end." Where
this is the case, the Lord promises as a reward of grace — not because of the works but according to them [97] — "power over the
nations." [98] This power is not exercised by anyone while he is still
here in time and on this earth, because he receives it only after
his "end." Having gone to heaven, he there rules with Christ over
the nations, that is, the heathen, as is evident from what follows.

"He shall rule them with a rod of iron." [99] In Rev. 2:27 the
word for "rule" refers to tending a flock.[100] But the picture is not
that of a gentle, tender shepherd. We may think rather of "black
sheep," or to use another picture in Scripture, of goats (Ezek.
34:16b, 17; Matt. 25:31-46), and how the Shepherd deals with
them. As not everyone who says to Him, "Lord, Lord," will enter
into the kingdom of heaven (Matt. 7:21) so will not everyone
who says, "The Lord is my shepherd," stand on His right hand
with the sheep. Many will find that the Lord and His saints, who

94 The delicate shade of meaning in the construction of the Greek verb, which
leaves the time of His coming indeterminate, is untranslatable into English. Also
see Mark 13:32; Rev. 3:3; 1 Cor. 4:5.

95 See the notes on Rev. 2:7.

96 John 3:21. Also see Phil. 1:11; Heb. 13:21.

97 Ps. 62:12; 2 Cor. 5:10; Rev. 2:26: "give," unearned, undeserved.

98 This introduces a reference to Ps. 2:8, 9 which continues into Rev. 2:27.
"Power over the nations" is symbolized by thrones in Matt. 19:28; also see 1 Cor.
6:2, 3; Rev. 3:21; 20:4.

99 See the notes on Rev. 1:6.

100 Moffatt: "He will shepherd them." Luther: "Er soll sie weiden." In Ps.
2:9 the Hebrew means "break." But the LXX, which Rev. 2:27 quotes, means "to
shepherd."

rule with Him, will "shepherd" them "with a rod of iron." So the picture changes. The rod, being iron, becomes a scepter, and the Shepherd is a king. His word is law. Those who break it, remain impenitent, will themselves be broken! (Matt. 21:44; Luke 20:18)

"As the vessels of a potter [101] shall they be broken to shivers!" In his incomparable *Messiah* George Frederick Handel captured the dramatic scene in music and painted it with a melody line, in an air for tenor, which includes pairs of notes poised high, followed by descending spans of full octaves, and these followed in turn by a series of rapid notes ascending and descending. The potter holds a vessel which he made. His eyes (Rev. 2:18) need but a glance to examine it and discover an imperfection which makes the vessel useless. In his anger he raises it high for a moment and in the next instant hurls it to the ground, with the small potsherds flying as tiny fragments in all directions. His heel grinds them into the dust.[102] The Lord and His saints overcome their enemies with the same ease and speed with which a potter destroys forever one of his vessels. (Ps. 110:1, 2)

The ascended Christ is absolute Ruler over the nations.[103] He "received" power over all things not according to His divine nature, according to which He always had all power, but according to His human nature (Matt. 28:18). He is able to give His faithful followers "power over the nations" (Rev. 2:26), and "the morning star" too (Rev. 2:28; 22:16). The latter expression, like "a white stone" (Rev. 2:17) has well-nigh become the despair of commentators. The reference seems to be to some special bright and beautiful reward which we shall have as kings ruling with the King of kings.[104]

101 Or "as earthen vessels" (Rev. 2:27).

102 Rev. 2:18; also see Ps. 18:39 in Luther's translation: "Ich will sie zerschmeiszen . . . sie müssen unter meine Füsze fallen."

103 Some editors and translators, including Luther, begin a new verse (28) with the words "Even as I received of My Father," giving this verse a balance similar to that in Luke 22:29. The RSV supplies the word "power": "Even as I Myself have received power from My Father." Moffatt similarly supplies the word "authority."

104 For comment on Rev. 2:29 see the notes on Rev. 2:7.

Rev. 3:1-6: Letter to the Church in Sardis

Sardis   At Sardis there was a dead church (Rev. 3:1) in a dead
             city. Not that Sardis was already a "ghost city," but its
greatest glory lay in the past. At one time it had been one of the
few great cities on earth. The Greeks long regarded it as the
greatest of all cities, and its coins, the oldest of all known coins,
bore the proud inscription "Sardis, the First Metropolis of Asia and
of Lydia and of Hellenism." [1] It was the most important manu-
facturing center in the early Lydian kingdom.

The city probably dates from about 1200 B. C., with the beginning of the kingdom of Lydia. It was about 65 miles inland east
of Smyrna, perhaps a little farther northeast of Ephesus by way
of a winding road,[2] and about 30 miles [3] southeast of Thyatira.
Built on a small plateau, from 950 to 1500 feet high, the original
city was accessible to the outside world only from the south by
a steep winding road on a narrow neck of land. On every other
side the natural rock walls on which it was built were nearly
perpendicular and generally considered unscalable. Because it
was so secure, and because it commanded the entire Hermus
Valley, Sardis was naturally the capital city of the kings and
princes of Lydia, whose welfare and fate depended on the valley.
But as time went on, the plateau, with its natural limitations, be-

[1] Ramsay, p. 358.

[2] In both cases a three-day journey in ancient times.

[3] Thirteen hours on foot.

came too small for the capital of an empire, and a lower city was
built, to the north and west on the plain at the foot of the
plateau, on the river Pactolus. The old portion of the city served
as an acropolis — much like Athens [4] had its acropolis.

Sardis was a war-torn city. Cyrus the Great of Persia captured
it from the fabulously rich King Croesus in 546 B. C. The
Athenians burned it in 490 B. C. In 334 B. C. it surrendered to
Alexander the Great of Macedonia. Antiochus III (the Great),
a Seleucid king of Syria, took it in 214 B. C. and lost it to the
Romans in 190 B. C. Finally, A. D. 17, it was destroyed by an
earthquake and has never again been of great importance, although
it was rebuilt. At the time of St. John it had definitely become
a city whose glory had departed. There was nothing in view for
it except inevitable decay. In the 14th century it was completely
destroyed in the invasion of the Turks. Today little is left of
old Sardis except a small settlement called Sart (or Sert-Kalessi),
consisting of shepherds' huts in the area.

Church   We know nothing certain about the church at Sardis
at Sardis at the time of John except what is in Rev. 3:1-6. Its
             history was in some respects similar to the history of
the church at Ephesus (Rev. 2:1-7). Both had made a good
beginning, but had left their first love. Sardis, however, had de-
generated more than Ephesus.

Address   At Sardis the church as a whole was dead. Only
Rev. 3:1a a few remained faithful and would continue so to
             the end (3:4). With spiritual wreckage all around
them, their hope and salvation lay in the power of God's Holy
Spirit. For their comfort and encouragement "the seven Spirits
of God" [5] are mentioned. Let not the faithful few at Sardis fear
that they are out of His hand or beyond His reach and power
to save.

[4] A plural name, like Sardis.

[5] See the notes on Rev. 1:4; also Rev. 3:6; 4:5; 5:6.

How the pastor of the church at Sardis must have read and reread for himself the words "These things saith He that hath . . . the seven stars"! [6] He was one of those seven stars. He belonged to Jesus. With that thought fixed indelibly on his heart and mind he could take all the discouragement at Sardis in his stride. Inseparably involved is also a reminder to the members of the church that their pastor belongs to God, who gave him to the church (Eph. 4:11). They are to receive and regard him accordingly.

Message to Sardis   "I know thy works,[7] that thou hast a name
Rev. 3:1 b-4   that thou livest." The church at Sardis was
                     a "name" church. It had a reputation for being very much alive. But reputation is not always accurate. Dead faith can only produce dead works. The only life that is worth striving for is "to be dead indeed unto sin but alive unto God through Jesus Christ, our Lord." [8]

Admonitions   "Be watchful," literally: "Become watching!" —
Rev. 3:2, 3 a   implying that they were not watchful at the
               moment (Eph. 5:14). There is a note bordering on impatience in the words, as though the speaker shook his hearers by the shoulders and said: You're sleeping! Wake up! Open your eyes, and see what is happening to your congregation. It is dying — practically dead! Do something about it. Don't just sit there so smugly as if everything would be all right. "Strengthen the things which remain, that are ready to die." [9] Check the deadly, creeping paralysis, or cancer, or spiritual dry rot, before it is too late.[10]

---

[6] See the notes on Rev. 1:16, 20.

[7] See the notes on Rev. 2:2.

[8] Rom. 6:11. Also see Eph. 2:1, 5, 6; Heb. 9:14; the story of the prodigal son, especially his father's glad words "My son was dead and is alive again" (Luke 15:24).

[9] Or "that are at the point of death."

[10] 2 Tim. 2:17; Matt. 26:41; Ezek. 34:4, 16; Luke 21:36; 22:32.

"For I have not found thy works perfect before God," rather "before My God." Christ's judgment is God the Father's judgment.[11] Such works as there were on the part of the church of Sardis made for a good reputation among men. We may think not only of church services but also of other activities and a general humming and buzzing, with many wheels going around fast, as it were, so that the people in the sister congregations would be moved to say, "They've really got something over there at Sardis!"

Yet something was radically wrong there. Spared the suffering of persecution and the strife and dissension of heresy, the church was dying from the inside out. If the heart is not right with God, nothing else can be "perfect" or "complete" with Him.[12] "Remember therefore . . . !" "Memory" is "again the lever for repentance." [13]

The next word has been variously translated: *"how* thou hast received," *"that* thou hast received," or *"what* thou hast received." The meaning is clear. "The Lord knocks at the door of their memory. Let them think back to the days of their young faith. With what grateful wonder had they once listened to the story of God's love for them in Jesus Christ! And with what holy zeal had they reached out for their heavenly pardon and had eagerly seized it, as a famished beggar clutches to his breast the bread that is handed him! Do you not remember those days? Jesus means to ask." [14]

Now, therefore, "hold fast!" Don't let go of the Word of God, but "keep" it, observe it, follow it. Make it a living, active, practical part of your life.[15] This also means that you will "re-

11 Also see John 10:30; Matt. 27:46; John 20:17; Rev. 3:12.

12 Cf. Col. 2:10: "Ye are complete [the same word which is translated "perfect" in Rev. 3:2] in Him," that is, in Christ. Also see 1 Sam. 16:7.

13 James Moffatt, in the EGT, V, 364, on Rev. 3:3. Cf. Rev. 2:5.

14 W. H. T. Dau, in *Concordia Pulpit,* XVI (St. Louis, 1945), 622. Also see Gal. 4:13-15.

15 Rev. 1:3; 2:26; 3:8, 10; 12:17; 14:12; 16:15; 22:7, 9. A different word is used in Luke 11:28 and Rev. 3:11.

pent," for all sins need to be repented of — also the insidious cooling off of the heart in faith and love.[16] The only effective prescription against spiritual death in time and everlasting death in eternity is repentance — contrition, that is, sorrow for sin and saving faith in Jesus Christ. (Mark 1:15)

A Warning   "If therefore thou shalt not watch, I will come on
Rev. 3:3b   thee as a thief, and thou shalt not know what hour
               I will come upon thee." [17] This may be a subtle reminder of the way Sardis on the plateau had twice fallen victim to invaders. The enemy scaled the forbidding walls at night at a point where no watch was kept because it was felt there surely was no danger there. For the church at Sardis, this was not only a solemn and impressive warning to be prepared for Judgment Day at the end of the world but also a warning of a special, preliminary judgment which would overtake it. Among the lonely ruins of Sardis, silent witnesses to the truth of God's Word, are a few remains of a Christian church, built before the fourth century. When the hour of judgment has struck, every hope of averting or forestalling it is vain.

Exceptions   The inhabitants of Sardis were known for their
Rev. 3:4   voluptuous life. Living in pleasure, they were spir-
                itually dead while they lived (1 Tim. 5:6). Even so, "even in Sardis" there were a few "names," that is, individuals,[18] who had not given themselves to these sins. They had not "defiled their garments," and did not hold that "what everybody does is all right." In matters of sin the majority point of view does not make a matter right.

The "few" in Sardis would surely find life everlasting. Jesus promises them: "They shall walk with Me in white" (Cf. Luke

16 See the notes on Rev. 2:5; also Rev. 2:16; etc.

17 Rev. 2:5; 1 Thess. 5:2-6; 2 Peter 3:10; Rev. 16:15.

18 As in Acts 1:15.

23:43). White garments are symbols of purity [19] and of festivity (Eccl. 9:8). The "few" are "worthy" of this reward, not because of their own goodness or righteousness but because of their faith in the worthy Lamb that was slain and redeemed them to God by His blood (Rev. 5:9,12). Faith, which makes a person righteous, or "worthy," in the sight of God, also shows itself in a life of good works, as in the case of the "few" in Sardis.[20]

Conclusion　"He that overcometh,[21] the same shall be clothed
Rev. 3:5, 6　in white raiment,[22] and I will not blot out his name
　　　　　out of the book of life." [23] The book of life is not a literal book. The expression is figurative.

The fact that some [24] names are written in the book of life is reflected in 2 Tim. 2:19: "The Lord knoweth them that are His." [25] They are the elect. "Those that are written in the book of the Lamb . . . the elect of God, will enter the heavenly city, where they will have complete and perfect salvation." [26] "Names that are written in the book of life will not be blotted out. If the hand of God records them there, who can obliterate them?" [27]

"He that overcometh" is assured of a favorable judgment because Jesus Christ the Righteous (1 John 2:1) "will confess his

[19] Rev. 4:4; 6:11; 7:9-17; also see Luke 9:29.

[20] Rom. 1:17; 1 Cor. 1:30; James 2:17.

[21] See the notes on Rev. 2:7.

[22] The better MSS read: "shall be so clothed in white raiment." See the notes on Rev. 3:4.

[23] The phrase "book of life" occurs in Rev. 3:5; 13:8; 17:8; 20:12, 15; and 21:27. In Rev. 22:19 the best MSS read "tree of life." Outside the Book of Revelation the phrase occurs only in Phil. 4:3. "The book of the living" occurs in Ps. 69:28. Other similar or related references: Ex. 32:32; Ps. 56:8; Is. 4:3; Dan. 12:1; Mal. 3:16; Luke 10:20.

[24] The rest are not written in the book of life. See Rev. 13:8; 17:8.

[25] The Lutheran Confessions speak of Christ as the Book of life. Formula of Concord, Epitome, XI, 6, 12; Thor. Decl., XI, 13, 66, 70, 89. *Triglot Concordia* (St. Louis, 1921), pp. 833, 835, 1067, 1085, 1093.

[26] Kretzmann, *Popular Commentary* (St. Louis, 1922), on Rev. 21:27.

[27] Barnes, on Phil. 4:3.

name," as He says, "before My Father and before His angels" (Rev. 3:5). Jesus will testify that He "knows the name of the overcomer, written in the book of life, as the name of one of His own and that therefore the person named belongs to Him, the Lord, and on this account shall have part in the glory of His kingdom." [28] "In a solemn hour the exalted Lord Himself will fulfill the promise which He once gave to the circle of His disciples on earth (Matt. 10:32), a promise which now applies to all the disciples of Christ." [29]

Rev. 3:7-13: Letter to the Church in Philadelphia

Philadelphia   Built about the middle of the second century B. C., Philadelphia [30] was named after its founder, Attalus II Philadelphus, who succeeded his brother Eumenes II [31] as king of Pergamos in 159 B. C. It was located about 80 miles nearly due east of Smyrna (105 miles by railway), nearly 100 miles southeast of Pergamos, and about 28 miles southeast of Sardis, at the eastern foot of Mount Tmolus, in the plain of the river Hermus. Because of its festivals and temples it came to be known also as "Little Athens." Situated at the western edge of a highly volcanic district, it was frequently rocked by earthquakes, a fact which lends added significance to the stability and permanence of a firm and solid "pillar." (Rev. 3:12)

Church at   Beyond Rev. 3:7-13 nothing is known of the early
Philadelphia   history of the church in Philadelphia.

Address   With the word "holy" the Author of this letter recalls
Rev. 3:7   one of the most familiar names of God in the Old
                  Testament, "the Holy One of Israel" (2 Kings 19:22;

---

[28] Meyer, quoted in *Concordia Pulpit* for 1945, XVI, 626.

[29] Lilje, p. 91. — For comment on Rev. 3:6 see the notes on Rev. 2:7.

[30] Modern name, Alashehr, or Alasehir.

[31] See the notes on Rev. 2:12.

etc.). The reason for the reference to the Old Testament in the address of this letter lies in the success which the church at Philadelphia was to have in its mission work among the Jews (Rev. 3:9). The Holy One of Israel was to be the Savior (Is. 43:3), the Messiah. Jesus is not a false Messiah, as the Jews declared, but "He that is true." [32] He is the One who was to come. We are to look for no other.[33]

He "hath the key of David" (Rev. 3:7). This is not the "key to the Scriptures" in Mrs. Eddy's *Science and Health*, p. 499 ff. The reference is to Is. 22:20-22. Eliakim, with his authority over the doors of the palace of King Hezekiah, was a type of Christ, the Messiah who was to come. This was to be noted especially by the Jews who were brought under the saving influence of the Gospel in the loving outreach of the Christians at Philadelphia. The Lord has both, "the keys of hell and of death" (1:18 KJV) and "the keys of the kingdom of heaven" (Matt. 16:19). He "openeth and no man shutteth, and shutteth and no man openeth" (Rev. 3:7). No man can limit or interfere with His power to admit into His kingdom and to exclude from it. The Lord has, indeed, given the Office of the Keys to His church on earth, but this office can be properly exercised and administered only at His command, by His power, and according to His Word. (John 20:21-23; Matt. 18:18)

Message to   "I know thy works;[34] behold, I have set before
Philadelphia   thee an open door." The picture of an open door
Rev. 3:8-11   is used repeatedly in the New Testament in speaking of opportunities for Christian missions.[35] We can enter only where the Lord Himself opens the door (John 3:8;

[32] Literally, "the True One," "the Genuine One," a favorite expression of John, occurring 23 times in his writings and only six times in the other New Testament books.

[33] Matt. 11:2-6; 1 Cor. 3:11; Acts 4:12.

[34] See the notes on Rev. 2:2.

[35] Acts 14:27; 1 Cor. 16:9; 2 Cor. 2:12; Col. 4:3.

Acts 16:6-13). When He does, man cannot close it, though he may neglect to go through it. On the Day of Judgment, having neglected an open door, no man will be able to excuse himself before God by saying that he had no opportunity. At Philadelphia the mission opportunities were especially among the Jews. (Rev. 3:9)

By way of encouragement to continue to go forward in mission work, the Lord adds His reason for setting an open door before this congregation: "Thou hast a little strength, and [and yet] hast kept My Word, and hast not denied My name" (Rev. 3:8). Strong praise! Though weak, the congregation had proved itself loyal. The Lord commends it and rewards it with favorable mission opportunities. So His grace is sufficient for it, and His strength is made perfect in its weakness.

We do not know what the weakness was which made for "little strength" in the church at Philadelphia. Perhaps the church was small and its leader not particularly prominent. But both pastor and people were quietly steadfast and faithful to the Lord; they did not forsake Him and his Word in spite of temptation at the hands of enemies of the Gospel.

Weak as it was, the congregation at Philadelphia was to be an instrument in the hands of God for the salvation of some who were at the moment still "of the synagog of Satan, which say they are Jews and are not, but do lie." [36] It is a lie to claim to be a Jew when you are not, even as it is a lie to claim to be an apostle when you are not (Rev. 2:2). The Jews claimed to be God's real, beloved people. But because they had rejected knowledge, God also rejected them (Hos. 4:6). Now only Christians are God's own people. (1 Peter 2:9)

Yet there is hope also for Jews. At least some of those in Philadelphia were to come under the saving influence of the Gospel. The first part of Rev. 3:9 can be translated: "Behold, I will cause some of them to come out of the synagog of Satan"

[36] Rev. 3:9. See the notes on Rev. 2:9. Also see Rom. 2:28, 29.

(2 Cor. 6:14-18; 1 Kings 18:21). The last part of the verse is even more specific in its clear, positive promise: "Behold, I will make them to come and worship before thy feet," that is, bow down before you, as in homage, reverence, respect, or repentance, or to make a request. They would come humbly to the Christians. This points to repentance, a change of heart, on the part of these Jews for their former enmity and opposition against the Christians. Ordinarily no Jew would have thought of going humbly to a Christian. They hated the Christians. But some would come to know that God loved the Christians. "I will make them . . . to know," says God, "that I [emphatic] have loved thee." [37] These Jews were to learn what many others, Jews and Gentiles, never learn: God's love is not limited to one people. (John 3:16)

As for success in Gospel mission work, God's promise is sure (Is. 55:10-13). When success crowns our efforts, it is His doing, not ours. He says, "I will make them . . . " (Rev. 3:9b). It is always God who converts men.[38] We can only be His instruments in effecting the contact between men and the Word. Rev. 3:9 is a promise concerning a certain place and time. This promise was a special reward to the faithful congregation at Philadelphia. We must not read into this text the false, millennial notion of a general conversion of the Jewish race as such, Israel according to the flesh, before the end of the world.

"Because thou hast kept the Word of My patience, I also will keep thee." [39] The church at Philadelphia seems to have passed through a period of trial which included the temptation to deny the Word or let it go. But it did not yield to the temptation. It held fast to the Word — "the Word of My patience," [40] says

---

[37] Rev. 3:9. Cf. Jer. 31:3. See the notes on Rev. 1:5.

[38] Phil. 2:13; Jer. 31:18; Hos. 13:9.

[39] The reader who has an eye and ear for the niceties and subtleties which combine to form music and beauty in language will appreciate in this passage the play on words which occurs also in the original. It is not always possible to preserve plays on words in translation, but here we have one: "kept . . . keep" (Rev. 3:10).

[40] Or patient endurance, suffering. The RSV translation "My Word of patient endurance" does not closely follow the Greek in placing the word "My."

Jesus, that is, the word of the Passion and death of the suffering Messiah, the atoning Savior in His work of redemption (Heb. 12:2, 3) the Word of the Gospel, the essence of Christianity.

The church at Philadelphia had "kept" (Rev. 3:10; cf. 3:8) this Word. Therefore the Lord promised that He would also "keep" (Rev. 3:10) that church, that is, guard it, preserve it from all real harm, and deliver it "from the hour of temptation," or trial by severe testing, which was to come "upon all the world, to try them that dwell upon the earth," that is, in the Roman Empire of that time (Luke 2:1; Acts 11:28). "Those that dwell upon the earth" is an expression which we may take to refer to those whose home is not heaven but earth and who desire no other home.[41]

We hold that the Book of Revelation was written A. D. 95 or 96 and that the "hour of temptation" (Rev. 3:10) is not the "great tribulation" of Matt. 24:21, the destruction of Jerusalem A. D. 70. Church history gives us good reason to look for the fulfillment of Rev. 3:10 in the persecution under Trajan, who became Roman emperor A. D. 98, and perhaps also in the many other persecutions which followed. The church at Philadelphia continued to exist through the centuries. "It is interesting to note that the church in Philadelphia survived the Ottoman invasions, and the town still has a bishop and about 1,000 Christian inhabitants. The historian Gibbon reports that among the seven churches, only Philadelphia remained erect, a column in a scene of ruins." [42]

At every step along the way the church was to remember the final coming of the Lord, who says: "I come quickly." [43] For the church on earth He is constantly the Coming One.[44] Human

[41] Rev. 3:10. Also see Rev. 6:10; 8:13; 11:10; 12:12; 13:8, 12, 14; 17:2, 8. Cf. Phil. 3:19; 1 Tim. 6:9, 10. A different Greek word is used in Rev. 14:6; Luke 21:35.

[42] H. H. Wernecke, *The Book of Revelation Speaks to Us* (Philadelphia, c. 1954), p. 62.

[43] Or soon. Rev. 3:11. Also see Rev. 22:7, 12, 20.

[44] Ps. 50:3; Is. 40:10; 59:20; 66:15; Zech. 14:5; Mal. 3:1; 4:6; Rev. 2:25.

standards and definitions do not apply to the word "quickly" or "soon" and cannot determine the moment of His coming. (2 Peter 3:3-10)

The thought of the Lord's coming is to encourage and console the believers and move them always to be ready and prepared to meet their God (Amos 4:12; 2 Peter 3:11-14). This verse refers not only to the coming of Christ at the end of the world but also to every previous point of time in which the Lord comes to set an individual before Him in judgment (Heb. 9:27). As the world continues to stand, it may seem that the Lord has not kept His promise. But ask both the saints and the damned, and they will agree that the Lord does indeed come soon. The world continues to stand only because God is patient with those who live on earth and deals with them in His mercy. (2 Peter 3:9)

"Hold that fast which thou hast, that no man take thy crown" (Rev. 3:11) is a favorite confirmation verse. Saving faith lays hold on the righteousness of Christ (Rom. 3:21-26). Through such faith we have forgiveness of sins, life, and salvation (John 3:36; 5:24). One who continues in this faith to the end shall be saved.[45] There is danger of losing this faith and its final reward; otherwise there would be no point to the admonition "Hold fast" and to the warning "that no man take thy crown!"

A Christian's assurance of salvation is not an absolute assurance; it is an assurance of faith; and the moment his faith ceases, the assurance of salvation and salvation itself is lost. The believer has the crown; it is *his* crown, his inheritance, reserved for him in heaven, ready to be revealed in the last time, 1 Peter 1:4-5. Yet if he does not in faith and loving loyalty toward his Savior hold fast what he has, he will be deprived of it; his enemies will succeed in taking that crown from him. Therefore cling to it! Let your faith and loyalty never waver! The crown prepared for you is worth the struggle.[46]

45 Matt. 10:22b; 24:13; Rev. 2:7, 10, 11; etc.

46 Th. Laetsch, in Concordia Pulpit, XVI (St. Louis, 1945), 634. Also see 1 Cor. 9:24, 25; 2 Tim. 4:7, 8.

Conclusion   "Him that overcometh [47] will I make a pillar"
Rev. 3:12-13   (Rev. 3:12; cf. Gal. 2:9). The picture of a pillar
                  is used here perhaps because Philadelphia was sub-
ject to frequent earthquakes. Strong, solid pillars were symbols of
permanence. They endured and continued to stand when flimsier
construction was shaken into wrack and ruin.

More than that. He who overcomes will be a pillar "in the
temple of My God," [48] that is, in heaven.[49] In distinction from
this everlasting temple in heaven there was a temple of God on
earth in the Old Testament, the temple of Solomon, which also
had some beautiful pillars (1 Kings 7:13-22). In the course of
time that temple was destroyed and its pillars removed. But the
temple of God in the heavens is eternal, and he who is a pillar in
it shall never be removed. "He shall go no more out!" (Rev.
3:12). Once we are in heaven, it is ours forever! (Ps. 16:11)

He who is saved is signed and sealed with three names which
the Lord Himself will write on him (Rev. 3:12): First, "the
name of My God." He belongs to God as a member of His family
and household.[50] Second, "the name of the city of My God, which
is New Jerusalem, which cometh down out of heaven from My
God." This is the permanent address of the saved (Phil. 3:20).
To the faithful Jews there was no other city on earth equal to the
old Jerusalem. Some Jews were to become Christians at Philadelphia (Rev. 3:9). They were to look away from the departed
glory of the old to the abiding glory of the new.[51] Third, "My
new name." We are not told what this new name is. Some suggest that it is Savior Victorious.[52]

[47] See the notes on Rev. 2:7.

[48] Rev. 3:12. Speaking as a man, according to His human nature, "as a brother
to his brethren" (Th. Laetsch, op. cit., p. 636). Jesus calls God *"My* God" four
times in this verse. Cf. Ps. 22:1, 10; John 20:17; Heb. 2:11-18; also see the notes
on Rev. 3:2.

[49] Rev. 7:15; 11:1, 2, 19; 14:15, 17; 15:5, 6, 8; 16:1, 17; 21:22.

[50] Eph. 2:19; 1 John 3:1; Gal. 4:5; Rev. 14:1.

[51] For a further description of the new heaven and the new earth and the New
Jerusalem see Rev. 21:2 to 22:5.

[52] In view of Rev. 5:5; also see Rev. 2:17; 22:4.

We belong to Christ and to God (1 Cor. 3:23) because He makes and keeps us His own. It is all His work in us and for us. He who said, "I will keep thee from the hour of temptation" (Rev. 3:10), also makes a man a pillar in the temple of his God and writes upon him the three names mentioned in Rev. 3:12.[53]

Rev. 3:14-22: Letter to the Church in Laodicea

Laodicea   About 40 or 50 miles southeast of Philadelphia, and about 100 to 115 miles east of Ephesus, lay ancient Laodicea, named after Laodice, the wife of Antiochus II. The modern city, near the ruins of the old, is called Denizli and has a population of about 17,000. It is only about 15 miles west of old Colossae.

Quite a few Jews lived in and around Laodicea, the chief city of Phrygia, a center of banking and financial transactions, and one of the richest cities of Asia. A fine kind of wool, soft and glossy black, grew on the Laodicean sheep. The manufacture of fine cloth, carpets, and various kinds of garments was the chief occupation of the city. Among the other things at Laodicea which are reflected in Rev. 3:14-22 were a mint and a medical school whose doctors prepared powder for a widely used eye salve. Across the river Lycus, not far to the north, lay Hierapolis, with springs of water which issued hot from the earth. "The water flows over a rocky ledge exactly opposite Laodicea, leaving behind it deposits of lime which turn into shining cascades of pure white stone; in its fall the river loses its heat, and the water becomes lukewarm." [54]

Church at Laodicea   The church in Laodicea is mentioned in Col. 2:1 and 4:13-16. Epaphras, a companion of Paul, may have been its first leader (Col. 4:12, 13) and Archippus (Col. 4:17) may have been one of its teachers.

[53] Also see Phil. 1:6; 2:13. — For comment on Rev. 3:13 see the notes on Rev. 2:7.
[54] Lilje, p. 100.

Address   "And unto the angel of the church in Laodicea[55]
Rev. 3:14   write: These things saith the Amen, the faithful and
                    true Witness, the Beginning of the creation of God."

1. "The Amen" recalls Is. 65:16, where God is called, literally, "the God of Amen." "Amen" is here equivalent to "the
Truth."[56]

2. "The faithful and true Witness" explains "the Amen."[57]
Three things are necessary in a "true witness": (a) to have personally perceived that of which he speaks; (b) to be able to tell it
to others; (c) to speak truthfully. Jesus met these three requirements.

3. "The beginning of the creation of God"; not "the first
creature," for He was not created. He Himself is the Creator, the
Beginner, or Beginning, of creation. It was He who brought all
created things into existence.[58]

There is a reason for using this threefold designation in addressing the church in Laodicea. "Amen," or "truth," is closely
related to sincerity, while lukewarmness of heart (Rev. 3:15, 16)
is related to insincerity. Again, though they may not like it, the
Laodiceans must admit that all things which "the faithful and
true Witness" says, His accusations, threatenings, advice, and
promises, are completely correct. Finally, excessive riches usually
create a feeling of self-sufficiency which forgets the Creator. The
Laodiceans had fallen victim to this snare and delusion of riches.
(1 Tim. 6:9, 10; Rev. 3:17)

Message to Laodicea   "I know thy works,[59] that thou art neither
Rev. 3:15-20   cold nor hot." The "cold" are those whose
                                hearts are not set on fire by the Gospel.

---

[55] The wording of the best MSS.

[56] John 14:6. Also see Rev. 1:6, 7; 2 Cor. 1:20.

[57] On "the faithful Witness" see the notes on Rev. 1:5. "True" is added here.
Cf. John 14:6: "I am . . . the Truth," and see the notes on Rev. 3:7: "He that is
true." Also see John 18:37; Ps. 89:37; 1 Cor. 10:13; Rev. 19:11. An example of
Jesus as a "true" witness is referred to in 1 Tim. 6:13 (Christ before Pilate).

[58] John 1:1-3, 10; Col. 1:15-18; Rev. 4:11; Prov. 8:22-30.

[59] See the notes on Rev. 2:2.

The "hot" are those who follow the Lord in fervent faith and burning love and zeal. Somewhere between are those who wish to claim the blessings of Christianity and be counted among the followers of Jesus, but who are not ready or willing to share and carry the responsibilities and obligations which that involves. They hope somehow to ride into heaven on the coattails of the church.

Lukewarm indifference — being neither cold nor hot over against Christ — presents one of the most difficult of all church problems. Many a pastor says with his Lord to an indifferent church member: " 'I would thou wert cold or hot' (Rev. 3:15). Be one or the other. If you want to be one of us, then come and help us do the work of the Lord. The way through this world divides at the cross of Christ. You cannot go to the right with your faith and to the left with your life."

God was quickly coming to the point of decisive action in dealing with the Laodiceans. "So then," He said, "because thou art lukewarm, and neither cold nor hot, I will spue thee out of My mouth (Rev. 3:16). That is, I am about to spew thee out. The act itself was still pending for the moment, but not for long. The Lord was simply giving the Laodiceans a final time of grace; He was waiting in His divine patience to see if perhaps, before it would be too late, they would warm up to Him and His work. There is a line of eternal demarcation on God's thermometer. The spiritual temperature at the moment of physical death, as observed by the divine Physician, shows definitely whether or not the patient will live — forever. A "lukewarm" reading falls on the "cold" side of the line and indicates eternal death.

The pastor of the church at Laodicea was apparently included in the Lord's censure. Pastors should remember that lukewarmness on their part comes under the same, and even worse, condemnation as does indifference and indecision on the part of church members. (Ezek. 3:17-21; 33:7-9)

"Thou sayest, I am rich." [60] The specific reference here is to

60 Rev. 3:17; cf. Hos. 12:8; Luke 16:14, 15; 18:10-12.

the spiritual condition and attitude of self-satisfaction and self-sufficiency. The material wealth of Laodicea may have entered into the picture in a secondary way.[61] Spiritual complacency often grows with the increase of material riches, but it can develop also in a congregation that is poor in this world's goods.

In the case of the Laodiceans riches had moved in and taken possession of the heart. They said not only, "I am rich," but also "and increased with goods," repeating it and thus emphasizing the abundance of their wealth. And on the basis of that they drew the conclusion "and have need of nothing" (Rev. 3:17). They neglected the one thing which alone is really needful (Luke 10:38-42). Their heart was not set on things above (Col. 3:2). Their treasures were of the kind which moth and rust corrupt and which thieves break through and steal. (Matt. 6:19-21)

No doubt they felt that they had the best of everything — also as far as religion was concerned. In a sense they were right. Nothing is better than the Gospel of Jesus Christ, which had been given to them (cf. Ex. 8:10). But pride in religion is sinful when it is blind and boastful self-delusion. The truth in such a case is stated vividly and graphically in the last half of Rev. 3:17: "And knowest not . . ." People who are in this condition do not recognize their state for what it really is.

The Laodiceans did not know that they were "wretched, and miserable, and poor, and blind, and naked" (Rev. 3:17). "Wretched" means miserable, distressed (Rom. 7:24). "Miserable" means pitiable, pitiful (1 Cor. 15:19). "Poor" means beggarly, needy, destitute. Philo the Jew [62] had enough understanding and sufficient insight into the real nature of things to write: "No one is enriched by secular things, even though he possessed all the mines in the world; the witless are all paupers." [63] Without true wisdom no one can be truly rich. The beginning of wisdom

---

[61] Matt. 19:24; Prov. 30:8, 9; Ezek. 28:4, 5.

[62] Jewish philosopher of Alexandria at the time of Christ.

[63] Quoted by James Moffatt in the EGT, V, 371, under Rev. 3:17.

is the fear of the Lord (Ps. 111:10); this was lacking in the church at Laodicea. It was "blind," not physically but spiritually (Is. 59:10), and "naked," not having on the garments of Christ's righteousness.[64]

Such people must first be told how they really stand over against God. Then they must be told what should be done about it. Jesus did that for the Laodiceans. The first necessary plain words had already been spoken. He had, so to say, laid down the Law. Now He goes on with the Gospel (Rev. 3:18) to point out what the Laodiceans needed to do for their spiritual health. In his advice he speaks of three things: (1) gold; (2) clothing; (3) eye salve.

1. The gold is not the gold of the mint and of the banks of Laodicea but rather "gold" in the sense of the riches of heaven (Rev. 21:18, 21), obtained only after the refining fires of tribulation. There may be a hint here that the church at Laodicea had escaped persecution by compromise and maneuvering. This would fit into the picture of its lukewarmness. The first part of the counsel would then amount to this: Stand your ground! The road to heaven leads through tribulation. You must be ready and willing to endure it. (Acts 14:22)

The Laodiceans were to "buy" gold from Jesus (Rev. 3:18; Is. 55:1). But the riches of heaven, which can be obtained only from Jesus, are all free! Jesus said "buy" to help prod the people out of their complacency and move them to action — to impress on them that there was something they needed which they had not yet bought and without which they were not rich. Until they would acquire these riches, they would be a rich poor church, in distinction from the poor rich church at Ephesus.

2. "White raiment" (Rev. 3:18) is mentioned as distinct from the beautiful, luxurious, glossy, soft black cloth made from the wool of the sheep of Laodicea, of which the city and its people were proud. "The best raiment you can produce," says Jesus in effect, "is not good enough. You need the white raiment which

[64] Rev. 16:15; 2 Cor. 5:3; Matt. 22:11-14; Luke 12:15-34; Rev. 17 and 18.

only I can give you." White garments are symbols of rejoicing in the righteousness of Christ.[65]

Before God they were naked in sin and shame — in spite of the best clothing that money could buy. Nothing less than the robe of Christ's righteousness could cover them properly before His eyes, so that the shame of their nakedness would not appear. (Rev. 16:15; 2 Cor. 5:3)

3. "Eye salve" (Rev. 3:18). This is the only place in the Bible in which this expression occurs. Apparently it is used here because of the preparation for eye treatment which was made in Laodicea and which helped to give the city a good reputation. But good as it was, says Jesus, it was not good enough to cure the spiritual blindness of those who, having eyes, do not see (Mark 8:18). They need the eye salve of the Word of God, which opens the eyes of faith. (Is. 35:5)

How tenderly Jesus deals with the lukewarm Laodiceans! His first words to them (Rev. 3:15-17) were indeed sharp and severe. But they needed to be said. Now, lest some take offense at his Gospel counsel and ask: "Isn't our gold, our clothing, our eye salve good enough?" Jesus assures them that he was speaking the truth in love.[66] In love he reproves them for their lukewarmness, false pride, and indifference, and "chastens" them (Rev. 3:19a). Chastisement emphasizes the result of education and improvement by discipline. The Lord is not primarily interested in having the Laodiceans suffer for their wrongdoing; but He is interested in having them bear the fruits of righteousness. (Phil. 1:11)

"Be zealous therefore," he says, "and repent" (Rev. 3:19). These are not two separate steps, following one after the other. Rather, as Luther says, our whole life should be one continuous zealous repentance.[67] "Behold, I stand at the door and knock" (Rev. 3:20). The "door" is the tightly shut door of every natural

[65] Is. 61:10; Matt. 22:11; Eccl. 9:8; Rev. 3:4, 5; 4:4; 6:11; 7:9-17.

[66] Rev. 3:19a; cf. Prov. 3:11, 12; 1 Cor. 11:32; Heb. 12:5, 6; Job 5:17.

[67] Cf. the first of the Ninety-five Theses, in the *Lutheran Cyclopedia* (St. Louis, c. 1954) under "Theses, Ninety-five, of Luther."

human heart. Our Lord reminds the congregation at Laodicea that he is outside that door knocking and awaiting admission. Besides knocking He also calls that His voice might be heard and recognized and the door be opened so much the more quickly and eagerly. No one, however, can by his own power open the door of his own heart to the Savior. It takes the power of God in the Gospel call to do that. (Rom. 1:16; Phil. 1:6; 2:13)

"I will come in to him," says Jesus, "and will sup with him, and he with Me" (3:20). This is a picture of intimate communion and close fellowship between Christ and the Christian (John 14:23; 15:5; 1 John 2:24-28). Its full meaning can be appreciated only by one who has himself personally experienced it.

Conclusion   "To him that overcometh[68] will I grant to sit
Rev. 3:21-22   with Me in My throne." This is a promise of
                 a free gift of divine grace, to be fulfilled in the
life to come. The exalted Christ is speaking here.[69] "He that overcometh" will sit with Him in His throne. Royal fellowship with the King of kings! Death itself pales into insignificance, for "if we be dead with Him, we shall also live with Him"; and suffering loses its terror, for "if we suffer, we shall also reign with Him!"[70] He that promised is our faithful Forerunner (Heb. 6:20), who Himself went before us on the way of suffering, death, and victory over death and hell, into heaven. "Even as I also overcame," He says, "and am set down with My Father in His throne." (Rev. 3:21; 22:3)

We will not argue the number of thrones mentioned in this verse, whether there be two or only one. We are dealing here with one of heaven's sublimest matters, which cannot be fully set forth in the language and concepts of earth. To help us understand the scene which is portrayed here, attention has been drawn

[68] See the notes on Rev. 2:7.

[69] In distinction from Christ in His humiliation (Matt. 20:23b); see Heb. 1:3; Ps. 110:1; Heb. 1:8.

[70] 2 Tim. 2:11, 12; cf. Rev. 22:3, 5.

to the fact that the thrones of eastern kings are often large and wide seats that will hold many persons; such thrones are intended to seat also those whom the king delights to honor by placing them close beside himself.[71] They are on his throne and yet are not his equals. Be that as it may, our final, blessed goal is assured by Him who has prepared a place for us (John 14:2, 3). God the Father has accepted the sacrifice of His Son for the reconciliation of the world and "set Him at His own right hand in the heavenly places" (Eph. 1:20-23). Our Lord has also said: "Fear not, little flock; for it is your Father's good pleasure to give you the Kingdom" (Luke 12:32). Here is the highest fulfillment and final grand climax of what it means for the children of God to be made "a kingdom" (Rev. 1:6, literally). There is no finer summary of what the Bible teaches concerning all of this than the close of Luther's explanation of the Second Article of the Apostles' Creed. Christ "has redeemed me . . . that I may be His own and live under Him in His kingdom and serve him in everlasting righteousness, innocence, and blessedness, even as He is risen from the dead, lives and reigns to all eternity. This is most certainly true!"

"He that hath an ear, let him hear what the Spirit saith unto the churches." [72]

[71] Sadler, p. 47.

[72] Rev. 3:22; see the notes on Rev. 2:7.

Rev. 4: The Throne in Heaven

Introduction   Revelation 4 begins the second major portion of
Rev. 4:1-2a   the book. At this point we pass from matters
                   which are comparatively easy to understand to
such as are more difficult, and the scene shifts from earth to
heaven.

John saw heaven's door open and heard a voice which spoke
to him. Apparently he saw no one, but he recognized the voice
as the first one which he had heard and which sounded "like
a trumpet" (Rev. 1:10 RSV). It was the voice of the Lord Jesus
Christ,[1] inviting John to come up and see "things which must
come to pass after these things."[2] Since the voice said, "Come
up," this part of the vision seems to have shown John an open
door in the sky.

John immediately accepted the invitation not with a physical
ascension to heaven but "in the spirit."[3] His prompt and favorable reaction was a result of the power of God working in him
(Phil. 2:13). He did not put himself into a trance. Peter and
Paul had similar experiences. (Acts 10:10; 2 Cor. 12:1-4)

John describes his glimpses of heaven in the language of
earth. His words must therefore not be taken in their usual sense

1 See the notes on Rev. 1:10-18.

2 Rev. 4:1, literally; cf. "soon," Rev. 1:1 RSV.

3 Rev. 4:2. Also see the notes on Rev. 1:10.

under the limitations of space and time. "The heaven of the angels and saints is not a created locality, but the condition of the blessed vision of God." [4] The "throne" is not a physical piece of furniture, etc. Rather God here condescends to the forms and terms of this present world in order to convey to us, as far as possible, some idea of the realities of heaven, which, in their full glory and splendor, are inconceivable to us now.

The Vision Itself   "Behold, a throne was set in heaven" (Rev.
Rev. 4:2b-11   1:4; 3:21). There is no greater or higher
                 symbol of power and authority, dominion
and rule, than a throne in heaven. Small wonder that it caught John's eye at once. However, he does not describe the throne in detail, but gives us instead a swiftly unfolding picture of the entire scene.

John does not specifically identify the One who sat on the throne, but from the description and the action which follows it is clear that it was God the Father.[5] Here, then, is a passage in which God the Father is pictured as exercising supreme rule. His appearance reflected the beauty and glory of His high office. To look upon, He was "like jasper [diamond] and a sardine ["carnelian" RSV] stone" (Rev. 4:3), precious gems suggested, very likely, by the brilliant radiance of divine majesty and judgment. (Rev. 21:11, 18-20)

Round about the throne was a rainbow. Here we must think of its shape rather than of the usual colors of a rainbow. It did not have all the colors of an ordinary rainbow, but was green, "in sight like unto an emerald" (Rev. 4:3). Green is a color of comfort, standing for grace, hope, and peace. A rainbow is a symbol of God's rule of spiritual peace and of His faithful promises.[6]

[4] Pieper, I, 471.

[5] In Rev. 4:5 He is distinguished from the Holy Spirit, and in Rev. 5:5-7 He is distinguished from the Son.

[6] Gen. 9:8-17; Luke 2:14; Ezek. 1:26-28; Ps. 93:1, 2.

"Round about the throne[7] were four and twenty seats"[8] (Rev. 4:4). On these thrones sat 24 elders. Inasmuch as they were human beings, in distinction from the four "living ones" (4:6ff.) and the angels (5:11), we may regard them as having some connection with the human race in their symbolism, specifically as regards the worship of God (4:10). Some take the number 24 to be symbolic of the people of God in the Old Testament, with their 12 patriarchs, and of the New Testament church, with its 12 apostles; in that case, John would see himself represented in one of the elders.

There is another number 24 with which Rev. 4:4 might be compared, namely, the 24 courses of priests (1 Chron. 24:3-19). This supplements the picture of "a kingdom [thrones and crowns] and priests" (Rev. 1:6; 5:10). The duties of the priests included leading the people in worship and teaching them the Word of God. We may, then, take the 24 elders to represent the ministry of the Word. As the types of the Old Testament priesthood found their fulfillment in the New, so the symbolism of the elders (Rev. 4:4ff.) is not limited to the Old Testament but has reference to all time.

The elders sat on their thrones, exercising ruling power. They were "clothed in white raiment;[9] and they had on their heads crowns of gold," symbols of victory, but perhaps also of royalty and of the glory of their office.

There was awe-inspiring action in this vision. "Lightnings and voices and thunderings"[10] came out of the throne, a display of God's almighty power and of His right to speak with final authority.[11] There were also seven lamps, or torches,[12] of fire

7 In a circle or semicircle, a most impressive setting.

8 Or "thrones," the same word as in vv. 2, 3.

9 See the notes on Rev. 3:4.

10 Rev. 4:5, following the order in the best MSS.

11 Also see Ex. 19:16; Rev. 8:5; 11:19; 16:18; Ps. 29, esp. vv. 3, 4.

12 Not the same word as in Rev. 1:12, 13, 20, etc.

burning before the throne; they were "the seven spirits of God" (Rev. 4:5), that is, the sevenfold Holy Spirit.[13]

"Before the throne there was a sea of glass like unto crystal" (Rev. 4:6; 15:2). As a matter of fact, we are not told that John saw a vast expanse of glass, a "sea of glass," or even that he saw a sea which looked like glass. But the entire expression, including the "sea" itself, is properly qualified, as in the RSV, *"as it were a sea of glass,"* or "before the throne it was *like* a sea of glass." John is using a comparison in order to describe what he saw. The words "like crystal" indicate that the reference to "glass" seems to be with regard to transparency rather than smoothness.

Since the Bible does not tell us what the "sea of glass" represents, we may leave it unexplained, like other impenetrable mysteries in the Book of Revelation. However, many have tried to discover its significance. Perhaps the best among their suggestions is that which regards the "sea of glass" as a type of the providence of God. Like the sea it encircles the earth. To us its depths are dark and mysterious (Rom. 11:33-36), but from the viewpoint of heaven it is all crystal clear.

Rev. 4:6b-9 puts "the Sphinx of Revelation"[14] before us in the "four beasts."[15] More than 20 different interpretations have been suggested to explain these "living ones." The Bible simply speaks of them, but does not tell us what they stand for.[16] They are simply types and symbols as part of this vision. In Revelation the number four seems to refer in some way to the earth, the

13 See the notes on Rev. 1:4; see also Acts 2:3; Rev. 5:6.

14 Lenski, p. 179.

15 Rev. 4:6 KJV; better translated "four living ones." "Beasts" — a different Greek word from that in Rev. 11:7; 13:1 — is an unfortunate word in this passage for our modern English-speaking world. John Wyclif used it in this passage in 1380, in the first English Bible. It was perpetuated in the KJV. Most modern English translations use the expression "living creatures." (See ch. 11, n. 23; ch. 13, n. 1.)

16 The four "living creatures" of Ezek. 1 are identified as cherubim in Ezek. 10. But the "living ones" of Rev. 4:6 are distinguished from the angels in Rev. 5:11.

world, and man.[17] Perhaps, then, we shall not be far wrong in following the suggestion that the four "living ones" symbolize the living earthly agencies or instruments of God's providence, which serve him in his dealings with the world.

The four "living ones" were "in the midst of the throne (Rev. 5:6; 7:17) and round about the throne" (Rev. 4:6). This is the language of visions, and must not be understood in the usual relationships of space. " 'Amid the throne' . . . indicates that the four living ones are immediate agencies of the rule and power that uses them. 'Encircling the throne' indicates agencies that are used by this rule all around on every hand. In other words, God's providential rule and dominion radiates out from a *center* . . . in an unbroken *circle* . . . of agencies." [18]

The four "living ones" were "full of eyes before and behind" (Rev. 4:6). God's providence does not overlook anything. Some of the eyes were turned to God, to search out His will; the rest were turned toward the world of creatures in search of ways and opportunities to carry out God's providential will.

The first "living one" was like a lion, the second like a calf or ox, the third had a face like a man, and the fourth was like a flying eagle (Rev. 4:7). The church was not slow in drawing on this verse for some of the earliest Christian symbols. Irenaeus [19] held that the face of a man signified the human nature of Christ; the lion represented His royal character, since the lion is the king of beasts; the calf, as an emblem of sacrifice, referred to His priestly office; and the flying eagle signified the grace of the Holy Spirit, which was ever upon Him. However, Christ has His own symbol, a lamb (Rev. 5:6), in this vision. Therefore some have interpreted the four "living ones" by associating them with the

[17] See Rev. 7:1; 20:8; also the notes on Rev. 1:4.

[18] Lenski, p. 182.

[19] The most eminent teacher of the church in the second half of the second century.

four evangelists.[20] But there is no obvious connection between this verse and the four evangelists.

If we regard the four "living ones" as agencies of God's universal providence, we may take the lion as representing the wild places of the earth, the calf (or ox) as representing the cultivated parts, the human countenance as representing the cities and towns, and the flying eagle as representing the whole expanse of air and sky.[21]

Each of the four "living ones" had six wings (Rev. 4:8), symbols of speed in doing the providential will of God. Perhaps the number six finds its proper explanation in Is. 6:2: two to cover the face in reverence, two to cover the feet in modesty, and two for flying.

The many eyes of the four "living ones" are mentioned again in Rev. 4:8 (4:6), this time as being "all round and within." [22] Nothing escapes the eyes of divine providence; they make no mistakes and overlook nothing.[23]

"They [the four living ones] rest not [never pause or cease] day and night" (Rev. 4:8; 7:15) to serve and glorify God. "Day and night" is an interesting expression in this connection, because there is no night in heaven (Rev. 21:25; 22:5). It simply refers to an unbroken round of activity. The purpose of divine providence is not simply to provide what is necessary for God's creatures but also to bring about what results in the glory of God.[24]

---

[20] The evangelists have at various times been associated in various combinations with the four "living ones." Most familiar among us is the following: Matthew — the man, because he begins his Gospel by tracing the human descent of Christ. Mark — the lion, because he begins his Gospel by describing John the Baptist, who was the voice of one crying in the wilderness. Luke — the calf (or ox), because he gives a very full account of the sacrificial death of Christ. John — the eagle, because he soars, as it were, on eagle's wings to the very throne of heaven.

[21] Cf. Lenski, p. 183.

[22] According to the RSV, which takes the words "all round" with the eyes, rather than with the wings, as the KJV does.

[23] See Matt. 10:29, 30; Luke 12:6, 7; Ps. 34:15; 37:25.

[24] Ps. 19:1; 29:1, 2; 96:7, 8; 99; Rev. 11:17.

The four "living ones" sang the praises of God, giving Him glory, honor, and thanks.[25] Their hymn (Rev. 4:8b) consists of three parts, each of which, in turn, consists of three parts. The triple "holy" is a reference to the three Persons, Father, Son, and Holy Ghost. God is holy Himself, and He makes us holy by faith in Jesus Christ. Besides the triple "holy" there is also the triple name: "Lord God Almighty." [26] He is Lord, inasmuch as He is the Ruler of the universe. He is God, worthy of all worship. And He is almighty.[27] The third part of the hymn, "which was, and is, and is to come," echoes Rev. 1:4, 8.[28] It is a hymn of glory to God; it acknowledges the sum total of His divine attributes; it gives Him the honor, or reverence, which is properly His; and it offers Him thanks for all that He is and does.[29] He "liveth forever and ever!" [30]

The four "living ones" are always joined in their worship of God by the 24 elders. Whatever God does in the world serves in one way or another to accomplish the purposes for which His Word is preached. The ways of His providence and the ministry of His Word redound to His honor and glory. As the 24 elders fell down in worship, they "cast their crowns before the throne" (Rev. 4:10). As in Rev. 4:4, the "crowns" are trophies of victory, symbols of success, indicating that the ministry of the Word accomplishes what God pleases (Is. 55:11). In casting their crowns before the throne the elders disclaimed all honor for themselves. (Ps. 115:1)

As do the four "living ones" (Rev. 4:8), so also the 24 elders express their worship and adoration in a song of praise: "Thou

25 Rev. 4:8, 9; cf. Is. 6:3.
26 See Rev. 11:17; 15:3; 16:7; 21:22.
27 See the notes on Rev. 1:8.
28 See the notes on Rev. 1:4.
29 See Ps. 103:19-22; 111:7-10; 145.
30 Rev. 4:9. See the notes on Rev. 1:18.

art worthy, our Lord and God,[31] to receive glory and honor and power" (Rev. 4:11). These are properly offered to Him, ascribed to Him, and accorded to Him as Lord, Ruler over all things, and God. Without Him we are nothing — nothing would even exist. It is fitting that the story of creation in the first book of the Bible (Gen. 1, 2) should be referred to also in its last book. The mention of creation also helps us to understand why the elders sing of "power" in their song. (Cf. Heb. 1:1-3)

The last part of Rev. 4:11 is easily misunderstood in the KJV: "For Thy pleasure they are and were created." The meaning is not that creation was intended to give God pleasure, or make Him happy, but rather that all things came into existence *by the will* of God.[32]

This is one of the Bible's strongest and most direct passages that give the lie to all man-made theories of the origin of the universe. The universe did not simply "happen." It is a product of God's creative will, which is so powerful that when it found expression God simply said: "Let there be . . . " — "and there was. . . !" (Gen. 1:3). Rev. 4:11 carries us back to the word "create" in Gen. 1:1. All created things received their existence by the will of God. "Create" in Gen. 1:1, then, means to call into existence out of nothing.

[31] RSV, following the best MSS.

[32] RSV: "By Thy will they existed and were created."

CHAPTER

5

Rev. 5: The Scroll and the Lamb

The purpose of Rev. 4 and 5 is to prepare for Rev. 6 and 7 (the opening of the seals of the scroll) and in a larger sense to help provide a background and basis for Rev. 6—22. At every point and step along the way through time into eternity the church and its members do well to remember these two chapters and remind themselves that, come what may, as children of God following His Word they are completely safe in the hands and under the providence of the Almighty (Rev. 4:8) Creator (4:11), Redeemer (5:5-14), and Sanctifier.[1]

Rev. 5:1-5: The Scroll

Rev. 4 and 5 presents one vision, with the focus, or center of attraction and attention, changing as the vision unfolds. John saw a dynamic situation, not a series of static scenes. The words "And I saw" (Rev. 5:1) simply mark an advance in the action: something new with added significance, that caught the eye of the divine seer.[2]

He that sat on the throne (Rev. 5:1) is God the Father.[3] His right hand is the hand of His divine power and majesty (Rev. 1:16). He had a "book" in His right hand (Rev. 5:1) — not

[1] The Holy Spirit, Rev. 4:5.

[2] Cf. Rev. 6:1, 2, 5, 8, 9, 12, etc. Sometimes John uses another phrase for the same purpose, e. g., "and when," Rev. 6:3, 5, 7, 9.

[3] See the notes on Rev. 4:2, 3.

a bound volume but a roll, or scroll, of writing material.[4] This help us to understand how it was "written within and on the backside" (Rev. 5:1). Usually scrolls had writing only on one side. But when a scroll was not long enough for all the writing to go on that side, the scribe often simply turned his scroll over and finished his writing on the "backside."

The scroll which John saw was "sealed" (Rev. 5:1). Its writing was completely finished, and it was of such importance that it was fastened shut with seven seals (Rev. 5:1). Without breaking a seal no one could even turn down a corner of the scroll to see a word or two of the writing within; and with the scroll rolled up and sealed with seven seals and held in the hand, very little could be seen of the writing on the backside.

We are not told what the writing was about, or that it was read by anyone in the vision. But we have reason to say that the scroll contained a full statement of "things which must be hereafter" (Rev. 4:1), for we see the unfolding of events with the opening of each of the seven seals. Such a scroll, then, in the hand of the Almighty, is a symbol of God's omniscience. Even the angels and the Son in His state of humiliation do not know the future (Mark 13:32). Only so much of it becomes known to us as He reveals to us.[5]

In this vision St. John saw the future unfold in a general series of symbols and events as one seal after the other was opened. In its significance the series covered the entire remaining span of time until the end of the world. The end itself is specifically connected with the sixth seal (Rev. 6:12-17). The number of the saved is completed (ch. 7). The seventh seal brings the silence of heavenly peace (Rev. 8:1), in strong contrast to the noise of battle and conflict and the tumult and turmoil of war. The Church

---

[4] The oldest books as we know them were made in the early part of the second century of the Christian era (Kenyon, *Our Bible and the Ancient Manuscripts* [New York, 1951], pp. 12, 13).

[5] See the notes on Rev. 4:2a.

Militant has then at last become, completely and forever, the Church Triumphant.

The symbolized passage of time does not begin until the seals are opened. The opening of the seals, then, is equivalent to venturing forward into the future. Who can do this safely and properly? This question was asked in the vision by "a strong angel." [6] Though he was strong, he did not venture to open the scroll himself. His strength was necessary for the task to which he was assigned: to proclaim (publish, announce) with a voice loud enough to be heard through all creation: "Who is worthy to open the book and to loose the seals thereof?" [7] The question is not: Who is *bold* enough, or who is *strong* enough, or who is *willing,* etc., but rather: Who is "worthy," that is, completely and fully qualified, and so "able" (Rev. 5:3), that is, equal to the challenge of the situation and its reward.[8]

"No one [9] in heaven, nor in earth, neither under the earth was able to open the book" (Rev. 5:3). The reference to heaven includes the angels there. "In [on] earth" means among living mankind. "Under the earth" includes all who had died, but not as though they were in an intermediate place between heaven, earth, and hell. The word *Hades* does not occur here, and it should not be read into the meaning of the text. Here is simply a series of sweeping phrases *including* all men, saints, and angels whom anyone might regard as "worthy," and *excluding* them all from opening the scroll, or even looking thereon ("into it" RSV), that is, to read it.[10]

The very fact that no one was found worthy to open the scroll or read it was enough to move John to many tears. He "wept much" (Rev. 5:4) in sorrow over the unworthiness and inability of anyone to come forward in response to the angel's

6 Rev. 5:2; see Ps. 103:20; Rev. 10:1.

7 That is, to open the book by unfastening its seals (Rev. 5:2).

8 See the notes on Rev. 3:4 and 4:11. Also see Rev. 5:4, 9, 12; 16:6.

9 KJV, "no man." Luther: *niemand.*

10 Ps. 14:2, 3; 53:3; Is. 53:6; 64:6; Rom. 3:22, 23.

question, and in disappointment at the prospect of not seeing any
of the "things which must be hereafter." (Rev. 4:1)

But man's extremity is God's opportunity. In this case He
caused one of the "elders" [11] to speak comfort to the heart of
John. "Weep not!" [12] Heaven is no place for tears. (Rev. 7:17;
21:4)

The end of John's sorrow was found in Him who alone can
make a final end of all sorrow, "the Lion of the tribe of Juda, the
Root of David" (Rev. 5:5), that is, Christ.[13] The names which
the elder uses in referring to Christ are significant. The lion is
king in his world, a victor, conqueror, and ruler. "Root of
David" also points to royalty (Luke 1:32, 33). Both expressions
are Old Testament references to the Messiah. The elder, as an
agent of the Word, properly reaches back into the revealed Word
in pointing to the Messiah, the incarnate Word. He also makes
it clear that these Old Testament prophecies had actually been
fulfilled. Christ "hath prevailed." [14] The outcome of His warfare
is not, and never was, in doubt (1 Peter 1:18-21). He was successful in His mission, according to the Word and will of God,
and He is therefore the One who is able and worthy to "open the
book and to loose the seven seals thereof." [15] For Him there is no
cause or reason for fear in it. The revelations which it contains
can only deal with the results of His victory in the final and complete overthrow of His enemies on the one hand and of the triumphant course of His church and Kingdom on the other. These are
the things which "must be" (Rev. 4:1) in view of the battle
which He fought and won. Let the Champion Himself therefore
come forward to open the book in which they are written and
loose its seals!

[11] An agent of the Word. See the notes on Rev. 4:4.

[12] Rev. 5:5; see Luke 7:13; 8:52.

[13] Gen. 49:9, 10; Hos. 11:10; Is. 11:1, 10; Rom. 15:12; Heb. 7:14; Rev.
22:16.

[14] Rev. 5:5; lit., has conquered; see Gen. 3:15; Rev. 3:21.

[15] Rev. 5:5; see the notes on Rev. 5:2.

Rev. 5:6, 7: The Lamb Takes the Scroll

How eagerly the eyes of the divine seer must have looked for the action to suit the words of the elder! (Rev. 5:5). He was not disappointed. "I beheld," he says, "and lo, in the midst of the throne and of the four beasts, and in the midst of the elders, stood a Lamb as it had been slain. . ." (Rev. 5:6). Yes, the Lion is also a Lamb.[16] There is no contradiction in this, because each picture has its own meaning. The combination of various names in this passage leaves no doubt as to the identity of the One to whom they refer and who now begins to hold the center of attention.

The Lamb was "in the midst of the throne, etc." (Rev. 5:6): not in the sense of physical location in space [17] but rather as being directly and closely related to the throne and its power, divine providence, and the ministry of the Word. In fact, as the center of all these, He actually rules as King: exercising full, divine power with God the Father (John 10:30), directing and controlling the dispensations of Providence (Eph. 1:20-23), and, as Prophet, through the preaching of the Word, revealing Himself as the Son of God and the Redeemer of the world. (Luke 10:16)

The Lamb "stood" (Rev. 5:6) ready for action.[18] It was remarkable that the Lamb was standing, in view of the fact that it appeared "as it had been slain" (Rev. 5:6) and as such might be expected to lie prostrate. Dead, yet alive again! (Rev. 1:18). He was crucified, dead, and buried, but the third day He rose again from the dead, and now lives and reigns to all eternity.

The Lamb had "seven horns" (Rev. 5:6). *Seven* is a symbol of perfection, and may also be taken as a symbol of God's dealing with men.[19] Horns are a symbol of power and might,[20] here

[16] Rev. 5:5, 6 has given the church the symbol of a lamb with a banner of victory. Also see John 1:29, 36; Acts 8:32; 1 Peter 1:19; Is. 53:7.

[17] Also see the notes on Rev. 4:2 b, 6.

[18] See Luke 1:19; Acts 7:56; Rev. 8:2.

[19] See the notes on Rev. 1:4.

[20] Dan. 7:7, 20; 8:3; Luke 1:69; Rev. 12:3; 13:1, 11; 17:3, 7, 12, 16.

a reference to Christ's kingdom of power, in which He, according to His human nature, as the God-man, in His state of exaltation now rules with His almighty power over all creatures (Matt. 28:18). Nothing is out of His control or ever out of hand.

The Lamb has "seven eyes," which are immediately explained as signifying "the seven Spirits of God," that is, the Holy Spirit,[21] "sent forth into all the earth" (Rev. 5:6; Zech. 3:9; 4:10). God not only knows all things, but also sees all things. The number *seven* may here be taken as referring to completeness or perfection in God's dealing with men. He overlooks nothing and no one.[22] Our Lord, the Lamb, shares not only in the majesty of God the Father but also in all the powers of the Holy Spirit. (Rev. 3:1)

He it was — the Lamb, strong Victor! — who came in response to the angel's call (Rev. 5:2) and "took the book out of the right hand of Him that sat upon the throne" (Rev. 5:7). It was not refused Him, for He had every right to take it. In giving it to Him God the Father [23] fully recognized the right and claim of His Son, the Lamb, to it. This was in further confirmation of what was already established by the resurrection and the ascension of Christ: God the Father accepted the sacrifice of His Son for the reconciliation of the world, highly exalted Him (Phil. 2:9-11), set Him at His own right hand in the heavenly places, put all things under His feet, and gave Him to be Head over all things to the church.[24]

Rev. 5:8-14: Three Doxologies

When the Lamb had taken the scroll, the four "beasts" [25] — agents of divine providence — and the 24 elders — agents of the Word — "fell down before the Lamb" (Rev. 5:8) in worship

21 Also see Rev. 4:5 and the notes on Rev. 1:4.

22 Ps. 139:1-16; Gen. 16:13; Rev. 4:6, 8; 1 Cor. 2:10, 11; Rev. 2:23.

23 The One who "sat upon the throne" — see the notes on Rev. 4:2.

24 Eph. 1:20-23; also see Ps. 110; Heb. 1:1-9; 2:9; Rev. 3:21.

25 Rather "living ones"; see the notes on Rev. 4:6.

and praise. This was entirely fitting and proper, because the Lamb is true God with the Father and the Holy Ghost.[26] Divine providence and the ministry of the Word are to serve this one purpose: to glorify God, especially our Savior Jesus Christ.

The four "living ones" and the 24 elders all had harps,[27] stringed instruments whose tone quality provides a wonderful background for singing, well suited to the "new song." (Rev. 5:9 ff.)

Besides harps the four "living ones" and the 24 elders also had "golden vials (bowls) full of odors (incense), which are the prayers of the saints" (Rev. 5:8, lit.). "Golden," precious, highly regarded. Never despise prayer, nor think lightly of it (James 5:16b). Here incense is a symbol of prayer.[28] The "saints" who offered the prayers symbolized by the incense were not in heaven; no saints in heaven had entered into the picture which John saw. Much less does Rev. 5:8 tell us that the saints in heaven pray *for us*. Nor are the 24 elders or the four "living ones" called saints. But there are "saints," or "righteous men," on earth (Col. 1:2), and they pray (James 5:16b). We therefore take this verse as speaking of the prayers of believers on earth. We are not even told that the elders in the vision carried the incense of prayer to God. Prayers ascend directly to God. This is in accord with the pattern of divine providence and a result of the ministry of the Word. There is nothing here, or anywhere else in the Bible, which gives us reason to pray to saints in heaven.[29] A Christian on earth can come as close to God in prayer as does the greatest saint in heaven.

"They sung a new song" (Rev. 5:9), the first of three grand doxologies in Rev. 5 (cf. Rev. 5:12, 13). The old song, by way

26 John 5:23; Heb. 1:6; Phil. 2:10; 1 John 5:20; Rev. 5:12, 13; John 10:30.

27 Or zithers, lyres (Rev. 5:8). They come into the picture of heaven again in Rev. 14:2 (where we see them actually come into play) and in Rev. 15:2. This is significant in view of the fact that some religious bodies will not have any musical instruments of any kind connected with their worship.

28 Cf. Ps. 141:2; Luke 1:10. See the notes on Rev. 8:3, 4.

29 Also see the notes on Rev. 8:4.

of contrast, was that of a Redeemer who was to come — the Old
Testament theme, with its typical lambs (Ex. 12:3; etc.). The
new song was the song of redemption accomplished — the New
Testament theme dealing with the Lamb of God that was slain.[30]

Music in   This is the first mention of music in the Book of
Heaven   Revelation.[31] How we wish that we could know what
              the melody and harmony was! But God the Holy
Ghost did not move St. John to tell us any more about the music
itself, lest, perhaps, our attention be diverted from the words.

"Thou art worthy." [32] It is a song of worship.[33] Christ, the
Lamb of God, is worthy to take the book, or scroll, and to open
its seals. Here is the answer to the question in Rev. 5:2 — an answer which is now complete both in words and in action.
(Rev. 5:7)

"For Thou wast slain and hast redeemed us [34] to God by Thy
blood" (Rev. 5:9). He is worthy not only because He was slain.
Many a man has been slain, some of them in what the world calls
the "supreme sacrifice," giving their lives in devotion to a high
and noble cause. Yet "none of them can by any means redeem
his brother" (Ps. 49:7), in fact, he cannot even redeem himself.
Christ alone did redeem men. He bought them for God, from
whom they had been separated by sin. The price of their redemption called for His blood and He gave it.

Christ died for all (2 Cor. 5:15). But Rev. 5:9, 10 speaks
only of those redeemed ones who accept their Redeemer in saving
faith.[35] That is the reason for the phrase *"out of* every kindred,
etc." [36]

30 John 1:29; Rev. 5:9, 10, 12; Ps. 96.

31 Also see Rev. 14:2, 3; 15:3.

32 Rev. 5:9; see Rev. 4:11; 5:12.

33 Originally, "worth-ship." Also see the notes on Rev. 14:7.

34 Supply the word "men" instead of "us."

35 In Rev. 5:10 the best reading is: "and hast made *them,*" etc.

36 Rev. 5:9. Also see Rev. 14:4. Compare John 3:16: "God so loved the
world," with Eph. 5:25: "Christ loved the *church* and gave Himself for it."

"Kindred" means tribe, one of the smaller groups of the human race having a common ancestor. "Tongue" means language. "People" refers to a larger group with common interests. "Nation" means those who are joined in political unity.[37] None of these categories presented insurmountable barriers to Christ in His work of universal redemption. All will be represented in heaven. What a thrilling encouragement for the work of world-wide Christian missions! [38]

Those who come to saving faith He made "unto our God kings [lit., a kingdom] and priests." [39] The agents of Providence and of the Word call Him *our* God." They do not forget whose they are and whom they serve. (John 20:28; Acts 27:23)

Millennialism? "They [40] shall reign on the earth" (Rev. 5:10).
No! This does not mean that the church will exercise a physical rule over this present earth with Christ for 1,000 years. A thousand years are not mentioned in this passage, and we should not read them into it. Besides, the Bible tells us that the church will be under the cross to the end of time.[41] Furthermore: note the future tense "shall reign." This points forward, beyond the spiritual reign which the saints exercise on this present earth, to the more glorious rule which shall be theirs on the new earth of Rev. 21:1ff.

Before the enraptured eyes of St. John the vision continued to unfold as there now fell upon his ears "the voice of many angels round about the throne and the beasts [living ones] and the elders." There were exceedingly many angels — "ten thousand times ten thousand, and thousands of thousands" — more than could be counted.[42]

---

[37] There are in all seven lists like this in the Book of Revelation: 5:9; 7:9; 10:11; 11:9; 13:7; 14:6; 17:15.

[38] Is. 55:10, 11; Rev. 21:24.

[39] Rev. 5:10. See the notes on Rev. 1:6.

[40] This is the reading of the best MSS. KJV, "we."

[41] Acts 14:22; John 16:33; etc. See the notes on Rev. 20.

[42] Rev. 5:11; see Heb. 12:22; Dan. 7:10.

The angels in heaven are deeply interested in the works of God (1 Peter 1:12). They sang together and shouted for joy at the creation (Job 38:7). They sang glory to God when the Savior was born (Luke 2:13,14). They rejoice whenever a sinner repents (Luke 15:10). And they all join their voices in worship (Heb. 1:6) and praise of "the Lamb that was slain." [43]

The number *seven* comes to our attention again [44] in the doxology of the angels as they sing of (1) power, (2) riches, (3) wisdom, (4) strength, (5) honor, (6) glory, (7) blessing. Three of these, glory, honor, and power, are also in the song of praise which the four "living ones" and the 24 elders raise to God (Rev. 4:9-11). "Power" is almighty power, evident, for example, in the creation of the world and in the overthrow of Satan. "Riches" includes all wealth, silver and gold (Hag. 2:8), the beasts of the forest and the cattle upon a thousand hills (Ps. 50:10), also God's own people in a special way, because of redemption (Is. 43:1; 1 Cor. 6:19), etc. "Wisdom" is divine wisdom, evident in all of the works of God, for example in creation, preservation, ruling over all things, dealing with sin and its results; in redemption, sanctification, justification, glorification of the saints, and in the eternal condemnation of the lost with the devil and his angels. "Strength" is might, "strength as a possession, whether it is put forth in action or not." [45] Take it as a synonym of "power," if you wish. "Honor" is high regard, and in the case of God (as here) it includes reverence. "Glory" is credit — as in the expression "All the credit belongs to Him" (cf. Ps. 115; Rev. 4:10, 11) and as in the hymn "All Glory Be to God Alone!" "Blessing" involves wishing someone well. Rev. 5:12, however, is more than a mere wish. It ascribes to Christ the worthiness to receive all the honor, love, respect, obedience, homage, etc., which can ever be given Him, because it is rightfully His.

[43] Rev. 5:12. See the notes on Rev. 5:6, 9.
[44] See the notes on Rev. 1:4; etc.
[45] Lenski, p. 210.

In the third and last doxology of Rev. 5 the multitude of angels was joined by all the other creatures of God throughout the universe.[46] There is no special or mysterious meaning connected with any one of the four places which are mentioned: in heaven, on earth, under the earth, and on ("in" KJV) the sea. Taken together, they are simply a comprehensive reference to all of God's creatures everywhere. In such a vision as this the powers of perception are greatly enlarged and expanded.

It is significant that the universal doxology in Rev. 5:13 [47] sings praises not only "unto Him that sitteth upon the throne" [48] but also "unto the Lamb," Jesus Christ, the Son of God. It is a very pointed example of what is meant by John 5:23: "All men should honor the Son even as they honor the Father."

This doxology first takes up the last word of the angels' doxology ("blessing," Rev. 5:12), and also repeats the chant of "honor" and "glory." [49] "Power" is mentioned, but it is a different Greek word from that which is in Rev. 5:12. In Rev. 5:13 "power" means might as it is put to use.[50]

In all of the world's literature there are not many passages which even begin to approach the three grand doxologies of Rev. 5 in the full scope and sweep and forceful impact of their theme. It remained for George Frederick Handel to rise successfully to the challenge of setting the choruses in Rev. 5:12, 13 and the "Amen" of Rev. 5:14 to the tremendous climax of instrumental and vocal music which brings his majestic and magnificent oratorio *Messiah* to an overwhelming close. No one who has ever been thrilled by an understanding performance of that world's master-

[46] Rev. 5:13; cf. Phil. 2:10; Rev. 5:3; esp. also Ps. 148.

[47] The RSV follows the better MSS in the order of thoughts, beginning the doxology with the words: "To Him who sits upon the throne and to the Lamb," etc.

[48] God the Father; see the notes on Rev. 4:2.

[49] See the notes on Rev. 5:12.

[50] For comment on "forever and ever" see the notes on Rev. 1:6. — In Rev. 5:14 the words "four and twenty" and "Him that liveth forever and ever" are not in the attested Greek MSS, but were interpolated by Erasmus.

piece, involuntarily rising to his feet with the final "Amen," can ever forget the experience. Living in his memory, the echoes of it are a constant reminder of that great and eternal hymn of praise which is sung by all creation and supported by the very harps of God in heaven. Small wonder that in the vision which John saw the four "living ones" chanted their "Amen" and the elders fell down and worshiped! [51]

[51] Rev. 4:10; 5:8, 14; 19:4; 22:8.

Rev. 6: Six Seals Opened

Chapter 6 begins a new section in the Book of Revelation. The next four sections are parallel to each other in point of time:

Rev. 6:1 to   8: 5: Seven Seals
       8:6 to 11:19: Seven Trumpets
     12:1 to 15: 4: Seven Visions
     15:5 to 16:21: Seven Bowls

Rev. 6 tells of the opening of the first six of the seven seals of the scroll which Christ, the Lamb, took out of the right hand of God the Father, who sat on the throne (Rev. 5:1-7). With the opening of each seal John saw a separate vision, dealing with events on earth, in time; in this respect they differed from the vision in Rev. 4 and 5, in heaven. For this reason much of the study of the Book of Revelation has been directed to Rev. 6 ff., in the hope of discovering a helpful key and guide to future events in the history of the world.

The first four seals are related in such a way that each of them reveals in its accompanying vision a horse and rider; each horse, however, differs from the others in color.

Rev. 6:1, 2: The First Seal and the White Horse

The expression "four horsemen" has become proverbial. But many who use it do not know its origin in the Book of Revelation. Though many questions arise in connection with Rev. 6:1-8 which are not definitely and clearly answered in the Bible, note that also this part of Scripture, deep and mysterious as it is, was written for our learning.

Rev. 6:1 may be translated as follows: "I saw when the Lamb opened one of the seven seals, and I heard one of the four living ones saying as with a voice of thunder, 'Come!' " [1] If this "living one" was the first "beast" of Rev. 4:7, which was "like a lion," the sound of his voice fitted his appearance.

Because John was already close enough to see, we hold that "Come" was addressed to the one who sat on the first horse (Rev. 6:2). One of the agents of God's providence calls this horseman into action.

"I saw, and behold, a white horse!" (Rev. 6:2). White is a symbol of holiness. In ancient times conquerors and rulers rode on white horses. Horses were associated with war, conquest, and triumph.[2] In his painting of Christ's triumphal entry into Jerusalem Plockhorst shows Jesus riding on a white animal.

The white horse in Rev. 6:2 had a rider whom some regard as Christ. However, Christ, as the Lamb, plays a different role in the action. He opens the seals of the scroll. Rev. 19:11-16 is a different vision, and therefore does not help identify the rider in Rev. 6:2. In both cases it is the Word. But there it is the incarnate Word, while here we take it to be the inspired Word. "Horse, rider, and what is said of him, are a composite symbol," in which is set forth "the whole Word of God as Jesus speaks of it in John 12:48b." [3] The Word of God goes out into all the world (Matt. 24:14) and triumphs over every enemy.

The one on the horse "had a bow" (Ps. 45:5), an instrument of war which was deadly effective at a distance.

"A crown was given unto Him" (Rev. 6:2) — literally, a wreath of the kind given to victors. There was no question as to

[1] The best MSS read simply "Come" here and in Rev. 6:3, 5, and 7, not "Come and see" as in the KJV.

[2] See, for example, Job. 39:19-25; Rev. 19:11-14.

[3] Lenski, pp. 221, 222.

the outcome of his warfare; his victory was assured before his first arrow sped on its way. (Is. 55:11)

"He went forth conquering": a symbol of the Word successfully at work in the world; "and to conquer" (Rev. 6:2) points to the final victory of the Word over all opposition.

The first horseman, accordingly, does not represent only one period of world history, but his symbolism covers the entire span of time which still remains before the end (Matt. 24:14), a rich source of comfort and encouragement for all who trust and believe the Word.

Rev. 6:3, 4: The Second Seal and the Red Horse

The second horse was "red," literally: "fiery," the color of fire and blood and a symbol of war and bloodshed (Matt. 24:6, 7; Zech. 1:8). "Power was given to him that sat thereon to take peace from the earth, and that they should kill [4] one another; and there was given unto him a great sword." [5] This horse and rider do not represent only one period of world history or one war or series of wars. Sin and the wild passions of the wicked abroad in all nations constantly precipitate wars. In the midst of these wars and in spite of them the Lamb brings His kingdom to its triumphant consummation. The symbolism here does not simply refer to spiritual conflict, but it applies to real wars and bloodshed at various times and places, covering the entire span of time still remaining before the end. God is a God of peace (Rom. 15:33). But He is also just and punishes sin. War is one of the results of sin (Lev. 26: 21-25; James 4:1, 2). God sends it as a scourge on the wicked. Occasionally He permits it to fall also on His children in order to draw them to Himself. (Rom. 8:35-37; Heb. 12:5-11)

Rev. 6:5, 6: The Third Seal and the Black Horse

The third horse was black and is commonly taken to represent famine. However, the hunger and starvation which are involved

[4] Or "slay," "slaughter"; see Rev. 5:6, 9, 12; 13:3, 8; 18:24.
[5] Rev. 6:4. On the sword see also the notes on Rev. 2:12.

here do not arise out of a lack of available food but rather out of economic disparity and imbalance which stand in the way of its distribution according to need. The market price of wheat is "a measure" [6] for a "penny." [7] That is about 12 times the normal price. Three "measures" of barley are equal to one "measure" of wheat in nourishment and sell for the same price. This reduces many a man to the bare subsistence level, living from one day to the next, from hand to mouth. Not that there is no more food, but he cannot pay for more. He cannot even provide for his other needs or those of his family. We are not told that the rider of this horse used the "pair of balances" which he had in his hand, but the implication seems to be that the grain is to be very carefully weighed out.

When difficult times of this kind arise, God is not unaware of them, nor has He lost control as though He were helpless. The market prices which are mentioned here are set under the providence of God. The "voice" which announced them came from "the midst of the four beasts" (Rev. 6:6). All four of them are involved and concerned.

The situation is not cured by flexible government price supports or by a free food distribution program. The roots of the difficult situation lie in sin. As long as sin continues, to the end of the world, so long will the black horse and its rider be abroad in the world.

"See thou hurt not the oil and the wine" (Rev. 6:6). These words are not easy to understand. Though the second person singular is used, we are not told who is addressed. It is usually held that the rider on the horse is addressed and so directed to moderation in his mission. As to the oil and the wine, there is no agreement as to whether or not these were luxury items that only the rich could afford in times of economic crisis. Nor is there agreement as to what extent they were to remain available for the

---

[6] About a quart; the ordinary daily allowance for one man.

[7] Lit., a "denarius," that is, about a day's wages (Matt. 20:2).

refreshment of the sufferers. Perhaps they were not to be "hurt" [8] because they were used to aid in healing (Luke 10:34). This much is clear: this affliction is limited. God is at all times still in control. He "sets bounds to all calamities beyond which they cannot go." [9]

Rev. 6:7, 8: The Fourth Seal and the "Pale" Horse

The fourth horse was "pale" (Rev. 6:8), that is, yellowish or pale green, the ghastly color of death. It is very fitting that the rider of this horse is called Death. Death seizes and claims the mortal body.

"Hell followed with [after] him" (Rev. 6:8). "Hell," literally, Hades, is a general word for the state of immortal souls before the resurrection of the body.[10] We are not told how it was symbolized in this vision.

The word "death" (in the last part of Rev. 6:8 in the KJV) is rendered "pestilence" in the RSV. This avoids redundancy.[11]

The span of time conveyed by the activity of the fourth horseman extends to the end of the world.

"The fourth part [one fourth] of the earth" (Rev. 6:8), more than a small area, is given into his hands. We must not take "the fourth part" literally, as if only 25 per cent of all people were lost (Matt. 7:13, 14). However, the fact that only a fraction is involved shows that there are limits and bounds to the work of this horseman.

Rev. 6:9-11: The Fifth Seal and the Souls Under the Altar

John "saw under the altar the souls of them that were slain for the Word of God and for the testimony which they held"

---

8 Adversely affected, or prohibitively priced.

9 Little, p. 66.

10 See the notes on Rev. 1:18; 20:13, 14.

11 Ex. 5:3. On "sword," "famine," and "death" (or pestilence); also see Jer. 14:12; 21:7, 9; 24:10; 27:8, 13; Rev. 2:23.

(Rev. 6:9). His vision [12] was not restricted by limitations of time and space.

He saw an altar, of which he immediately speaks as "the" altar, though he has not mentioned it previously. This is graphic language, much like that of a child who sees with his mind's eye an event which he describes, beginning, for example: "I saw this boy running down the street . . . ," without first stopping to say which boy.

John does not describe the altar, but says immediately what he saw "under" the altar: "the souls of them that were slain [slaughtered] for the Word of God" (Rev. 6:9). Their blood had been shed. In the Old Testament the priest poured all the blood of the sacrificial bullock "at the bottom of the altar of the burnt offering" (Lev. 4:7). Perhaps there is a connection between that and John's vision. These saints, whose souls John saw, had been slaughtered; they made the "supreme sacrifice" for their faith.

They had been slain because they held fast the faithful Word and boldly and steadfastly let their faith be known (Rev. 20:4). Stephen and James, the son of Zebedee, and Antipas were among them (Acts 7:54-60; 12:2; Rev. 2:13); so were the Christians who died as living torches in Nero's gardens.

"They cried [out] with a loud voice" (Rev. 6:10), raising their voices in a fervent prayer of appeal. The souls of these martyrs were not in a "soul sleep," but were awake and aware of a number of things.

Their cry was addressed to God as absolute sovereign "Lord" (Rev. 6:10). This is the only time this word is used in the Book of Revelation. It is related to the word "despot" and expresses the thought that the Lord is supreme. Now then, these souls would say, since He is supreme, absolute, sovereign, how long would it be before He would take appropriate action? How much longer

[12] He was "in the spirit" (Rev. 1:10; 4:2)

will He delay who is also "holy and true" (Rev. 6:10), who hates sin and is faithful to His promises? [13] How long until He would judge and avenge their blood on them that dwell on the earth? They know *that* He will do it — but *when?*

This is a cry not for revenge upon those who had slain them but rather for an expression of divine justice upon "them that dwell on the earth." [14] Those who had suffered without just cause (1 Peter 3:14) ask first that God would "judge" (Rev. 6:10). This word in itself does not mean to condemn but simply to pronounce an opinion concerning right and wrong. Then they ask that God would "avenge their blood" (Rev. 6:10), that is, exact the penalty of the crime which had been committed in their death. Finally, they specify of whom the penalty is to be exacted: of "them that dwell on the earth" (Rev. 6:10). This cannot include the godly who are still on this earth, since they are not guilty of the death of the saints. It must mean the ungodly, "who have no home but earth and want no other home." [15] The judgment, condemnation, and execution of punishment takes place on the Last Day. This prayer of the saints is therefore also a prayer for the end of the world. It does not contradict the spirit of Jesus in Luke 23:34 and of Stephen in Acts 7:60, but is rather in harmony with the spirit of Jesus Himself (Matt. 23:34-36; Luke 11:49-51), and of John in the prayer with which he closes the Book of Revelation: "Come, Lord Jesus." (Rev. 22:20)

Each one of the "souls" (martyrs, Rev. 6:9) received a white robe,[16] symbolizing holiness. They were also asked to wait quietly and patiently for a while, "to rest yet for a little season" (Rev. 6:11). We are not told who said that, but the message must have come from God, who alone knows what is to come.

[13] See the notes on Rev. 3:7; also see 1 John 5:20.

[14] Rev. 6:10. The cry is answered in Rev. 19:2; cf. Rev. 18:20.

[15] Lenski, p. 236. See also the notes on Rev. 3:10.

[16] Lit., "stole," a long, loose garment reaching to the feet (Rev. 6:11). See Mark 16:5; Rev. 7:9-14. A different word is used Rev. 3:4, 5, 18; 4:4.

It was not yet time for the end of time. There still remained
"a little season" (6:11). The same expression is used in connection with the loosing of Satan at the end of the 1,000 years
(20:3). But the two periods of time which are called a little
season (6:11; 20:3) are not coextensive. In the case of Rev.
20:3 Satan would no longer be able to do anything to the saints.[17]
In either case we have no way of calculating the exact time of the
"little season." If we take the souls which John saw as representing those who had gone to heaven up to the time of John's vision,
then the "little season" of Rev. 6:11 would be the rest of the
New Testament age, which may seem long to us here on earth
but which is short from the point of view of eternity in heaven.
God here accommodates Himself to human language and concepts. Since there will be no measurable time in heaven, the concept of "a little season" has application only to us who are still
on earth.

The souls under the altar were to await, as it were, the arrival
in heaven of all "their fellow servants also and their brethren
that should be killed as they were" (Matt. 24:9). All who are
Christ's are "fellow servants" and "brethren" of these martyrs
(Rev. 1:1, 9). It is a sobering thought that to the end of time
children of God will die for their faith. Self-preservation is one of
the first laws of nature, but it yields, as necessary, when one is
convinced in the full assurance of faith that there is an eternal
life to come and that to save one's life here on earth would mean
to lose heaven and be forever lost in hell.

When the number of martyrs is complete, then shall the end
come. Then "the souls under the altar" will have the final and
complete answer to their question: "How long. . . ?" In this sense,
and not in any false, millennialistic, or Zionist sense, are we also to
understand such other passages of the Bible as Joel 3:17-21.

17 See the notes on Rev. 20:7, 9.

Rev. 6:12-17: The Sixth Seal and the End of the World

One of the many Bible passages about the end of the world is Rev. 6:12-17.[18] Vv. 12-14 speak of things; vv. 15-17 speak of people.

In the vision which John saw "there was a great shaking."[19] Heaven and earth, the entire created universe,[20] will be "greatly" shaken, down to the very foundations. It will be a universal upheaval and overthrow.

"The sun became black as sackcloth of hair" (Rev. 6:12). Humanly speaking, physical life depends on the light of the sun. If that light is extinguished, Egyptian darkness (Ex. 10:21-23) envelopes the universe. We may think that with the light of the sun its heat too departs, leaving the universe in the grip of the ultimate in extreme cold. Actually, however, the text does not say this. (Also see 2 Peter 3:10, 12)

In John's vision the sun was darkened, literally, "became black" (Rev. 6:12). This was not an ordinary eclipse, but one of the signs immediately preceding the end. The degree of darkness is described in the words "black as sackcloth of hair" (Rev. 6:12). Evidently sackcloth [21] was of a very dark color.

"The moon [lit., the whole, or full, moon] became as blood," that is, red like blood, perhaps as a result of the fading away of the light of the sun, certainly as a sign of imminent calamity and catastrophe.

"The stars of heaven fell unto the earth" (Rev. 6:13; see Is. 34:4). It may be true that the stars are beyond the earth's perceptible pull of gravity. We are simply told here what John

18 Some others are Joel 2:1-11; 3:14,15; Matt. 24:29-31; Luke 21:25-27; 2 Peter 3:10-12; Rev. 16:17-21. Also see Is. 13:6-13.

19 Rev. 6:12. KJV, earthquake. Lit., commotion, upheaval. Cf. Matt. 8:24, a great "shaking" in the sea, that is, a tempest.

20 Heb. 12:26; Mark 13:31; Luke 21:33; Ezek. 38:19,20; Is. 13:13; Joel 2:10; Hag. 2:6; Matt. 24:29; Rev. 16:18.

21 Of which we read also in Matt. 11:21; Luke 10:13; Rev. 11:3; and in many passages in the Old Testament, esp. Is. 50:3.

saw in his vision as one of the signs of the end. The why and
the how of it, both in John's vision and at the end of the world,
are separate questions, the answers to which lie in the will and in
the almighty power of God.

The falling of the stars must have been a highly impressive
picture unfolding before the eyes of John. In order to convey
some of its force to his readers, he compares it to the falling of
"untimely" [22] figs when a mighty wind shakes the tree. Unseasonal figs grow under the leaves during the winter. They do
not ripen to maturity, but dry up and fall to the ground in the
winds of spring (Is. 34:4). If wind can do that, who are we to
doubt that the power of God can make the stars fall on the earth?
It is the part of wisdom for us not to ask unnecessary, curious
questions but rather to be properly prepared for the great Day of
the Lord.

As John's vision of that day continued, he saw how "the
heaven departed as a scroll when it is rolled together" (Rev.
6:14). The "heaven," that is, the expanse of the sky, is here
thought of first as being like an unrolled scroll (Is. 34:4).
A scroll is a roll of writing material. When a scroll has served
its purpose, it is rolled up and put away. So when the end of all
things is at hand, the sky is made to depart; it is put away. It will
have served its purpose; it will be replaced by a "new heaven."
(Rev. 21:1)

"Every mountain and island were moved out of their places"
(Rev. 6:14). Mountains and islands are usually places of refuge
and safety in days of distress, but not on the Last Day. Then the
mountains will tremble, and all the hills will be moved. There
will be no place to hide in all creation, no solid stronghold on
land, no isle of assurance in the waters of the sea. But though the
earth be removed, and though the mountains shake and be carried
into the midst of the sea, yet will not he fear who has God for his
Refuge and Strength, as a very present Help in trouble.[23]

22 Or "unseasonal." Rev. 6:13. See Nahum 3:12.
23 Ps. 46:1-3. Also see the notes on Rev. 16:20.

John describes the effect of the cataclysmic events (Rev. 6:12-14) on six classes of men: (1) "The kings of the earth," rulers over their nations; (2) "the great men," lords (Mark 6:21); (3) "the rich men," the wealthy; (4) "the chief captains," generals, men high in the councils of military strategy and authority; (5) "the mighty men," those who are strong and powerful; (6) "every bondman and every free man," "an expression that is taken from the Roman world of John's time, takes in the entire lower class of men. The whole world had multitudes of slaves and thus also multitudes of slaves who were released freedmen." [24]

These six classes represented different levels in society. But in the extremities of the Last Day the differences among them vanished as they "hid themselves in the dens [caves] and in [among] the rocks [crags] of the mountains" (Rev. 6:15). Death is a great leveler. So is the very prospect of imminent eternity. In John's vision scarcely any king, having entered a cave, would have refused a slave entrance also.

The desperate action and the despairing cry of the people in this vision show that they were ungodly. They ran to hide and cried to the mountains and rocks, "Fall on us" (Rev. 6:16). This is the voice of despair. Anything, even being crushed to death, which they apparently thought would end everything for them, seemed to be better than to live through the end of the world and be taken straight out of it for the even more fearful experience of falling into the hands of a just, angry, and living God (Heb. 10:31). "Hide us," they cry to the mountains and rocks; "conceal us from the face of Him that sitteth on the throne [25] and from the wrath of the Lamb." [26]

Rev. 6:17 is also a part of the cry of those who are lost in their despair. They recognize and admit the fact that "this is it,"

[24] Lenski, p. 242. RSV: "and everyone, slave and free." Some count this as two classes, making a total of seven instead of six.

[25] That is, God the Father; cf. Rev. 4:2; etc.

[26] That is, Jesus Christ. Rev. 6:16; cf. Rev. 5:6; etc.; Hos. 10:8; Amos 9:1-4; Luke 23:30.

as we would say. "The great day of His [their] wrath is come,"
that is, the wrath of God and of the Lamb. This single, final fact
gathers together in fulfillment, once and for all, the many prophecies of that day.[27]

"Who shall be able to stand?" [28] It is significant not only that
the ungodly in this vision are hopeless, as this question shows,
but also that they are obviously familiar with the Bible. They use
the language of the Bible. But it is not enough to know what
is in the Bible and to be able to quote from it or use its language.
Pray God that you may so hear, read, learn, and inwardly keep
the Holy Scriptures that you will find your Savior there. Abiding
in Him, you can abide the day of His coming. Standing in faith
on this Rock, you will, by the grace of God, continue to stand also
when earth and heaven shall pass away!

[27] Mal. 4:1,5; Matt. 7:22; Luke 17:24; 1 Cor. 1:8; 1 Thess. 5:2; 2 Peter 3:10,12;
Rev. 16:14.

[28] Rev. 6:17. Cf. Ps. 76:7; Joel 2:11b; Mal. 3:2.

Rev. 7: The Church

The word *church* means "of, or belonging to, the Lord." But not everything that men call church is necessarily the Lord's. All believers, and only believers, are members of "the holy Christian church, the communion of saints," of which the Third Article of the Apostles' Creed speaks.

Rev. 7 speaks of the church without using the word. The chapter divides as follows: vv. 1-8 speak of the church on earth, the Church Militant (the church at war), the kingdom of grace (of which we become members only by the grace of God and over which Christ rules with His divine grace). Vv. 9-17 speak of the church in heaven, the Church Triumphant, the kingdom of glory.

Rev. 7:1-8: The Church on Earth

Because the Bible speaks of "the four corners of the earth" (Rev. 7:1) some ancient mapmakers drew the world rectangular. They also put fantastic beasts into the four corners, such as they thought might live there. However, the words "the four corners of the earth" do not refer to a flat earth with four literal corners but to the four points of the compass, the complete extent of all the earth.[1]

The angels standing on the four corners of the earth held "the four winds of the earth," that they "should not blow on the

[1] Also see the notes on Rev. 20:8.

earth, nor on the sea, nor on any tree" (Rev. 7:1). They were not free to exercise their power except by the permission and at the direction of God, who sent another angel to them with specific instructions (Rev. 7:2, 3). Even the wind cannot blow without God's permission. The winds in this vision are universal (Matt. 24:31); they might be felt by men on earth or be "seen" in the waves of the sea (Matt. 14:30) and in any tree. Rev. 7:2, 3 indicates that damage can result from these winds.

These winds have been understood either as actual winds, gentle or severe, or as symbolical winds of war (Jer. 49:36-38), persecution, or adversity of any kind. This we know, that not a single leaf of "any tree" can stir in the breeze without God's permission. Nor can anything of a larger and more serious nature occur to hinder His plan and purpose to save the elect.[2]

An angel was sent with a restraining order to the four angels mentioned in Rev. 7:1, forbidding them for the present to hurt either the earth, or the sea, or the trees. This fifth angel "ascended [went up] from the east," literally: from the rising of the sun, "the quarter from which light comes, i.e., the most glorious quarter of the heavens."[3] Until the day of grace is ended and the church stands completed with its last living stone in place, the angels with the winds were to hurt nothing.

The angel who brought this order to the others came equipped with "the seal of the living God" (Rev. 7:2). This seal, whatever it was and looked like, is God's special identification placed upon those who are His, setting them apart from the world and for Himself.[4] He is "the living God,"[5] the only true God.

There is no particular significance in the fact that the angel messenger "ascended"; for the purposes of the vision the four angels who held the winds were no doubt pictured as being in the sky, from where the winds often seem to come. Nor is there any

[2] Rev. 7:3; Rom. 8:29, 30; John 10:27-29.

[3] Sadler, p. 88.

[4] 2 Cor. 1:22; 2 Tim. 2:19; Eph. 1:12-14; 4:30.

[5] Rev. 7:2; see Deut. 5:26; 1 Cor. 15:20.

special meaning in the fact that he "cried with a loud voice" (Rev. 7:2), other than that it would take a loud voice to reach to the "four corners of the earth." We may, however, note that in view of his loud voice he must have been another "strong" angel.[6] Nor is it important that "a tree" is not mentioned at the end of Rev. 7:2 as it is at the end of Rev. 7:1; this is "only abbreviation." [7]

The message of the fifth angel to the other four is: "Hurt not the earth, neither the sea nor the trees" — creation is to stand and continue — "till we have sealed the servants of our God . . ." (Rev. 7:3). "We" means the angel who is speaking and those for whom he is speaking. To seal the servants of God is a part of the work and ministry of the good angels.

"The servants of our God" [8] are the faithful, who serve God with holy works (1 Peter 2:5). Among them were Moses (Rev. 15:3), the prophets,[9] James (James 1:1), Peter (2 Peter 1:1), Jude (Jude 1:1), and all who say with Joshua, "We will serve the Lord" (Joshua 24:15), and with Paul, "Lord, what wilt Thou have me to do?" [10]

All the servants of God are to be "sealed . . . in their foreheads," [11] the noblest part of man's body, where the seal could easily be seen (Rev. 22:4). Those who are touched by the seal are fellow servants of God with the other saints and the angels. They belong to God (Acts 27:23; 1 Cor. 6:19, 20). In the light of Rev. 14:1 we may add here that the seal put the name of Christ and of His Father on their foreheads.

John heard "the number of them which were sealed" (Rev. 7:4), that is, saved. Perhaps it was mentioned by the fifth angel

6 See the notes on Rev. 5:2.

7 Lenski, p. 249.

8 Rev. 1:1; 2:20; 19:2, 5; 22:3, 6.

9 Rev. 10:7; 11:18.

10 Acts 9:6. Also see Acts 27:23.

11 Lit., the space between the eyes (Rev. 7:3).

in speaking to the other four. The number 144,000 [12] is a symbolical number, made by multiplying 12 times 12 times 1,000. It is a misinterpretation of this number to take it literally and include in it those who are found worthy to establish God's rule in a type of millennium [13] or to hold that the number includes only Jewish Christians. 144,000 is a number which represents completeness. It stands for all of God's people. None of them are left unsealed (Rev. 7:3). Rev. 7:2-17 is very appropriately an Epistle for All Saints' Day, Nov. 1.

The 144,000 sealed are drawn from "all the tribes of the Children [sons] of Israel," (Rev. 7:4), 12,000 out of each tribe. The list of tribes in Rev. 7:5-8 cannot be based on the nation of the Jews in its later days, because by then 10 tribes had been lost, and the remaining two had lost their national independence. Nor is it based entirely on the nation of Israel in its earlier days. Neither Dan (Joshua 19:40-48) nor Ephraim (Joshua 16:1-10; 17:13-18) are mentioned in Rev. 7. On the other hand, Joseph and Levi are mentioned, although Joseph died in Egypt (Gen. 50:22-26), and his name does not occur as the head of a tribe in Joshua 13-19, and Levi's tribe was charged with the care of the sanctuary (Num. 1:50-53; etc.) and is not listed among the 12 tribes which received a portion of the Promised Land (Joshua 13:33; etc.). Nor were all the 12 tribes the same size. Under these circumstances we cannot identify the list in Rev. 7:4-8 with the Jewish believers only. Too many inconsistencies and difficulties are involved. The solution lies in taking these verses in a spiritual sense.[14] "These 144,000 are God's great nation, an ordered and organized people. And as being all sealed with the sealing of the servants of God, they constitute the whole number of the saved." [15]

[12] Cf. Rev. 14:1, where John says that he also saw the 144,000.

[13] Also see the notes on Rev. 20.

[14] Gen. 22:18; 32:26-28; Rom. 9:6—11:26; 2:28, 29.

[15] Little, p. 75.

Rev. 7:9-17: The Church in Heaven

John saw the church in heaven, the Church Triumphant, the kingdom of glory — more saints than you can count, innumerable as the stars and as the sand on the seashore[16] — the sum total of the saved, who, while they were on earth, lived in all parts of the world (Rev. 5:9). The fact that no man could number them is one reason why we do not take the figures in Rev. 7:4-8 literally. The fact that it was "a great multitude" (Rev. 7:9) should encourage us when our efforts to win souls for Christ seem to be in vain. And the fact that "all nations, and kindreds, and people, and tongues" (7:9) were represented in the great multitude should move us to engage in worldwide Christian mission work to the fullest extent possible.[17]

The multitude which John saw was "standing." They were "erect, confident, triumphant." [18] The throne before which they stood represents the power and authority, rule and dominion of God.[19] The Lamb is Jesus Christ, the Savior, who sacrificed Himself on the altar of the cross.[20] The "white robes" (Rev. 7:9) the multitude is clothed in are symbols of holiness, righteousness, and festivity.[21] We can stand before God only in such white robes, which become ours when we take them and put them on. That is done when we accept and trust in Christ as our only and all-atoning Savior from sin, death, and hell.

The multitude had "palms in their hands" (Rev. 7:9) as a symbol of festive joy in final and complete victory over every enemy (John 12:13; 1 Cor. 15:26). An old custom puts a little palm branch into the hands of a departed Christian at his burial, as a symbol of his faith and hope.

16 Gen. 15:5; 22:17; 32:12.

17 Is. 55:10-13; Matt. 24:14; 28:19, 20; Mark 16:15, 16. Also see the notes on Rev. 5:9.

18 James Moffatt, in the EGT, V, 398, on Rev. 7:9. Cf. Luke 21:28.

19 Also see the notes on Rev. 1:4; 4:2.

20 John 1:29; Heb. 7:26, 27; Rev. 5:6.

21 See the notes on Rev. 3:4.

The song of the church in heaven (Rev. 7:10) is a hymn of praise: "Salvation to our God which sitteth upon the throne and unto the Lamb!" All credit and glory for our salvation belongs to Him! He is both the Author and the Finisher of our faith and salvation (Heb. 5:9; 12:2). Moffatt puts it this way: "Saved by our God . . . and by the Lamb!" We are not saved by our own good works. They do not even help us get to heaven. Salvation is entirely a free gift of God's grace in Christ Jesus.[22]

In heaven there will be an eternal Christmas and Easter. The song of the redeemed exalts the praises of God the Father, whose love gave the world a Savior, and of God the Son, the Lamb, who defeated the last enemy, which is death (1 Cor. 15:26), in His resurrection.

As the saints stand and sing (Rev. 7:9, 10), the angels, who "stood round about the throne and about the elders and the four beasts" (5:11), fall on their faces in an attitude of worship (11:16; Lev. 9:24). Their song (Rev. 7:12) begins and ends with "Amen," that is Yea, it shall be so! (5:14). Their doxology is very similar to the chants in Rev. 5:11-13, adding only "thanksgiving."[23] Blessing, glory, etc., are again[24] ascribed to God as properly belonging only to Him.

While John saw this vision, one of the elders in it asked him: "What [who] are these which are arrayed in white robes? And whence came they?" (Rev. 7:13). John replied respectfully, "Sir [my Lord], thou knowest" (Rev. 7:14). He did not say, "I do not know." Perhaps he could have given an answer. But he was ready and willing to listen to words of wisdom higher than his own. He courteously stepped back from the question and suggested that the elder himself give the answer. He recognized his limitations — and so should we. It is not necessary for us to answer every question that is raised in the field of religion. Some-

---

22 Rom. 3:19-28; Eph. 2:4-9. — On the words "which sitteth upon the throne" and "the Lamb" see the notes on Rev. 4:2, 3; 5:6.

23 Included in Rev. 4:9.

24 As in Rev. 4:9-11; 5:11-13.

times the highest wisdom consists in placing a finger on the lips of our small knowledge and quietly, humbly, awaiting the answer of the One who really knows — waiting patiently, if the answer is not immediately given.

The elder gave John a twofold answer (Rev. 7:14-17):

1. "These are they which came out of great tribulation." [25] Some think this means a special, great tribulation at the end of time, just before the final coming of Christ. But Dan. 12:1, cited as proof, really speaks only of the climax of the great tribulation, and Matt. 24:21 speaks of the destruction of Jerusalem, a type of the end of the world. Besides, the final climax of the great tribulation will not strike the entire church, which John saw in heaven, but only those of the faithful who will be alive on earth at the time of the end. We therefore take the expression "the great tribulation" in Rev. 7:14 to mean the suffering through which the children of God in all ages pass before they enter into the eternal kingdom of God. (Acts 14:22; 1 Peter 3:14)

2. "These are they which . . . have washed their robes and made them white in the blood of the Lamb." [26] This is a highly concentrated figure of speech. The blood of Christ, shed for the forgiveness of our sins, is red. A garment washed in blood would become red. But when our sins are forgiven we are holy, and white is the symbol of holiness, purity, and forgiveness.[27]

The robes are washed and made white by those who are saved. They do this by repentance and faith (Mark 1:15). In Baptism the Word of God and faith work forgiveness of sins, deliver from death and the devil, and give eternal salvation. It is a "washing of regeneration" (Titus 3:5; Acts 22:16). Though Baptism is performed only once in our lives, it is of daily significance. We should renew our baptismal vow daily. In this sense every day is washday in the life of a Christian. This washing is

[25] Rather, "the great tribulation" (Rev. 7:14).

[26] Rev. 7:14. See the notes on Rev. 22:14.

[27] Also see Is. 1:18; Phil. 3:9; Heb. 9:14; 1 John 1:7-9; Rev. 7:9.

not in any sense work or effort on our part. For all labor on our part in this washing has been made unnecessary by Him who does all for us. (Rom. 3:28; Eph. 2:8,9)

"Therefore," because they are saved alone by the blood of Christ, they are "before the throne of God," face to face with Him in His blessed presence,[28] and "serve Him day and night in His temple" (Rev. 7:15), or sanctuary, heaven.[29] There the saints "serve" God, not in drudgery, as slaves, but in that perfection of which the worship and service of the church on earth is to be a type.[30] They serve Him "day and night," though there is no literal night in heaven (Rev. 21:25; 22:5). "Day and night" means "continually, constantly, without ceasing."

"He that sitteth on the throne shall dwell among them."[31] There is much more here than the simple thought of God living among, or with, the saints in heaven. The verb is related to the word for tent, or tabernacle, and literally means that God will spread his tent, or tabernacle, over the saved in heaven, so that they may dwell in safety and security under its cover and protection.[32]

Rev. 7:16, 17 tells of the final, complete, and perfect fulfillment of Christ's promises in Matt. 5:6 and John 6:35. In heaven the saints "shall hunger no more, neither thirst any more" (Rev. 7:16a), neither physically nor spiritually. Hunger and thirst, and the burning light of the sun, and scorching, painful heat (Rev. 7:16b), represent the various trials and afflictions which the children of God suffer on earth because of their faith. All to-

---

[28] 1 Cor. 13:12; Ps. 16:11; 17:15.

[29] See the notes on Rev. 3:12.

[30] See Ps. 100, esp. v. 2, compared with Rev. 7:10, 15. Also see Rev. 22:3.

[31] Rev. 7:15. The 1941 Catholic translation: "dwell with."

[32] For similar or related thoughts see Deut. 33:12; Ps. 91:4; Ezek. 37:26, 27; Rev. 12:12; 13:6; 21:3. The RSV expresses the sense very well: "He will shelter them with His presence."

gether, they are "the great tribulation" of Rev. 7:14. These things are forever past for the saints in heaven.[33]

The saints in glory, under the direct, personal, loving care of the Son of God, are free from every evil. "The Lamb which is in the midst of the throne[34] shall feed them."[35] As their Shepherd He will "lead them unto living fountains of waters."[36] For those who drink of the waters of life forever at their very source and fountainhead there is no more death, or sorrow, or crying, or pain — and no more tears! (Also see Rev. 21:4; Is. 25:8; 49:10.) "God shall wipe away all tears from their eyes" (Rev. 7:17; cf. Ps. 126). When God wipes tears away, they are wiped away forever. Nor does He wipe only some tears away from the eyes of the saints, but "all tears!"[37]

[33] Also see Rev. 21:1: "no more sea," and 21:4.

[34] See the notes on Rev. 5:6.

[35] Rev. 7:17. Lit., "He will be their Shepherd." See Is. 40:11; Ps. 23; John 10:11-16, 27-29; Heb. 13:20; 1 Peter 2:25; 5:4.

[36] Rev. 7:17. Lit., "to the fountains of the waters of life." See John 4:14; 10:10; Rev. 21:6; 22:1.

[37] Lit., "every tear."

Rev. 8 concludes the series of visions in which the Lamb opens the seven seals of the scroll (cf. Rev. 6:1, 3, 5, 7, 9, 12). The chapter begins a new series in which seven trumpets are sounded by seven angels. (Rev. 8:7, 8, 10, 12; 9:1, 13; 11:15)

Rev. 8:1: The Seventh Seal Opened

"Silence in heaven!" This impressive hush of reverence and expectancy[1] is in strong contrast to the resounding hymns of praise with which the saints and angels had filled heaven (Rev. 7:10, 12). The calm helped provide a most effective setting for what followed, for it was shattered by the crash of thunder and "voices."[2] The calm lasted about half an hour. Since there is no time in the eternity of heaven, this mention of time is an adaptation to the language and concepts of earth. Time seems to pass slowly when there is complete silence. Added to the suspense of the vision itself, that fact may have made the half hour seem long.

Rev. 8:2: Seven Angels with Seven Trumpets

John speaks of "the" seven angels as if he had already referred to them. Therefore some think here of the "seven spirits" (Rev. 1:4; 4:5; 5:6). Others point to the apocryphal book of

---

[1] Cf. Ps. 46:10; Hab. 2:20; Zeph. 1:7; Zech. 2:13.

[2] Phillips "noises" (Rev. 8:5).

Tobit: "I am Raphael, one of the seven holy angels which present the prayers of the saints and go in before the glory of the Holy One" (Tobit 12:15). But Rev. 8:2 merely uses vivid, graphic language, similar to that in Rev. 6:9.

There were seven[3] angels in this vision. They "stood before God," ready for action, to carry out His commands at His beck and call.[4] Seven trumpets were given to them; we are not told by whom, nor are the trumpets further described. John here mentions only what is essential. Then the angels and their trumpets yield the center of attraction and attention (until Rev. 8:6) to "another angel."

Rev. 8:3-5: The Angel with the Golden Censer

"Another angel" (Rev. 7:2; 14:18; etc.) appeared on the scene. He stood at "the" altar which appeared in this scene.[5] It was a golden altar, used for the burning of incense (Ex. 30:1-8), "before the throne," in the presence of God. (Ex. 30:6)

The angel had a golden censer, a vessel for holding incense while it is being burned.[6] He did not supply the incense himself, but it was given to him. "It is given to him by Christ, whose meritorious obedience and death are the incense, rendering the saints' prayers well-pleasing to God. . . . Christ alone is the Mediator through whom, and to whom, prayer is to be offered." [7] The smoke of the incense is "Christ's special intercession for His believing people, adding power and efficacy to their prayers." [8]

The incense is associated with prayers (Ps. 141:2; Luke 1: 9, 10). There was "much" of it "because the occasion was one

---

3 The number *seven* may be regarded as referring to God's dealing with the world of men. See the notes on Rev. 1:4.

4 Ps. 103:20, 21; Matt. 18:10; Luke 1:19; Heb. 1:14.

5 The same vivid manner of expression as in Rev. 6:9; 8:2.

6 1 Kings 7:50; 2 Chron. 4:22; Heb. 9:4.

7 Jamieson, Fausset, and Brown, on Rev. 8:3. Cf. Eph. 5:2.

8 Little, p. 81. See 1 John 2:1; Rom. 8:34.

on which many prayers might be expected to be offered"[9] and because it was to accompany the prayers of "all" saints.

The mission which this angel stood ready to perform was to offer ["mingle" RSV] the incense with the prayers of all saints upon the golden altar. As he went about this task, the smoke of the incense went up with the prayers of the saints out of his hand before God (Rev. 8:4; Lev. 16:12, 13). Both the incense and the prayers were acceptable to God.

Note (1) the incense in this vision is not a symbol of the prayers of the saints. It accompanies their prayers. (2) The angel does not bring any prayer to God. Prayers ascend directly from the saints to God. The angel handles incense and adds it to the prayers as a sweet smelling savor. (3) The angel himself does not pray. The prayers are those of the saints — not only some of the saints but "all" of them. Everyone who is a child of God by faith in Christ Jesus is a saint (2 Cor. 1:1; etc.) and has the privilege of addressing God in prayer. (4) This passage does not say that the angels and saints in heaven pray for us or carry our prayers to God; nor does it give us any reason to believe that we should pray to them.[10]

The tranquil scene at the altar of incense was interrupted when the angel took the censer and filled it with fire from the altar and threw it (the fire) on the earth (Rev. 8:5; Ezek. 10:2), as a symbol of God's wrath (Rev. 20:9). It is God's answer to "all ungodliness and unrighteousness of men, who hold the truth in unrighteousness" ["suppress the truth" RSV] (Rom. 1:18) and also an answer to the prayers of the saints.[11]

There were also "voices [loud noises, blasts, rumblings], and thunderings [peals of thunder], and lightnings [flashes of lightning], and an earthquake."[12] God has the final word. His over-

---

[9] Barnes, on Rev. 8:3.

[10] Also see the notes on Rev. 5:8.

[11] See the notes on Rev. 8:7; 15:1.

[12] Lit., "a shaking," not necessarily confined to the earth. Rev. 8:5. See Ps. 29 and the notes on Rev. 6:12.

ruling power prevails. His judgments are just and inescapable. The scourges of destruction which He sends on the earth are warnings of their climax in the final Judgment. (Rev. 11:18, 19; 16:18)

Obviously there is a connection between the scene in Rev. 8:3-5 and the seven angels with the trumpets. The angel with the censer appears immediately after the seven angels with the trumpets have been introduced and immediately before they prepare themselves to sound. The scene of the angel with the censer is by way of background and preparation for that which is to follow. There had been silence in heaven for about half an hour (8:1), the seven angels with the trumpets had stood in silence, and the angel with the censer performed his ministration in silence until he cast fire from the altar on the earth. Then the silence was shattered (8:5), and the seven angels prepared themselves to sound. (8:6)

Rev. 8:6: The Seven Angels Prepare to Sound Their Trumpets

It was an impressive moment of tense anticipation as the seven angels prepared to sound. The visions connected with the seven seals had repeatedly spanned time and finally carried over into eternity. What would the seven trumpets bring?

In the scenes which follow, the trumpets sound singly, consecutively, each introducing a separate vision. The first four trumpets, like the first four seals, belong together. They are set off from the others by the angel (eagle) in Rev. 8:13.

Rev. 8:7: The First Trumpet

In this verse there is a mixture of things not normally found together: hail, fire, and blood. God can mix and mingle them, as He did in Egypt at the time of Moses (Ex. 9:23-25) and as He threatened against Gog.[13] Some believe that the picture described here is that of an unexpected, quick hailstorm with fiery

[13] Ezek. 38:22. Also see Ps. 18:12, 13; Joel 2:30.

lightning, the blood being that of its victims.[14] Hail brings sudden destruction (Ex. 9:18-31), as though stones were falling from heaven (Joshua 10:11). Fire causes devastation, with added suffering from its heat. Blood indicates physical injury and possible death for man and beast.

The combination of the three, "cast upon the earth," is a symbol of God's anger going into action.[15] The expressions in this verse are general and must not be limited to any specific application. The following thoughts, however, are suggested by the text. Those who stoned the faithful [16] would be stoned by God from heaven, though not necessarily with literal hail; those who burned the martyrs at the stake in the Christian persecutions would themselves suffer for it; those who shed the blood of the saints in any way (Heb. 11:33-38) would receive their own due reward. It has also been suggested that the events introduced by the first four trumpets symbolize religious delusions as a punishment of God upon those who reject the knowledge of the truth.[17]

The effects of the mingled hail, fire, and blood cast on the earth are mentioned in the last part of Rev. 8:7. Here Luther and the King James translators did not have the best Greek text. This part of the verse should read: "They were cast upon the earth, and the third part of the earth was burnt up, and the third part of the trees, etc."

Who can say with final authority what is signified by the fact that only a third [18] of the earth and a third of the trees was burnt up, while all of the grass was burnt up? Or why the destruction by fire is mentioned three times, while no damage by hail is mentioned? Or what the meaning of "earth," "trees," and "grass" is? Still less are we able to date the fulfillment of this vision by point-

14 *Hirschberger Bibel.*

15 Also see the notes on Rev. 8:5; 15:1.

16 Matt. 23:37; Luke 13:34; Acts 7:59; 2 Chron. 24:21.

17 Compare Rev. 8:7-11 with Hos. 4:6; Hag. 2:17.

18 The fraction "one third" occurs again in similar settings in Rev. 8:8-12; 9:15-18.

ing to any specific events in history. Here is simply a prophecy of God's terrible judgments. They will surely come. They affect more than a small portion of the earth. They will be completely carried out. There is no escape for the doomed.

With the unfolding of this vision we note also that an increasingly extensive part of creation is affected by the judgments of God until the seventh trumpet heralds the end of the world. The nature of some of these judgments reminds us of the Egyptian plagues (Ex. 7:19—12:30). But even Egypt with its darkness, both physical and spiritual, suffered nothing so fearful as this.

Rev. 8:8, 9: The Second Trumpet

The only other Bible passage which speaks of "something like a great mountain burning with fire" (Rev. 8:8 RSV) is Jer. 51:25, where God threatens to make Babylon "a burnt mountain." [19] Both passages speak of God's anger and judgments.

John saw how the great mountain burning with fire "was cast into the sea" (Rev. 8:8). Huge waves must have been caused when the mountain struck the sea with a hissing noise and the hot mass fell into the water. But John says nothing of this. His pen moves quickly to tell of another, altogether unexpected development: "the third part of the sea became blood" (Rev. 8:8), a vivid symbol and instrument of widespread death and destruction. One third of the creatures in the sea died. Why should they suffer? Did land animals die when the earth, trees, and grass were burned? The destruction wrought in this vision included one third of the ships too — no small number (Rev. 8:9). With those who were in them? Is there a connection between this verse and Rev. 20:13? Were the ships destroyed by the heat of the mountain's fire, or were they struck by it when it was cast into the sea? Were they driven on the rocks, did they collide, or did they founder in the high waves which resulted?

Had God wanted us to know, He would have told us. In what

[19] Ex. 19:18 speaks of fire on the mount, not of a mount on fire.

He does say we see a reflection of Heb. 10:31: "It is a fearful thing to fall into the hands of the living God!" Rev. 8:8, 9 sets before us in a few bold strokes a symbolic picture of the shape of some of the dreadful things to come before the end of time. It is far better to know how to escape these things than to learn by experience what they include.

Rev. 8:10, 11: The Third Trumpet

The star-spangled curtain of the heavens on a clear night apparently provided the backdrop against which the action in this vision took place. A large star, burning like a lamp, fell from heaven. It was not simply a shooting star, which burns out before reaching the earth. Even a meteorite, striking the earth, affects only a comparatively small area. But the star which John saw "fell on a third of the rivers and on the fountains of waters" (Rev. 8:10). The main thought is that of increasing and expanding destruction.

"The name of the star is called Wormwood [lit., Absinthe, Rev. 8:11]." Since there is no natural star by that name, we look for a clue to the meaning of this vision in the meaning of the star's name. "Absinthe," or wormwood (Luther, *Wermuth*), is a bitter herb. When the star fell on the waters, they became bitter (Ex. 15:25 in reverse). Absinthe is not necessarily a fatal poison, but it can become so when it is used in place of water. "Many died of the waters because they were made bitter" (Rev. 8:11). Calamity and destruction continue to increase and spread.

The language is symbolic. Its interpretation is difficult. Some think the star represents Lucifer, the devil.[20] Others say teachers and leaders in the church are associated with stars (Dan. 12:3; Rev. 1:20). A large or great star, bright as a torch, indicates an outstanding person. His falling from heaven means that he was rejected by God. The fact that men died of the waters which he made bitter refers to the soul-destroying effect of his false doctrine.

20 Perhaps because of Is. 14:12; Luke 10:18.

So they point, as Luther did, to Origen (about A. D. 185—254), who denied the physical resurrection and assumed the pre-existence and pretemporal fall of souls, an eternal creation, the final restoration of all men and fallen angels, etc.; or to Pelagius (about A. D. 360—420), who taught that man's nature is not depraved since Adam's fall; or to Arius (died A. D. 336), who denied the deity of Christ; or to Pope Gregory the Great (died A. D. 604). The "rivers" and "fountains of waters" are then understood as being the wellsprings of divine wisdom, knowledge, and truth, which are to provide relief and life for thirsty souls,[21] but which, being corrupted, become bitter and cause spiritual and eternal death.

Rev. 8:12: The Fourth Trumpet

Whatever it was that struck the heavenly bodies, the result was partial darkness, which affected both day and night. The light of the sun, moon, and stars was dimmed by one third. This weird phenomenon is not to be explained as an eclipse, which occurs either by day or by night, but not by both in immediate succession, or simultaneously, and which never affects one third of the stars.

Here, as in the previous visions, the important thing is not the possibility of the phenomenon but rather its significance and effects. Since there are three more trumpets to come, this fourth one and its accompanying vision cannot refer to the end of the world, as do the phenomena following the opening of the sixth seal (Rev. 6:12, 13). Neither is there any clear connection between this vision and any specific historical events nor is there any reason to interpret this vision literally, inasmuch as the entire context is figurative.

We have here, perhaps, a picture of the further effects of false doctrine and religious delusion. The Word of God is a lamp unto our feet and a light unto our path (Ps. 119:105). The Gospel has shined like the light of the sun (Luke 1:79; 2 Cor. 4:6).

---

[21] Cf. Prov. 18:4; Is. 12:3; 32:6; 55:1.

Jesus is the Sun of righteousness (Mal. 4:2) and the bright Morning Star (Rev. 2:28; 22:16; 2 Peter 1:19). Those who shut their
eyes to Him will find that they cannot see Him when they want to
(Matt. 13:13-15; Amos 8:11, 12). Without the Word of God
the foolish heart of man is darkened (Rom. 1:21), and he gropes
about as in darkness. This judgment of God is not localized or
limited to any one point of time or age, but it falls on all who
reject knowledge (Hos. 4:6). For those who are so left in darkness there is little comfort in the thought that they have lost only
one third of the light. "Terrible is the judgment when the light
of the Word is taken away to any degree." [22]

Rev. 8:13: Introduction to the Three Woes

This verse is a short interlude between the first four trumpets
and the last three.

According to the best manuscripts, John saw an eagle [not an
"angel," KJV] in this vision. An eagle appears repeatedly in the
Bible as a symbol of God's consuming judgments.[23] Here an eagle
flies in the midst of heaven, at its zenith, as though it were about
to plummet on its prey. At this very moment of high suspense
it cries a warning with a loud voice. So the eagle is here not an
instrument of death and destruction, but rather a prophet of
danger and doom, as if it shouted: "Look out below! The final
and most fearful judgments of God are about to fall on you!"
It is neither possible nor necessary to identify this eagle with any
one individual in history. The important thing is the warning
cry — and that we heed it!

The threefold "Woe" corresponds to the final three trumpets
(Rev. 9:12; 11:14; 12:12). "The inhabiters of the earth" is an
expression used repeatedly in the Book of Revelation for those
who reject the saving Gospel of Jesus Christ and are earthly
minded.[24]

[22] Lenski, p. 282.
[23] Deut. 28:49; Hos. 8:1; Hab. 1:8.
[24] See the notes on Rev. 3:10.

Rev. 9:1-12: The Fifth Trumpet and the First Woe

"I saw a star fallen [1] from heaven unto the earth" (Rev. 9:1). John does not say that he saw the star in its motion of falling, but speaks of it as a fallen star, personified, and as being able to act. (Rev. 9:2)

A key was given to him, that is, to the star; we are not told who gave the key, but it was given with God's permission or at His direction (Rev. 1:18). We therefore take the star as representing the fact that the judgment which takes place in connection with this trumpet comes from God. The key is the power to control the entrance to "the bottomless pit." [2] The star does not represent Satan, for he fell not "unto the earth" but into the abyss itself (Jude 6) as into a prison, and he has no key or power to open its shaft and release himself or any of his followers. (Rev. 20:7)

In Rev. 9:2 the pit is opened, and heavy, billowing clouds of thick smoke, pregnant with noisome, noxious locusts, burst forth. The smoke, "as the smoke of a great furnace" (Rev. 9:2), darkened the sun and the air (Gen. 19:28). Perhaps there is no better interpretation of this than that which relates it to the darkening

[1] Not "fall," as in the KJV. Luther, *gefallen*.

[2] Lit., "the shaft of the bottomless pit" (Rev. 9:1). There is no special significance in the fact that Rev. 9:1, 2 speaks of the "pit," or "shaft," of the abyss, while Rev. 20:1-3 mentions only the "abyss" itself. Obviously the thought in Rev. 9:1, 2 is simply that of an entrance into the abyss which widens as one goes into it. See the notes on Rev. 20:1-3, 10.

of the heavenly bodies which followed the fourth trumpet.[3] There
the light of the sun was dimmed. Here the air is affected, filled
with infernal smoke. One thinks instinctively of coughing, chok-
ing, sore eyes, etc.; but John mentions none of this — only a darkening pall which hung over the world, big with ominous fore-
boding. God's truth still shines, but men no longer see it. Their
minds are blinded. There is a veil on their heart.[4] It is a fearful
thing for man not to be able to see what he needs to see most
of all, the Sun of righteousness. (Mal. 4:2; also see Joel 2:2, 10)

In Rev. 9:3 the evil brood of the bottomless pit comes to life
in the smoke. Locusts, with "power" like that of scorpions, descend
on the earth. The smoke had screened their escape out of the
abyss. Now that they are at large, man cannot control them
(Joel 2:3-9). It is as futile to try to beat back a large swarm of
locusts in flight as to attempt to sweep back the ocean with
a broom. (Ex. 10:12-15)

"Power," that is, authority, or the ability to act effectively,
was "given" to the locusts. They could carry out their mission
only with God's permission. Their power was as that of "the
scorpions of the earth" (Rev. 9:3), which are mentioned by way
of comparison and as distinct from the locusts, which came out of
the bottomless pit.

The description of the locusts in the following verses clearly
points to a supernatural phenomenon, not to a natural plague or
scourge. We may think of an increasingly larger development
of the curse of religious delusion. The course of error in religion
is always this, that it first asks to be tolerated, then it demands
equal rights, and finally it insists on exercising controlling power.
It is not satisfied until it has blotted out the light of truth and
translated its own power into action.

Rev. 9:4 speaks of the victims of the locusts in the vision.
The locusts were forbidden to hurt the grass of the earth, or any

---

[3] See the notes on Rev. 8:12.

[4] Rom. 1:21; Eph. 4:18; Heb. 6:4-6; 2 Cor. 3:14, 15.

green growth, or any tree. This prohibition originated with God, who alone is able to control even the most powerful forces of evil and who sets limits and bounds beyond which they cannot go.

Grass appears in this vision, even though "all green grass was burnt up" in the judgment connected with the first trumpet sound (Rev. 8:7). This shows that these visions do not refer to consecutive events. They run parallel or simultaneously, each spanning the New Testament age in its own way.

The fact that the locusts were not to hurt any plant growth shows that they are not to be taken literally. Their victims were to be found only among mankind, more specifically, "only those men [people] which have not the seal of God in their foreheads" [5] Those who have "the seal of God in their foreheads" are the elect. God has elected them to salvation. In His providence God watches over them, defends them against all danger, and guards and protects them from all evil. Those who "have not the seal of God in their foreheads" have rejected the saving knowledge of the Gospel. Therefore God also rejects them (Hos. 4:6), so that they are left exposed and defenseless in the day of this judgment.

Not death but excruciating torment short of death is their lot (Rev. 9:5). Even in inflicting this pain their tormentors do not act by their own authority, but "it was given them," that is, they were allowed to do their evil work. They could proceed only by permission, and only so long as God let them, that is "for five months" (Rev. 9:5, 10), the usual length of the locust season. The scourge will run its full course. But while its duration is not short, it is definitely limited.

The nature of the torment is described as "the torment of a scorpion when he striketh a man" (Rev. 9:5). This implies the sting of a scorpion, which is not specifically mentioned until Rev. 9:10. The sting of some scorpions is worse in its painful effects than that of others, varying largely with their size.

All of this, however, is not the actual judgment itself, but

[5] Rev. 9:4; see Ezek. 9:4; Rev. 7:2, 3; 14:1; 22:4.

is merely a comparative, symbolic way of speaking. In casting about for an interpretation, one can scarcely avoid the thought of the agonizing, gnawing pangs of conscience (Rom. 2:15), which are an inevitable result of departing from the ways of God and which often scarcely permit a man to live even with himself.

"In those days shall men seek death and shall not find it, and shall desire to die, and death shall flee [flies, or flees] from them" (Rev. 9:6). Cf. Job 3:21. Many commentators leave this verse uninterpreted. We may, however, draw from it at least the thought of inconceivably excruciating torment, which drives its victims into despair and which cannot be relieved in any way, not even by death. Every human soul is immortal.

Rev. 9:7-10: A description of the locusts. The great detail in which this description is given suggests that this vision appeared to John in such a way that he saw the locusts at very close range. But being one of the elect, he was not hurt by them. This fact must have served to encourage and comfort him, not only as the vision was unfolding but also during the remainder of his life.

The details in the description of this vision suggest that there may be some special significance attached to each one of the various features. The Bible does not explain them (Joel 1 and 2). But this much is clear, that the plague of locusts is a unified picture, whose message and meaning must not be lost, destroyed, or obscured by overemphasis of some of its minor details. The principal feature lies in the over-all effect of horror, pain, and suffering. Only with this firmly and constantly in mind can we safely venture a brief, passing glance at the single, separate parts of this picture of devilish monstrosity let loose from hell to afflict unbelieving men.

First, the locusts are compared to "horses prepared unto battle" (Rev. 9:7), a symbol of power and struggle — a sight calculated to strike fear and terror into the heart of the enemy and a sight indicating the planning and preparation which preceded the attack.

"On their heads were, as it were, crowns like gold" (Rev. 9:7), symbols of victory, worn already before the battle is joined. Victory is assured. For the enemy there is no effective defense or escape.

The faces of the locusts "were as the faces of men," [6] adding to the deception of religious delusion. The suggestion to depart from the Word and will and ways of God draws for persuasive power on an appeal to human reason and man's intelligence.

"They had hair as the hair of women" (Rev. 9:8). Human hair fits naturally into the picture of human faces (Rev. 9:7). But the hair of women does not seem to fit in with going out to battle (Rev. 9:7,9). Some have suggested that this is a reference to seductiveness and indulgence of the base passions. Perhaps it is simply to add to the illusion of harmlessness.

"Their teeth were as the teeth of lions" (Rev. 9:8) — strong, sharp, and slashing; yet their purpose was not to kill but only to hurt (Rev. 9:5; Joel 1:6). A wild lion abroad is a great terror. (1 Peter 5:8,9)

"They had breastplates, as it were breastplates of iron." Many forget how brittle and ineffective are the lances of their vaunted, self-made character and how light and fragile are the arrows of their sudden resolution.

"The sound of their wings was as the sound of chariots of many horses running to battle" (Rev. 9:9), overrunning everything in their path (Joel 2:5). Horses and chariots were the power which usually turned the tide of battle in ancient days. The side which had the most of them held the balance of power and could not be successfully opposed. The locusts were innumerable. The noise of their wings, like that of many chariots with horses, spoke plainly of complete victory.

Rev. 9:10 reviews some of Rev. 9:5 and adds "tails" and "stings," implied in the previous description.

In all of this there was no killing but only hurting, or tor-

6 Rather, "like human faces," RSV (Rev. 9:7).

turing — torment as of a hell on earth. The way of the impenitent transgressor is hard.[7]

Rev. 9:11: the king of the locusts. Natural locusts have no leader. But the locusts in John's vision have a leader, literally, a "king," that is, one who rules over them with authority and influence. This "king" is not one of their own number but "the angel of the bottomless pit." This expression neither occurs nor is explained elsewhere in the Bible. Some hold that it refers to Satan, an angel whose home is the bottomless pit,[8] where he is head and chief.

John gives the name of the angel of the bottomless pit. In Hebrew he is called *Abaddon*[9] and in Greek *Apollyon*. Both names refer to destruction and perdition and so fit into the picture of soul-destroying delusions (1 Tim. 6:9, 10). He who bears them is to be marked and noted by both Jews and Greeks (or Gentiles). This is a part of the Old Testament picture as well as the New.

"One woe is past" (Rev. 9:12) marks the end of this vision. It has passed out of John's sight. Its fulfillment, however, extends over all of the remaining span of earth's time. "Behold, there come two woes more hereafter" (Rev. 9:12), that is, in the sequence of revelation given to John.

Rev. 9:13-21: The Sixth Trumpet and the Second Woe

Of the identity of the angel in this vision nothing more is known than of the other six in this series. Nor can the time of his sounding of the trumpet be identified with any specific latter-day date in history. The events prophesied by each of the first six trumpet visions take place during the New Testament age. (Eph. 6:12)

In this sixth vision in this series John "heard a voice" (Rev. 9:13). Apparently he did not see who spoke. He does not de-

---

[7] Also see Matt. 8:29; Mark 5:7; Luke 8:28; 16:23, 28.

[8] See the notes on Rev. 9:1, 2.

[9] See Job 26:6; 31:12; Ps. 88:11; Prov. 15:11.

scribe the voice. We may regard it as the voice of God, for only God can restrain and release the angels and send them into action. (Rev. 9:14)

The voice came "from the four horns of the golden altar which is before God." [10] The Bible does not attach any special symbolical meaning to the "horns." "From the horns of the golden altar" means from the center of the altar table, where the incense burned.

"Before God" (Rev. 9:13) corresponds to "before the throne" (8:3), that is, the golden altar is in the presence of God (Ex. 30:6). The voice goes out from the presence of God, and the judgment which follows takes place at His direction. In His holiness (Rev. 4:8) He condemns and punishes those who do not repent. (Rev. 9:20, 21)

The voice spoke to the angel of the sixth trumpet, saying, "Loose [release, set free] the four angels which are bound in [at] the great river Euphrates" (Rev. 9:14). This angel is the only one of the seven with an assignment besides that of blowing a trumpet heralding judgment.

The four angels at the Euphrates had been "bound" (Rev. 9:14). This may indicate that they were evil angels, held in check by the power of God.[11] They were bound at "the great river Euphrates" (Rev. 9:14). The Euphrates in southwest Asia is 1,700 miles long. It flows south through eastern Turkey, northeast Syria, and western Iraq to join the Tigris, which is east of it. In this area the great world powers of the Old Testament, Assyria, Babylon, and Persia, had their beginnings. By association with them the river Euphrates takes on the larger significance and symbolism of world domination in its grass roots. (Cf. Rev. 16:12)

At the direction of the voice the four angels were loosed (Rev. 9:15). They lost no time in going about their work. They "were

10 Rev. 9:13. Cf. Ex. 30:2, 3, 6; 37:25, 26; also see the description of the altar of burnt offering in Ex. 27:2; 38:2.

11 *Hirschberger Bibel.*

prepared" (Rev. 9:15), they had been made ready, and they were kept in readiness, to go into action at a moment's notice and for a period of time determined by God and known only to Him (Acts 1:7) — "an hour," etc. (Rev. 9:15). The best manuscripts read: *"the* hour, and day, and month, and year." God's plans are specific with regard to their timing. These angels were bound and could not move until God was ready for it.[12]

When loosed, they were "to slay the third part of men" (Rev. 9:15). Loss of human life was perhaps an incidental by-product in some of the previous visions in the trumpet series. But it is the specific scourge in this vision. One third (Rev. 8:7-12) of mankind falls under it.

The transition from Rev. 9:15 to 16 is very abrupt, reflecting the rapid sequence of events in the vision: the sound of the sixth trumpet, a voice from the altar, the four angels loosed at the river Euphrates, and now suddenly and without further introduction: a vast multitude of military horsemen, more than the world had ever seen assembled at one time. There were many more than John could easily or quickly count. Yet he is able to say how many there were — 200 million [13] — because he "heard the number of them" (Rev. 9:16). He does not say, however, who spoke the number, where the voice came from, or what it sounded like.

A common interpretation of this prophecy looks for its fulfillment in the hordes of the Saracens, or Mohammedans, whose waves of conquest engulfed much of Asia, Africa, and Europe and brought death also to countless Christians. Their havoc may have been in partial fulfillment of this prophecy, which speaks in a larger way of fatal punishment of the impenitent whenever and wherever God directs and permits.

In Rev. 9:17 John describes the cavalry as he saw it in the vision, both horses and riders. The horsemen had breastplates in colors of which at least two: fire (red) and brimstone (yellow),

---

[12] Also see the notes on Rev. 14:15.

[13] Literally, "twice ten thousand times ten thousand."

are associated with hell.[14] "Jacinth"[15] is a dark red-blue, border-ing on black. "The heads of the horses were as the heads of lions" (Rev. 9:17), conveying the impression of great courage and strength, coupled with a quick readiness for violent and bloody action.[16] Their appearance was enough to frighten and dismay the heart of the bravest enemy. But their real deadliness lay in some-thing which no lion or horse ever had: fire and smoke and brim-stone issuing out of their mouths. They could breathe out this hellish mixture, which men could not survive. Apparently the horsemen were not affected by it; perhaps this indicates that they, like the horses, were unnatural. The entire vision is a prophecy of a frightful, supernatural judgment.

"By these three plagues[17] was the third part of men killed, by the fire and by the smoke and by the brimstone which issued out of their mouths" (Rev. 9:18), that is, the mouths of the horses. The judgment ran its full course (Rev. 9:15). Those who fell in it had a foretaste and smell of hell in the ghastly course of delusions which brought them into final destruction and perdi-tion: atheism, materialism, false philosophy, "science falsely so called" (1 Tim. 6:20), the glittering attractions and pleasures of various sins (Heb. 11:25), and underneath it all: unbelief. The Saracens could kill only the bodies of their victims. But unbelief kills large masses in the full and final sense of the word, destroy-ing both their body and their soul in hell. (Matt. 10:28; Mark 16:16)

The carnage in the vision is not wrought by the riders but by the horses, which John describes further (Rev. 9:19). Their power to kill is in their mouths, which breathe death-dealing fire, smoke, and brimstone (Rev. 9:17, 18), and in their tails (Rev. 9:3-10). "Their tails were like unto serpents and had heads, and

14 See Rev. 14:10, 11; 19:20; 20:10; 21:8.

15 Lit., "hyacinth." RSV, "sapphire."

16 Cf. the description of the Gadites who followed David (1 Chron. 12:8).

17 This word is in the best MSS, but not in the KJV.

with them they do hurt." The scourge of the horses was much worse than that of the locusts, not only in the death which they inflicted through the poisonous breath of their mouths, but also in this, that while each locust had only one sting, each horse had a tail of numerous serpents with venomous stings. There was no successful defense against their attack, while they themselves were scarcely open to attack from any side. Even in apparent flight they were dangerous. Never trust the devil or any of his agents, no matter what position they take!

One third of mankind was killed in the judgment which was announced by the angel of the sixth trumpet. We may suppose that some of the rest of mankind had been "hurt" (Rev. 9:19), that is, they experienced some of the evil, painful effects of irreligion, or false religion. But they were not killed. We like to think that while there is life there is hope, especially for one who has learned by experience that his ways are not good or pleasant but evil and painful. Others, perhaps, had not yet felt the pain of any such hurt as the serpent tails of the horses inflicted, but had before their eyes the gruesome example of what had befallen the victims of this judgment. One might suppose that they would learn by the experience of others. But "the rest of the men . . . yet repented not" (Rev. 9:20). This is an incidental key to the meaning of the word "men" as used in this passage in Rev. 9:15, 18. It refers to the impenitent, both within and outside organized Christianity. It does not include the members of the true church, who are Christ's in penitent faith.

In view of all that has taken place in the first six judgments connected with the trumpet angels, it is a striking commentary on the persistent perverseness of the human heart that "the rest of the men which were not killed by these plagues yet repented not of the works of their hands," manifest transgressions against both tables of the Law, "that they should not worship devils [18] and idols of gold, and silver, and brass, and stone, and of wood, which

[18] Or "demons"; see the notes on Rev. 2:10.

neither can see, nor hear, nor walk; [19] neither repented they of their murders, nor of their sorceries, nor of their fornication [immorality], nor of their thefts." (Rev. 9:20, 21)

These sins are in widespread evidence, some of them even in "Christian" lands. Most of those who commit them remain brazenly impenitent (Matt. 7:13, 14). This is one of the signs of the times. The seventh and last trumpet, announcing God's final Judgment (Rev. 11:14-18), may sound at any moment.

[19] Ps. 115:4-7; 135:15-17; Dan. 5:23.

There are several parallels between the series of seven seals (Rev. 6:1—8:1) and the series of seven trumpets (Rev. 8:2—11:19). In each series the first four belong together. In each series the first six do not deal so much with the church [1] as with the unrepentant, unbelieving enemies of Christ and of His church. And in each case there is a special section about the church between the sixth and the seventh in the series. Rev. 10:1 to 11:14 corresponds to Rev. 7. Both sections cover the entire New Testament age in point of time and must not be thought of as picturing something that slips in somehow and takes place just before the end.

Rev. 10:1—11:14 divides into three parts:

Rev. 10: The Angel and the Little Scroll
11:1, 2: John Measures the Temple
11:3-14: The Two Witnesses

Rev. 10: The Angel and the Little Scroll

John saw "another mighty angel" (Rev. 10:1; 5:2). It was a good angel, for he "came down from heaven." [2] He was "mighty" (strong), as was evident in his appearance, size, and voice. As

---

[1] Only the martyrs are mentioned in Rev. 6:9-11.

[2] John saw this vision from the point of view of earth.

a special representative of Christ, he reflected His glory and bore some of His emblems.

The angel was "clothed with ["wrapped in," RSV] a cloud" (Rev. 10:1), as with a garment of majesty. He was not of average human size, but was a colossal figure. "A [the] rainbow (Rev. 4:3) was upon [over] his head" (Rev. 10:1). It was a beautiful scene — the colorful covenant sign of divine grace and an angel in the broad expanse of the sky. What comforting hope and promise of assurance! Storms may break all around, but God holds His rainbow before the eyes of the church and sends a messenger of peace! [3]

The face of the angel was like the sun in its bright glory (cf. Rev. 18:1). His feet (legs) were like pillars of fire: symbols of "power over the enemies of the church," [4] and by the same token, of the strong defense of the church. (Rev. 1:15)

"And he had in his hand a little book [scroll] open" (Rev. 10:2). It was in his left hand, as we take it, since he lifted his right hand up to heaven (Rev. 10:5). The scroll was small and open, unlike the larger scroll of Rev. 5, which was sealed. Because it was small it could be eaten by John (Rev. 10:10). It was open. Its contents were not hidden or concealed, but we are not told what it contained.

The whole world was involved in the mission and in the action of the angel. "He set his right foot upon the sea and his left foot on the earth" (Rev. 10:2). The church is to be found around the world, on land and sea (Rev. 7:9). So that all the world might hear, the angel "cried with a loud voice as when a lion roareth." [5]

"When he had cried, seven thunders uttered their voices." [6]

[3] See the notes on Rev. 4:3.

[4] Lenski, p. 312.

[5] Rev. 10:3. See Hos. 11:10; Amos 3:8; compare Jer. 22:29 and Micah 1:2, and note that there, as here in Rev. 10, it is not the voice of the Lord Himself but that of His messenger bringing His Word.

[6] Rev. 10:3; cf. Rev. 4:5; 6:1; 8:5; 11:19; 14:2; 16:18; 19:6; John 12:29.

We may take the number *seven* here [7] as referring to God's dealing with the world of men. By the thunder the Lord in His power and majesty endorsed the action of the angel and underscored his message.[8]

"When the seven thunders had uttered their voices," says John, "I was about to write." He was on the point of setting down "the things which the seven thunders uttered" (Rev. 10:4). The seven "thunders" were not simply a rumbling noise, but conveyed a message that could be expressed in words.

At this critical point, John, with his pen in hand, poised over the parchment, "heard a voice from heaven saying. . . . Seal up those things . . . and write them not" (Rev. 10:4). Since the voice came from heaven and spoke with authority, we hold that it was the voice of God, perhaps more specifically God the Holy Spirit, whom the Scriptures associate with the inspiration of the Bible,[9] here telling John what not to write — a kind of "inspiration of restraint." [10]

At least nine suggestions have been offered as to what the thunders said.[11] But as a matter of fact, this is one of many mysteries and secrets we do not need to know. Had God wanted us to know, John would not have been forbidden to write at this point. Perhaps the message of the thunders served to meet a special need in John's own life and work.

John continued to give his undivided attention to the angel, who "lifted up his hand[12] to heaven" (Rev. 10:5), the usual action in taking a solemn oath (Deut. 32:40; etc.). It was not simply another announcement this angel was to bring, but it was of such serious and outstanding importance that he called upon God at quite some length (Rev. 10:6) before he stated his message.

[7] As in Rev. 1:4 and elsewhere.

[8] Also see 1 Sam. 7:10; 2 Sam. 22:14; Ps. 18:13; 29:3.

[9] E. g., in 2 Peter 1:21.

[10] James Moffatt, in the EGT, V, 412, on Rev. 10:4.

[11] Listed by Biederwolf, who is referred to by Lenski, p. 314.

[12] Rather, "his right hand."

He swore by God as the everlasting Creator of all things (Rev. 4:11), "who liveth forever and ever (Dan. 12:7; Rev. 1:4-6, 18), who created heaven and the things that therein are, and the earth and the things that therein are, and the sea and the things which are therein" (Rev. 10:6; see Rev. 4:11; Gen. 1, 2; Acts 14:15). This answers the question of the origin of the universe. The account of creation in Genesis is confirmed, and by such confirmation every denial of it is condemned in Revelation. It is good for the church and its members to remember this whenever pseudo-scientific theories regarding these matters are propounded and disseminated. The fear of the Lord, who made all things, still is, and will continue to be, the beginning of true knowledge.

When the angel had taken his solemn oath, he spoke his message, brief but extremely important: "There should be time [RSV, "delay"] no longer" (Rev. 10:6). This is more than the simple thought that at the end of all things time also shall cease to exist. It includes the thought, with its built-in warning, that meanwhile time is slowly but surely running out. The universe we live in, vast and largely unknown and unexplored by man as it still is, exists, with regard to time, in a finite framework within the infinite reaches of eternity. God, who Himself had no beginning, called it into being at a point we call the beginning of time. Now time is running its course and will end, together with the entire universe in its present form, at a point already determined by God (Acts 17:31), who Himself has no end. The fact that the end has not yet come therefore does not mean that God is haphazard or undetermined. Still less does it mean that the end will never come or that there is no God. The angel's oath of confirmation is for every child of God an end of all strife regarding these things, for it settles the question once and for all beyond all shadow of doubt and establishes beyond all question the truth of 2 Peter 3:3-10.[13]

The end itself will come at the sound of the seventh and

13 For an application see 2 Peter 3:11-15.

last trumpet (1 Cor. 15:52). When that will be, no man knows, neither the angels of heaven, but only God (Matt. 24:36; Mark 13:32-37). We do know, however, that when it will come to pass "the mystery of God should be finished." (Rev. 10:7)

That "mystery of God" is God's plan of salvation. It is a complete mystery to natural man and is known to the children of God only by His revelation in His Word (1 Cor. 2:7-16). God "declared" (RSV, "announced") this mystery "to His servants the prophets" (Rev. 10:7). John counts himself among them (Rev. 1:1). He and the other prophets of God in the Old and New Testaments received their knowledge of the mystery of God by direct revelation and in turn proclaimed it to others.[14] The very last part of the mystery, so far as the church on earth is concerned, is mentioned by Paul in 1 Cor. 15:51-57. We shall all be changed. Then the kingdom of this world will become the kingdom of our Lord and of His Christ (Rev. 11:15). Thus "the mystery of God" will be "finished" in due time and in complete fulfillment of God's own Gospel promises.

It is interesting and profitable to note a reference to the Gospel in Rev. 10:7 which neither the KJV nor the RSV has preserved. The Greek word for "declared" (KJV) or "announced" (RSV) is related to the words "evangelical, evangelist, evangelize," etc. The "Gospel" is in Greek called the Evangel. Here John is not merely speaking of the prophets as bringing a message of some kind, but their message referred to here is specifically the Gospel, the "good news," as brought out in the ASV: "Then is finished the mystery of God, according to the *good tidings* which He declared to His servants the prophets." God has not merely given us the Scriptures as a record of things which were, and which are, and which are to come, but the Scriptures are specifically intended to make us "wise unto salvation through faith which is in Christ Jesus." (2 Tim. 3:15)

The voice that had spoken to John from heaven (Rev. 10:4)

[14] See, for example, Hos. 1:1,2; Heb. 1:1.

spoke to him again and said: "Go and take the little book [or scroll] which is open in the hand of the angel which standeth upon the sea and upon the earth" (Rev. 10:8). We might think that it would have been sufficient to say: "Go, take the scroll which is in the hand of the angel." But for emphasis the scroll is again (Rev. 10:2) described as "little" and "open" for all to read. The angel is for the third time described as standing on land and sea (Rev. 10:2,5). This emphasizes the fact that the Word is for the world.

John was to "take" the scroll. It was to come into his hands. He was to take a personal part in the vision. This gives us further insight into the nature of such a vision as this. John was not simply an observer of something that took place at a distance. He was not looking, as it were, at an old-style motion picture playing on a flat screen. Nor was he seeing a stage play. This vision had such depth in dimension that John himself is in it and part of it. It was even more than three-D motion pictures, which seem to draw the observer into their setting. It was more like a stage play in which the actors go out among the audience and draw the spectators into the action.

John went to the angel and said, "Give me the little book [scroll, Rev. 10:9]." The angel replied, "Take it, and eat it up [lit., down]," that is, digest it, make it a part of yourself. Compare the expression "to devour a book" and the Collect for the Word: "Grant that we may . . . inwardly digest the Holy Scriptures." (Also see Ezek. 2:8,9; 3:1-3)

The angel also told John how the little scroll would taste and what the effects of eating it would be. "It shall make thy belly [stomach] bitter, but it shall be in thy mouth sweet as honey" (Rev. 10:9). He ends on the more appealing note, perhaps, to persuade John to follow his directions, which must have sounded strange.

John again showed himself ready and willing not only to listen and hear but also to do. In this he is an example to the

church. When he took the little scroll and ate it, he found
the angel's words true. In his mouth the scroll was sweet as
honey (Ps. 19:9, 10; 34:8; 119:103), but when he had eaten it,
his stomach was bitter.[15] When the sweet Word has become an
inseparable part of you and of your life, there is also the bitterness of the things that must be endured as a result.[16]

The significance of this entire vision for John is expressed in
the words: "Thou must prophesy again before [17] many peoples,
and nations, and tongues, and kings." [18] A similar experience introduced Ezekiel to his prophetic office (Ezek. 2:8—3:3). In the
case of John, the last of the prophets, it served to open the final
phase of his work, beginning with the message he was to give
the world in the rest of the Book of Revelation, which speaks of
the weal and woe of the church to the end of time. The rich
and the poor meet together in it. The high and the low, princes
and paupers, devout men out of every nation under heaven, have
their part to play.

[15] Rev. 10:10. Here the natural sequence of events is observed: first the
mouth, then the stomach, as opposed to Rev. 10:9.

[16] John 16:2; Matt. 10:17-39; Acts 14:22; Rev. 1:9; 2:9, 10; 7:14; 1 Peter
3:14.

[17] Or "about." Cf. John 12:16: "These things were written of Him."

[18] Rev. 10:11. On "peoples and nations and tongues" see the notes on
Rev. 5:9.

Revelation 11 may be divided into three parts:

> Vv. 1- 2: Measuring the Temple
> 3-14: The Two Witnesses
> 15-19: The Seventh Trumpet

Rev. 11:1, 2: Measuring the Temple

Here [1] John is not simply a spectator of an unfolding vision, but is himself drawn into the action. There was given him "a reed like unto a rod." [2] He does not say who gave it him. [3] Since it was to serve as a standard in measuring "the temple [sanctuary] of God and the altar and them that worship therein" (Rev. 11:1), that is, the church (1 Cor. 3:16, 17), it must have come, directly or indirectly, [4] from God. Only He can set authoritative standards for His church.

John was told: "Rise, and measure the temple of God and the altar and them that worship therein. But the court which is without the temple [sanctuary] leave out, and measure it not" (Rev. 11:1, 2). There is only one God-given standard for measuring the church, drawing a line between those who are in it and

---

[1] As in Rev. 10:8-11.

[2] Or "a measuring rod like a staff," RSV (Rev. 11:1).

[3] The words "and the angel stood" are not in the best MSS. RSV: "Then I was given a measuring rod like a staff, and I was told, 'Rise. . . .'" (Rev. 11:1).

[4] In the light of Rev. 11:3 it appears that God Himself is speaking either directly or through one of His messengers.

those who are outside it.[5] That standard is the Word of God (John 8:31, 47; 12:47-50). We may therefore take the measuring rod as a symbol of the Word of God, which clearly shows that the church *in* the world is not *of* the world.

The church spoken of here is not the visible church as an organization with membership standards that may vary and be in error. The "reed" was "like unto a rod," straight and inflexible (Deut. 5:32; Mark 16:16). Its lines are drawn sharp and clear.

Outside the temple of God was a "court" which John was to leave out and not measure, "for it is given unto the Gentiles," or rather "heathen."[6] In Herod's temple at Jerusalem the court of the Gentiles was outside the sacred enclosure, which bore the inscription in Greek: "Let no Gentile enter inside of the barrier and the fence around the sanctuary. Anyone trespassing will bring death upon himself as a penalty."[7] However, in Rev. 11:2 the contrast is not between Jews and Gentiles but between the children of God and unbelievers. (Matt. 22:11-14)

The directions given to John were made completely specific by the use of both the positive and the negative: measure the temple; do not measure the court outside. Sometimes it is helpful when, for the sake of unmistakable clearness, the positive and the negative side of matters under discussion are set forth in antithesis. While the positive approach is essential, yet standing alone, it can at times be more indecisive than first appears. It is therefore to the point when doctrinal statements, for example, not only say "this" but also add "not that."

The "Gentiles" are spoken of in this passage as being outside the "temple," but they would be free to come and go and do as they please for a time in "the Holy City," which "they shall tread underfoot [Dan. 8:13] forty and two months (Rev. 11:2; cf. Luke 21:24). We may take "the Holy City" as referring in a typical

[5] Matt. 12:30; Mark 9:40; Luke 9:50; 11:23.

[6] Rev. 11:2. "Nations" (RSV) is perhaps not the best word, because many Gentiles "from every nation" (Rev. 7:9 RSV) belong to the church.

[7] Davis, *Dictionary of the Bible,* under "Temple — 3. Herod's Temple."

sense to the visible church, afflicted and oppressed in the world.[8] To "tread underfoot," or trample over, means to treat with insult and contempt (Dan. 8:13). When holy things are so treated, they are profaned, or desecrated.

We regard the "forty and two months" (Rev. 11:2; 13:5) as being the New Testament age. But many questions arise in this connection. For example: Why is the period of time here expressed in terms of months? Why specifically 42 months? In Rev. 11:3 and 12:6 "a thousand two hundred and threescore days" is about 42 months. But why the change from months to days? In terms of years it is three and a half. Is this why Rev. 12:14 speaks of "a time, and [two?] times, and half a time," so that "times" means "years"? In reply to such questions there have been many suggestions but no completely satisfactory answers. Nor do we need to know any more about them than what God Himself tells us in His holy Word, the Bible.

Rev. 11:3-14: The Two Witnesses

Rev. 11:3 begins literally: "And I will give unto My two witnesses. . . ." Some supply "permission" and translate: "I will allow My two witnesses. . . ."[9] Others supply "power."[10] Schonfield: "I will cause My two witnesses. . . ." We may also translate: "I will authorize My two witnesses. . . ."

The message in this passage comes from God.[11] He alone is able to move His[12] witnesses to prophesy and to give them the necessary power, permission, and authority for it. There are *two* witnesses here, so that their testimony may be above and beyond

---

[8] Cf. G. Göszwein, *Schriftgemäsze und erbauliche Erklärung der Offenbarung St. Johannis* (St. Louis, 1900), pp. 168, 169. — Kretzmann, on Rev. 11:1.

[9] Moffatt, *The New Testament. A New Translation.*

[10] KJV and RSV; see also Acts 1:8.

[11] Also see the notes on Rev. 11:1.

[12] Acts 1:8; lit., "Ye shall be My witnesses. . . ."

question.[13] Their "prophecy" is to extend over a period of 1,260 days. And they are to be "clothed in sackcloth." (Rev. 11:3)

"They shall prophesy" (Rev. 11:3) does not mean simply to foretell future events, but it means to bring the Word of God to bear on the world around them; not merely the *saving* power of the Word [14] but also the Word as rejected by those who will not listen and believe (Matt. 24:14; John 12:48). The church is not of the world, but it has the solemn task of telling the unbelieving, unheeding, profane world what God says. This is neither pleasant nor easy. But it must be done, and God gives His witnesses the necessary power and authority to do it. Their preaching of the Word to the world is to continue "a thousand two hundred and threescore days," that is, to the end of time.[15] They are appropriately "clothed in sackcloth" (Rev. 11:3), because repentance is the message of the church.[16]

From Rev. 11:4 it begins to appear that the "two witnesses" of Rev. 11:3 are not two individual persons but rather the entire church in its function of bearing witness. "These are the two olive trees and the two candlesticks [lampstands]." [17] It is only by the Holy Spirit that men become lights (1 Cor. 12:3; 2 Cor. 4:6). Only as we are constantly supplied with the oil of divine grace can the light of our Christian faith and life and testimony continue to shine.

The two olive trees and the two candlesticks are "standing before the God of the earth" (Rev. 11:4; Zech. 4:14). God's people serve Him in His presence, under His eye. He observes what they do and what is done to them.[18]

---

13 Deut. 17:6; 19:15; Matt. 18:16; John 8:17.

14 For all the saved are thought of as already being in the temple, or sanctuary (Rev. 11:1).

15 See the notes on Rev. 11:2.

16 Matt. 3:2; 11:21; Mark 1:15; Luke 13:3, 5.

17 Rev. 11:4. See Zech. 4:3, 11, 14, where two olive trees supply oil to the seven lamps on the candlestick, to keep the lamps burning. Cf. Ex. 27:20; Matt. 25:8. On the candlesticks, or lampstands, see Rev. 1:20, and cf. Matt. 5:14-16.

18 Deut. 10:8; 18:7; 1 Kings 17:1; 18:15; 2 Kings 3:14; 5:16; Jer. 15:19.

The carnal mind is still enmity against God (Rom. 8:7) and against all that are His (Matt. 24:9). Such enmity and hatred find expression at times not only in veiled opposition but also in direct action against God's witnesses. There are those who "will hurt them," that is, who want to do them harm.[19]

But "if any man will hurt them, fire proceedeth out of their mouth and devoureth their enemies; and if any man will hurt them, he must in this manner be killed" (Rev. 11:5; cf. Jer. 5:11-14). He is doomed to die in this way. The "fire" is the Word of God with its consuming judgments. No one can scorn or reject it with impunity (Luke 10:16). Those who speak it for the Lord are supported and protected by the power of God, against which no opposition can stand.[20]

As the symbolism in Rev. 11:5 reminds us of Jeremiah, so Rev. 11:6 calls to mind Elijah, at whose word there was no dew or rain for three and a half years,[21] and Moses, who brought 10 plagues on Egypt (Ex. 7:19 ff.) God's people are not helpless or powerless. Faith can do great things (Matt. 17:20). The angels of God in their strength serve the believers (Heb. 1:14). Prayer taps the power of God Himself. (Matt. 21:22; James 5:16b)

The wicked think that they can do as they please and harm the servants of God at will (Rev. 11:5). But they are at the mercy of the will of God, which is also the will of His witnesses and which can be carried out again and again without any effective let or hindrance. Two specific examples are mentioned in Rev. 11:6, and then the scope of the power given to God's witnesses is broadened so widely as to place at their disposal "all plagues, as often as they will." The very fact that more plagues are not described in detail but are simply referred to by a dusky hint makes this warning all the more impressive.

[19] Matt. 23:29-37; Heb. 11:24-27, 32-38.
[20] 1 Chron. 16:22; Ps. 105:15; Hos. 6:5.
[21] 1 Kings 17:1; Luke 4:25; James 5:17.

Nothing can stop the Gospel.[22] The testimony of God's witnesses will run its full course. "And when they shall have finished their testimony, the beast [23] that ascendeth out of the bottomless pit shall make war [do battle] against them." [24] The picture is that of an anti-Christian power. Its origin is in hell, its power and the scope of its influence and activity is worldwide, and it shall finally return to hell ("go into perdition," Rev. 17:8).

Among the suggested explanations are these: The "beast" is "the pagan world power" (Philippi), "the Roman Antichrist, personified in the pope of the Roman Church" (Kretzmann), "governmental authority fully in the hands of Satan" (Mauro),[25] pagan moralism, atheism, Modernism, naturalism, materialism, secularism, the religion of the lodge, Unitarianism, religious unionism, Christian Science. In this passage we must think not in individual but in comprehensive terms. This "beast" stands for everything, either within organized Christendom or outside it, which is either openly or subtly opposed to the Lord, to His Christ, and to His church. Whatever differences there are between these forces, they have this in common, that they aim to silence the Word of God, and to that end they "make war" (Rev. 11:7), or do battle, against His witnesses.

As the battle wears on, it does not always appear as if the beast of the bottomless pit will lose. In fact, he "shall overcome" God's witnesses (Rev. 11:7; cf. 13:7). This sounds like a prophecy of hopeless defeat for them. But it does not contradict Matt. 16:18. Though it is the same word used in speaking of Christ victorious over all His foes (Rev. 3:21; 6:2), it is not the last word in the

22 Matt. 16:18; 24:14; 28:18-20.

23 The Greek uses a different word here than in Rev. 4 and 5; 6:1-7; 7:11; 14:3; 15:7; 19:4; but it is the same word as in Rev. 6:8; 13; 14:9, 11; 15:2; 16—17; 19:19, 20; 20:4, 10. In all of these passages the KJV uses the one word "beast," while the RSV uses "living creatures" in Rev. 4:6 ff.; 5:8; etc., and "beast" in Rev. 6:8, etc. See ch. 4, n. 15; ch. 13, n. 1.

24 Rev. 11:7. Cf. Rev. 17:8. On the "bottomless pit" also see Rev. 9:1, 2; 20:1-3.

25 These three cited in Lenski, p. 342.

matter as it is used here in Rev. 11:7 of the beast. Nor is this the end of the story of the witnesses, that the beast "shall kill them" (Rev. 11:7-10). For them it is not a war ending in ignominious defeat, but a glorious war in which they shall finally conquer (11:11, 12; Rom. 8:28-39), and the beast will go down into perdition. (Rev. 17:8)

But meanwhile those who are killed by the beast will not receive a decent, Christian burial at the hands of their enemy. "Their dead bodies shall lie in the street" [26] for many to pass and see as public examples and object lessons. Nor is it simply on the main street of a small city or village where this most monstrous outrage that could be perpetrated against God's witnesses is committed, but it is in "the great city . . . where . . . our [better, "their"] Lord was crucified" (Rev. 11:8). Jerusalem, trodden underfoot by the Gentiles (11:2), and the scene of a complete rejection of Christ, is here used as a symbol of the crossroads of the world, where the beast, in his way, holds sway in his day. To all appearances his incessant attacks have finally been successful. God's Word is silenced. His witnesses lie dead and unburied, subject to the willful abuse and desecration of the profane passers-by. Godless Sodom (Gen. 18:16—19:9) and heathen Egypt in its abominable sin and shame were never worse than this. Therefore their names are "spiritually" ["allegorically," RSV, Rev. 11:8] also given to "the great city" in which God's witnesses will suffer the worst that the beast can do.

The dead bodies of God's witnesses will be exposed for the eyes of all the world to see.[27] They look on them not in sorrow and mourning but with the glint and gleam of pleasure and satisfaction. God permits this to continue for "three days and a half" (Rev. 11:9), a period of time not fixed and set by the beast and the other enemies of God's witnesses but by the Lord (Rev. 11:11). "Three and one half is the broken seven, the half of

26 Rev. 11:8; lit., "the broad street"; Lenski: "the city's 'Broadway,'" p. 343.

27 Rev. 11:9. On "people and kindreds and tongues and nations" see the notes on Rev. 5:9.

God's dealing with His slain witnesses." [28]   All this while their
bodies remain unburied, not by oversight but because their gloat-
ing enemies forbid and prevent their burial. "They shall not suffer
their dead bodies to be put in graves" (Rev. 11:9). They know
what they are doing, and they do it deliberately (John 16:2).
So much the greater their sin and condemnation. (Rom. 1:18-32)

In their perverted view "they that dwell upon the earth," [29]
the enemies of God's witnesses, feel that the occasion calls for
special celebration. Their rejoicing and merrymaking (Luke
15:23) includes the traditional exchange of gifts (Esther 9:22),
to mark what they regard as an especially happy and auspicious
occasion.

"These two prophets" (Rev. 11:3) had "tormented them that
dwelt on the earth" (Rev. 11:10), that is, the prophets had
bothered and annoyed them by preaching the Word of God, by
speaking against the errors and sins of the day, by calling for
repentance and a God-pleasing life, and by threatening God's
wrath and punishment on the impenitent. To the natural, un-
regenerated heart this is torment and torture, reflected in the expression "pangs of conscience." At least those who prodded the
conscience of "them that dwelt on the earth" were gone when
"these two prophets" were dead! But this did not really solve the
problem.

If the two prophets represent God's witnesses and are silenced
by death, with scoffers, mockers, and unbelievers surviving, will
there, then, be any living believers left at the end of time? Very
few.[30]

But all is not lost. "After three days and a half [31] the Spirit
of life [32] from God entered into" (Rev. 11:11) the "two prophets"
again. Physical death does not end all. God, the Author of life

28 Lenski, p. 346.

29 Rev. 11:10; see the notes on Rev. 3:10.

30 Compare 1 Thess. 4:15 with Luke 18:8.

31 See the notes on Rev. 11:9.

32 Or, "the breath of life." The reference is not to the Holy Spirit.

(Job 33:4; Ezek. 37:5-14), who breathed the breath of life (Gen. 2:7) into the first human being, will at the Last Day again breathe life into the dead and set them on their feet (Job 19: 25-27). We believe that this is the message and meaning of this verse rather than that God will continue to raise new voices to take the place of those which have been silenced, as Luther, for example, succeeded Huss. Accordingly, the sixth trumpet includes the resurrection of the body and the last Judgment.

The final reckoning will come when the victims stand alive again before those who put them to death. Not only will those who pierced Jesus see Him (John 19:34-37; Rev. 1:7), but all others who laid wicked, violent hands on any of God's people to put them out of the way will also see these dead alive again.

For God's witnesses it is the hour of the final redemption. "They heard a great voice from heaven saying unto them, Come up hither!" (Rev. 11:12). Their work on earth is finished, and they are called to enter into the joy of their Lord. Blessed of the Father, they are invited to inherit the kingdom prepared for them from the foundation of the world (Matt. 25:34). The "great" voice that called them spoke with full and final authority. "They ascended up to heaven in a cloud" (Rev. 11:12). God took them in the same way in which our Savior ascended. (Acts 1:9; cf. 1 Thess. 4:17)

The punishment of the wicked includes this, that they see the saved enter heaven. When God's witnesses "ascended up to heaven in a cloud . . . their enemies beheld them" (Rev. 11:12). What a picture for the lost to carry into the everlasting hopelessness and despair of their own damnation! There will be no more room for repentance for them, no "second chance," for then time comes to an end (Matt. 24:14). We must not think of the resurrection and ascension of God's witnesses as taking place before the final Judgment of God overtakes the rest. Both take place at the same time, "the same hour." (Rev. 11:13)

"There was a great earthquake,[33] and the tenth part of the

33 Lit., a great "shaking"; see the notes on Rev. 6:12.

city fell" (Rev. 11:13). "The city" is the headquarters of the
beast and of his followers (Rev. 11:2, 8). We find no further
meaning in the fraction "one tenth" than that it helps emphasize
the extent of the destructive power of the "earthquake" as a means
of striking fear and terror into the hearts of the inhabitants of the
city. When such a large part of a large city falls in that way, all
assurance of security is removed also from the rest. Eternal in-
security — another maddening factor in the fate of the lost.

"In the earthquake were slain of men seven thousand" (Rev.
11:13). This indicates a large number; we are not told if it was
one tenth of the inhabitants of the city. The death of so many
people would help impress on the rest an overwhelming sense
of catastrophe.

As for the difference between those who were killed and
those who remained, who can explain all the details in the Book
of Revelation? As well argue which is worse for the lost, a tor-
turing hopeless doubt or assurance of the worst. If any distinction
is drawn between the two, it is unimportant and shows only that
there are degrees of punishment. All the wicked, both living and
dead, fall under condemnation in the final judgment. (Rev.
11:18)

"The remnant were affrighted" (Rev. 11:13), or terrified, as
well they might be at such a demonstration of the final overruling
power of God. They "gave glory to the God of heaven" (Rev.
11:13), not in repentance and faith but as "the devils also believe — and tremble." (James 2:19b)

Out of World War II came the saying "There are no atheists
in the foxholes." It is also true that there are no atheists in hell.
"One thing is sure, hell contains no atheists, because the damned
actually experience God as the righteous Judge. There is no more
room in hell for the lie that there is no God." [34]

"The second woe is past, and, behold, the third woe cometh
quickly" (Rev. 11:14), so quickly, in fact, as to follow immediately upon the heels of the second woe.

[34] Pieper, III, 546.

Rev. 11:15-19: The Seventh Trumpet and the Third Woe

There are seven seals (Rev. 5:1 ff.), seven trumpets (8:2 ff.), seven visions (12:1 ff.), and seven bowls (15:7 ff.) The visions connected with each of these series of seven cover the same ground and time in the history of the world and of the church. These four series must not be thought of as taking place one after the other. In each case the seventh and last in the series announces the final climax, the end of all things. In the case of the trumpets, for example, the sixth carries us to the resurrection of the body and the last Judgment. The seventh introduces scenes which immediately follow the Judgment.

In Luther's day Michael Stiefel regarded himself as the "seventh angel" of Rev. 11:15.[35] Benjamin Purnell, founder of the communal religious colony known as the House of David, in 1895 claimed a revelation which told him that he was this angel.[36] Charles Taze Russell (1852—1916) not only claimed this honor for himself but also held that the first six "angels" were Paul, John, Arius, Waldo, Wycliffe, and Luther.[37] The human heart being what it is, we have probably not yet heard the last of such claims and counterclaims. But as a matter of fact, at least until this angel will sound his trumpet, we shall not know any more about him than the Bible tells us in Rev. 11:15; 8:2, 6.

John says that when the seventh angel sounded, "there were great voices in heaven" (Rev. 11:15). Because these voices spoke of "our Lord" (11:15), we may take them to be the voices of all the inhabitants of heaven, both saints and angels. They are great voices because they join to form a great chorus, including the elect from the four winds, from one end of heaven to the other (Matt. 24:31; also see Rev. 7:9; 19:1). This verse, with Rev. 19:6,[38] was such an inspiration to the composer Handel that it moved

35 Pieper, III, 517; Luther, SL, XXII, 1334.

36 F. E. Mayer, *Religious Bodies of America* (St. Louis, c. 1954), p. 444.

37 F. E. Mayer, *American Churches* (St. Louis, c. 1946), p. 77.

38 Also see 1 Tim. 6:15 and the notes on Rev. 17:14.

him to write the immortal Hallelujah Chorus in his oratorio
Messiah. After he had composed this chorus, his servant is said to
have seen tears streaming from his eyes. "I did think I did see
all heaven before me," Handel later confessed, "and the great
God Himself!" [39]

"The kingdoms [kingdom] of this [lit., "the"] world," that is,
kingship, or rule, over the world, "are [is] become the kingdoms
[kingdom] of our Lord," that is, of God, our Father, "and of His
Christ" (11:15). "The rulers of the darkness of this world"
(Eph. 6:12) have themselves been cast out into outer darkness
(Matt. 8:12; 22:13; 25:30). They no longer trample the Holy
City underfoot (Rev. 11:2), for Old Jerusalem has been replaced
by the New Jerusalem; and the first earth (Rev. 21:1), on which
the enemies of God's witnesses rejoiced and made merry (Rev.
11:10), has forever passed away. Now our Lord and His Christ
hold undisputed sway over all. "And He shall reign forever and
ever!" (Rev. 11:15). Here is a study in prophecy and fulfillment.[40] The "kingdom" and "reign" is not a rule on earth in
a millennium, or glorious 1,000-year period, but it is the kingdom
of heaven in eternity. (Rev. 21:1-5)

The 24 elders reappear in this vision (Rev. 11:16). They
represent the ministry of the Word in its effects after the end of
time. Those who received and believed the Word are saved. Those
who rejected the Word in unbelief are lost. In this vision the
line between the two is sharply, clearly, and permanently drawn,
and the elders, in a proper attitude of reverence, worship God and
give Him thanks for His mighty works (Rev. 11:17) and for
the justice of His judgments (Rev. 11:18)

"We give Thee thanks, O Lord God Almighty,[41] which art and

[39] Robert Manson Myers, *Handel's Messiah: A Touchstone of Taste* (New
York, 1948), p. 63.

[40] Cf. Ps. 2:1-6; Acts 4:25, 26; Ps. 10:16; Dan. 7:13, 14; Obad. 21; Luke
1:33; Rev. 12:10; 19:6, 16.

[41] See the notes on Rev. 1:8.

wast,[42] because Thou hast taken to Thee Thy great power and hast reigned" (Rev. 11:17). Not as though God did not previously have this power; it was His already before He "took it" in this way at this time. But now He took it up and put it to full use. No longer does He permit His enemies to roam at large, endeavoring to harm His church and its members and challenging His authority. For now He Himself wields His scepter over all things in such a way as to bring His sovereign power to bear effectively and completely over all.

"The nations [43] were angry, and Thy wrath is come" (Rev. 11:18). "The carnal mind is enmity against God" (Rom. 8:7). "A friend of the world is the enemy of God" (James 4:4). The heathen become angry at God's restraints, threats, and punishments and show their anger by flagrantly breaking His Law and persecuting, even killing, His people. But the sinful anger and opposition of men against the righteous wrath of God are ineffective. (Ps. 2:1, 4, 5; 46:6)

"All that are in the graves shall hear His voice and shall come forth" (John 5:28, 29), for "the time of the dead is come that they should be judged" (Rev. 11:18). The last Judgment does not reopen any cases for a new hearing, with possible change of verdict, but it confirms the verdict pronounced when the soul left the body, and it rejoins body and soul accordingly to be either in heaven or in hell forever. (Heb. 9:27; 2 Cor. 5:10)

For the servants of the Lord God Almighty, the prophets and the saints and those that fear His name, small and great,[44] there is in store the gift of a reward (Rev. 11:18). It is not a reward of merit but of grace. Heaven cannot be earned or bought (Rom. 3:28; 8:17; Eph. 2:8, 9; Matt. 25:34). It will be given as a free

[42] See the notes on Rev. 1:4. The words "and art to come" (KJV) are not in the best MSS in Rev. 11:17. God's final coming has already taken place before this point in the vision.

[43] Rather, "heathen"; see the notes on Rev. 11:2.

[44] See the notes on Rev. 20:12.

gift to all of God's people both of the Old and of the New Testament, young and old, high and low, rich and poor.[45]

But for those who are lost in their unbelief there is no comfort or hope. In their own way, directly or indirectly, deliberately or unknowingly, they all contribute to the effort of Satan and his followers to corrupt and destroy the earth (Rev. 11:18b), until at last, in even-handed justice, the tables are turned, and destruction overtakes them in a moment at the hand of God (Luke 19:27; Rev. 16:6). Their "destruction" is not annihilation but an eternal living death, suffering in hell beyond all human imagination and description.[46] Those who believe that Satan and all the wicked will be annihilated [47] will have a most rude awakening on Judgment Day. This is the third and final woe.

John's vision of the seven trumpets (Rev. 8:2—11:19) closes with a brief look into God's temple in heaven. "The temple of God was opened in heaven." [48] "Temple" refers to the Holy Place and the Holy of Holies. Since the ark of the "testament" (covenant) was in it, the symbolism of this vision is based not on the temple in Jerusalem at the time of Christ but on the old temple; the ark of the covenant was lost when the temple was burned in the destruction of Jerusalem in 587 B. C. Actually there is no temple in heaven (Rev. 21:22). But in this vision the temple serves appropriately as the setting for the ark of God's testament, or covenant. The ark of the covenant is a symbol of the faithfulness of God in keeping His gracious promises.

There were also "lightnings and voices and thunderings and an earthquake ("a great shaking") and great hail" (Rev. 11:19), as symbols of God's almighty power to carry out His threats of punishment.[49] Rev. 11:19 stands as a divine signature and seal at the end of this section of the Book of Revelation.

---

[45] Mal. 3:16; Mark 10:13-16; Luke 16:22; 23:40-43; John 3:16; Acts 2:39.

[46] Luke 16:23, 24; Dan. 12:2; Matt. 8:12.

[47] Seventh-day Adventists, Jehovah's Witnesses, and others; see Mayer, *The Religious Bodies of America*, pp. 439, 445, 457, 461, 516, 549.

[48] Rev. 11:19; cf. Rev. 15:5.

[49] Rev. 8:5, 7; 16:18, 21; 4:5; 6:12; 11:13; Ex. 9:18-31; 19:16-18.

Rev. 12:1—15:1 ff. speaks of three "signs" or "wonders" (12:1, 3; 15:1), which are presented in seven visions: (1) The Woman, the Child, and the Dragon (12:1—13:1); (2) The Beast of the Sea (13:1-10); (3) The Beast of the Earth (13:11-18); (4) The Lamb and the 144,000 on Mount Zion (14:1-5); (5) The Three Angels (14:6-13); (6) The Harvest of Mankind (14:14-20); (7) The Seven Angels with the Seven Last Plagues (15:1-4). These seven visions, like the visions of the seven seals (5:1 ff.) and the seven trumpets (8:2 ff.), portray the New Testament times to the end of the world and into eternity. Prominent in this series of pictures is the raging of Satan against Christ and against His church.

Rev. 12:1 to 13:1:
The First Vision — The Woman, the Child, and the Dragon

This chapter presents the first of the seven visions in Rev. 12:1 to 15:4. Rev. 12:1, 2 describes the first of the three "signs" or "wonders" in this section; it is called great (Rev. 12:1) because of its appearance and significance.

The Woman   The woman (Rev. 12:1 ff.) is the church, here represented not as the bride of Christ (Rev. 21:9; 22:17), but as the mother of the Messiah. She represents the people of God in both Testaments because she appears in the vision both before and after the birth of her child. She appears "in heaven" and in heavenly splendor.[1] "She is arrayed with the sun, the symbol of day. She has the light, the right knowledge of salvation. The moon is under her feet. The moon is the symbol of darkness. Night is the symbol of sin and death. She rules over sin and death and places them under her feet." [2] It is entirely fitting that the woman, as a symbol of God's people, should wear a royal crown,[3] and that it should be also the crown of a conqueror.[4] The 12 stars may be taken to represent the 12 tribes of the Old Testament and the 12 apostles of the New Testament (Rev. 21:12, 14). This woman is in no sense a symbol of the Virgin Mary. The details in this vision, except for her bringing forth a child, do not fit her.

The Child   The woman's child (Rev. 12:2 ff.) is Jesus Christ, our Savior. "The cry of travail fills the whole Old Testament. 'Oh, that Thou wouldest rend the heavens, that Thou wouldest come down!' Is. 64:1. It is the constant longing and 'waiting for the Consolation of Israel' (Luke 2:25), which is here represented as about to be fulfilled." [5]

The Dragon   The dragon (Rev. 12:3 ff.) is the devil, or Satan (Rev. 12:9; 20:2), here pictured as a "great" dragon, because he is powerful.

The red color of the dragon, a symbol of hellish anger, fire, and blood, refers to his murderous nature (John 8:44); it is not a specific prophecy speaking only of modern red Communism. The entire image of the dragon "expresses the extreme ferocious,

---

[1] Rev. 12:1; cf. Rom. 8:17, 18; Song of Sol. 6:10.

[2] Ludwig Fuerbringer, Mimeographed Classroom Notes on Revelation (Saint Louis, n. d.), p. 28.

[3] Rev. 12:1; see the notes on Rev. 1:6.

[4] Rom. 8:37; see the notes on the dragon's crowns in connection with Rev. 12:3.

[5] Lenski, p. 363; also see Gen. 49:18; Is. 7:14; 9:6; 25:9; Mark 15:43.

murderous, beastly, cruel power with the connotation of horror for men. . . . Gigantic strength, craft, malignity, and venom are combined in 'dragon.'"[6]

The dragon had seven heads.[7] When the number *seven* is associated with Satan it seems to mean that the devil claims for himself what properly belongs only to God in His relationship to the world of men. Other implications of seven heads are these: That the dragon is not easily slain; that it is not easy to escape him as he reaches out to kill and devour in many different directions at the same time; that his bloodthirstiness is not quickly satisfied; and that he is very cunning. But we must not try to draw a literal picture of this dragon, for though we are told that he has seven heads, yet Rev. 12:15, 16 speaks of only one mouth.

On his heads the dragon had seven "crowns," but they were merely the "diadems" (Rev. 12:3 RSV) of a usurper, while the woman's "crown" (Rev. 12:1) was of a type and style worn not only by rulers (Matt. 27:29) but also by victors and conquerors.[8]

The dragon also had 10 horns (Rev. 12:3). Since bulls and some other animals defend themselves with their horns and also do great harm in attacking with them, horns are a symbol of power and strength (Ps. 89:17; 1 Sam. 2:10). "Ten" is regarded by some as the number of completeness, and by others as the number of the world in prophetic language. In this vision the two thoughts combine. "He arrogates for himself divine power. He imitates divine works. He is the god and prince of this world."[9]

"His tail drew [10] the third part of the stars of heaven," that is, some of the angels followed him (John 8:44; Jude 6; Rev. 12:7). He was successful to a large extent in the supernatural world. The fact that he was effective with his tail recalls the fact that the

[6] Lenski, p. 364. Also see the notes on Rev. 9:11.

[7] Rev. 12:3. Regarding the number *seven* see the notes on Rev. 1:4.

[8] 1 Cor. 9:25; 2 Tim. 4:8. Two different words are used in the Greek.

[9] Fuerbringer, loc. cit.

[10] RSV, "swept down" (Rev. 12:4).

power of the locusts was in their tails (Rev. 9:10; cf. Is. 9:15). After he rebelled against God, he by his lies deceived and seduced many other angels to follow him and "cast them to the earth" (Rev. 12:4); they were banished from heaven. Then he set about to destroy other works of God, beginning with man, the crown of God's visible creation.[11] In his role as a "serpent" he can still do great harm.

He was not satisfied with the evil which he did in the Garden of Eden. Because God promised man a Savior from sin (Gen. 3:15), the dragon continued his war against God, taking the Savior Himself as his next target. He should have known better. He could not hurt the woman, the church, because she was at all times protected by the hand of divine providence (John 10:27-29; 14:2, 3, 19; Rev. 12:13 ff.). How much less could he hope to destroy her holy Child! (Matt. 2; Ps. 22:20, 21; Rev. 12:5)

No other dragon was ever made to look so ridiculous. There he stands, great and ferocious, with his seven heads and ten horns, before a woman who is helpless in the pains of childbirth. One would expect that he would lose no time in killing the mother before the child is born. But no — he must wait until she brings forth her child — a son, Jesus (Is. 9:6; Matt. 1:21). That must have been one of the bitterest pills which the devil ever had to swallow. But there was even worse to come for him. After the child was born, both the mother and the child escaped from him. If you want to laugh at the devil, read Rev. 12!

Instead of falling victim to the god of this world (2 Cor. 4:4), the child "was to rule all nations [12] with a rod of iron." [13] Christ's rule over the heathen extends throughout the entire New Testament age, from the time of His birth to the end of the world.

11 He "deceiveth the whole world" (Rev. 12:9; Gen. 3; John 8:44).

12 Rather "heathen," as in Ps. 2:8.

13 Rev. 12:5; on the word "rule" (lit., "feed," or shepherd") see the notes on Rev. 2:26, 27. The reference is to Ps. 2:9, where the KJV follows the Hebrew ("break"), while the Greek of Rev. 12:5 follows the LXX in using the word "feed," or "shepherd," for which our English uses the word "rule."

The dragon did indeed succeed in having the woman's Child killed on the cross (John 19:30), but he did not succeed in his plan to "devour" Him. "Her Child was caught up unto God, and to His throne" (Rev. 12:4,5). This is the exaltation of Christ.[14] "He descended into hell (in triumph); the third day He rose again from the dead; He ascended into heaven and sitteth at the right hand of God the Father Almighty; from thence He shall come to judge the quick and the dead."[15] The woman also, the church in the Old and New Testaments, escaped from the dragon.[16]

War in Heaven   Following the sequence of events in this vi-
Rev. 12:7-12   sion, we see that the dragon, in his presump-
                   tion, arrogance, and frustrated rage pursued
the Child as it was caught up to God and to His throne. He would have stormed after Him into heaven itself if possible. But he was met and successfully challenged by "Michael and his angels." "Michael" means "Who is like God?" Many Lutheran commentators [17] understand the name here to refer to Jesus, the Champion of His church.[18] Michael's angels are, of course, the good angels.[19]

The war between these two opposing hosts did not take place in heaven in the sense of Paradise (Luke 23:43). The serene peace of that abode of the blessed has remained undisturbed ever since Satan and his followers were cast out of it before the fall of man.[20] "Neither was their place found any more in heaven" (Rev.

14 Acts 3:21; Phil. 2:9-11; Heb. 1:4-14; 2:8,9.

15 The Second Article of the Apostles' Creed.

16 Rev. 12:6; see the notes on Rev. 12:14.

17 Luther's somewhat ingenious interpretation includes this: "heaven" is the kingdom of heaven on earth (Matt. 10:7), and Michael's angels are the Christians, the Church Militant. SL, X, 1066 ff.

18 *Lutheran Cyclopedia,* under "Michael."

19 Michael is also mentioned Dan. 10:13, 21; 12:1; Jude 9. — Regarding the dragon's angels see the notes on Rev. 12:4.

20 Luke 19:38; Col. 1:20.

12:8) must not be taken to mean that up to this time the dragon and his angels were actually in heaven. But let us rather think of Eph. 6:12, where Paul speaks of demons as "spiritual wickedness in high places." [21] Their power is broken as a result of the "war in heaven," and it is this result, or effect, which is emphasized here.

The dragon and his angels "prevailed not" — "neither was their place found any more in heaven" — "the great dragon was cast out [thrown down] . . . he was cast out into [thrown down to] the earth, and his angels were cast out [thrown down] with him" (Rev. 12:8, 9). In these three graphic statements we can first see the tide of battle turn, then the decisive rout, and finally the mopping-up action which disposed individually and collectively of each and every one of the rebels. Their leader is completely identified and unmasked as "that old serpent, called the devil and Satan, which deceiveth the whole world." [22]

In Rev. 12:10-12 a loud voice (11:15) in heaven proclaims the victory over the devil (12:10-12a) and sounds a warning for the earth and sea (12:12b). The pronoun *"our* God" includes John himself and his Christian readers. The "brethren" are their fellow Christians. (1 Peter 5:8, 9)

Rev. 12:10a: (1) "Salvation": full and complete redemption from sin, death, and the power of the devil, and the sum total of all blessings of the saved here in time and hereafter in eternity (Luke 3:6; John 19:30; Heb. 9:28; Rev. 7:10; 19:1). (2) "Strength" (or power): the mighty power of God which caught up the Child to His throne and which defeated and cast down the dragon and his angels (Eph. 1:19-23; Rev. 11:17). (3) "The kingdom of our God" is the kingdom in which He rules supreme in His love and grace over all that are His, who believe His holy Word and lead a godly life (John 18:36, 37).

---

[21] Lit., "in the heavenlies." RSV, "in the heavenly places."

[22] Rev. 12:9. See the notes on Rev. 2:9, 10; 12:3, 4. Also see John 8:44; 12:31; 2 Thess. 2:9-12; Rev. 20:2.

(4) "The power [or authority] of His Christ." "All power," says Jesus, "is given unto Me in heaven and in earth." [23]

The counterpart of this victory is the defeat of the devil, mentioned in the triumphant proclamation: "The accuser of our brethren is cast down,[24] which accused [accuses] them before our God day and night" (Rev. 12:10b). This is the devil's business: First, as a serpent he deceives, and then, as Satan, which means adversary, or opponent, he accuses his victims of the very sins he led them into. He gives them no rest, but accuses them "day and night" before God. He cannot make his accusations stick, however, because he is cast down (Rom. 16:20). The children of God, whom he accused, "overcame him (1) by the blood of the Lamb and (2) by the Word of their testimony." (Rev. 12:11a)

1. "By the blood of the Lamb" means "by reason of [because of] the blood of the Lamb." The Lamb is Christ.[25] His blood cleanses us from all sin.[26] This is "the expiatory cause" [27] why the devil cannot successfully accuse those who are in Christ Jesus.

2. The "mediatory cause" [28] is "the Word of their testimony," that is, "the Word of God and the testimony of Jesus Christ, which they held" (Rev. 1:9; 6:9). God's Word is truth (John 17:17), and by continuing in it in faith, word, and deed they were made forever free (John 8:31, 32), free from sin, from death — and from the power of the devil!

They conquered, though they died.[29] "Therefore rejoice, ye heavens, and ye that dwell in them." [30] It is an occasion to be merry. If there is joy in the presence of the angels of God in

[23] Matt. 28:18; also see Rev. 1:6; 5:13; 11:15; note the close connection between Rev. 12:10 and Ps. 2:2, 6.

[24] See the notes on Rev. 12:9.

[25] John 1:29; 1 Peter 1:18, 19.

[26] 1 John 1:7; Rev. 5:6; 7:14; 1:5.

[27] Lenski, p. 379.

[28] Ibid.

[29] Cf. Rev. 12:11 with 11:7-12.

[30] Rev. 12:12; also see the notes on Rev. 7:9, 10, 15.

heaven over *one* sinner who repents (Luke 15:7,10), what boundless joy must there be over *all* those who are saved! Heaven's eternal arches ring as saints and angels join in the celebration.

But how different on the earth and sea! "Woe to [the inhabiters of] the earth and [of] the sea!" [31] The reference here is not to the church on earth but to those who are earthly-minded, as distinct from those whose home is heaven. Their "woe" is that they fall into the hands of the devil, who "is come down . . . having great wrath, because he knoweth that he hath but a short time" (Rev. 12:12). "While the evil angels are all imprisoned (Jude 6), a certain freedom of movement and action has been left to them, which permits their activities here on earth. A man may be imprisoned in a penitentiary for life and yet be given the privilege of walking about in the prison-yard or even outside of it, certain conditions and restrictions being imposed on him." [32]

The devil came down to the earth and sea because he was cast down out of heaven (Rev. 12:9). When that took place, a limit was set on the short time at his disposal. He knows this, and it has made him angry. He is in a high rage and passion, determined to do his work as quickly as possible.

The Dragon Persecutes the Woman. Rev. 12:6, 13-17

The persecution of the church by the devil is introduced in Rev. 12:6 and spoken of at greater length in Rev. 12:13-17. Rev. 12:14 mentions again the woman's flight into the wilderness. [33] She was given "two wings of a great eagle." [34] On such swift and powerful wings the woman could safely escape and hide. She would not be wandering aim-

[31] Rev. 12:12. The words in brackets are not in the best MSS, but the meaning is the same as if these words were included. See the notes on Rev. 3:10.

[32] Wm. Arndt, *Does the Bible Contradict Itself?* (St. Louis, 1930), p. 108. See the notes on Rev. 20:3.

[33] Rev. 12:6. David fled from Saul into the wilderness (1 Sam. 23:14,15), and so did Elijah from Jezebel (1 Kings 19:4).

[34] Rather, "the two wings of the great eagle." The reference is not to the eagle in Rev. 4:7; 8:13, but rather to Ex. 19:4; Deut. 32:9-11; Is. 40:31.

lessly in the wilderness, but would go to a place prepared for her by God (Rev. 12:6), where she would have all necessary food.[35] She does not represent the visible church, which may cut a large and impressive figure before the world, but the invisible church, obscure and unseen, hidden from the eyes of man. The church on earth is the church under a cross.

If a "time" is taken as a year, the "time, and times, and half a time" (Rev. 12:14) corresponds approximately to the 1,260 days of Rev. 11:3; 12:6 and to the 42 months of Rev. 11:2.[36] All of these expressions refer to the New Testament age. To the end of time the church is safe, sustained and protected "from the face of the serpent," the devil. He can neither effectively strike nor fatally harm her. (Matt. 16:18)

In spite of his deep guile and great might, he is ridiculously helpless. Since the woman had been given the wings of an eagle (Rev. 12:14), he could not really expect to drown her in a flood. Yet he "cast out of his mouth water as a flood after the woman, that he might cause her to be carried away of the flood."[37] This is clearly one of the devil's greatest and most desperate efforts. The "flood" which the serpent cast out of his mouth may be understood either as persecutions, which God stays short of their intended effect (Ps. 32:6), or as lies and delusions calculated to separate the church from the truth as it is in Christ Jesus and His Word, the Bible; the world believes such lies and delusions (2 Thess. 2:11), but the church is not harmed by them.

Even the "earth" is against the devil. The woman does not even need her wings again. "The earth helped the woman, and the earth opened her mouth and swallowed up the flood which the dragon cast out of his mouth" (Rev. 12:16). In Rev. 12:4 the dragon stood before the woman. Now she is so far away that even a mighty, rushing flood could not catch up with her. The

[35] "They" should feed her (Rev. 12:6) is impersonal and means "she is to be nourished" (Rev. 12:14), sustained by Word and Sacrament.

[36] See the notes on this verse.

[37] Rev. 12:15; see the notes on v. 3.

dragon was completely foiled. Both the child and the woman escaped.

The serpent's mouth was not an inexhaustible fountain of flood waters. He was forced to abandon this effort to do away with the woman. Then his rage became altogether irrational. He "was wroth with the woman" (Rev. 12:17). We would expect him to be angry with the earth, which had helped the woman. And since he was, indeed, angry at the woman, we would accordingly expect to hear of further plots and plans against her. Instead, because he saw that the woman, the church, was obviously safe, by a transfer of emotions, he "went to make war with the remnant of her seed," [38] that is, her offspring, individual believers. In the hope of surely overcoming at least some of them, he engaged in an effort which is disproportionately large, considering the fact that his opponents now were only a few, a "remnant."

But even so he could do nothing. "The remnant of her seed . . . keep the commandments of God and have the testimony of Jesus [Christ]." [39] These "commandments" are not the Law, in distinction from the Gospel, but in a larger sense the Word of God.[40] To "have" the testimony of Jesus, the Gospel, means to believe it. Because the devil "makes war" against believers, they must "earnestly contend for the faith." [41] Though he may give some of the elect a bad time in this spiritual warfare, they come out of it more than conquerors (Rom. 8:37) through faith in Him who said, "I will build My church, and the gates of hell shall not prevail against it." (Matt. 16:18)

NOTE: Some editions of the Bible have the first words of Rev. 13 as the end of Rev. 12:17 or as Rev. 12:18. According to

[38] Rev. 12:17; see Is. 54:1-3.

[39] Rev. 12:17 KJV. "Christ" is not in the best MSS.

[40] Cf. Luke 11:28; also see John 14:15, 21, 23; 15:10; 1 John 2:3; Rev. 14:12. Regarding "the testimony of Jesus" also see 1 Cor. 2:1; 1 John 5:9-11; Rev. 1:2, 9; 6:9; 11:7; 12:11; 19:10; 20:4.

[41] Jude 3. Cf. 2 Tim. 4:7; also see the notes on Rev. 14:12.

the best manuscripts, these words read: "And he [42] stood upon the sand of the sea," where the sea and the earth meet. The place where he stood is significant in view of Rev. 12:12 [43] and because, in the following visions, the two beasts which come up, one out of the sea (Rev. 13:1-10), and the other out of the earth (Rev. 13:11-18), are the agents of the dragon, the devil. "He stood upon the sand of the sea" sets the stage for Rev. 13, where John continues: "And I saw a beast rise up out of the sea. . . ."

[42] That is, the dragon; not "I," as in the KJV.

[43] "Woe to . . . the earth and . . . the sea!"

Rev. 13 describes the second and third of the seven visions in Rev. 12:1 to 15:4: the beast of the sea (Rev. 13:1-10) and the beast of the earth. (Rev. 13:11-18)

Rev. 13:1-10: The Second Vision — The Beast of the Sea

Rev. 13 deals with the same things as Rev. 12:13-17, but at greater length. In Rev. 12:13-17 the devil himself tries to destroy the church and its members. In Rev. 13 he tries to do it through his agents, all anti-Christian powers in the world, represented by the two beasts. In point of time Rev. 13 covers the entire New Testament age, beginning with the exaltation of Christ.

The first beast [1] of Rev. 13 arose out of the sea. Like the dragon (Rev. 12:3) it had seven heads and ten horns. But, unlike the dragon, it had its crowns [2] on its ten horns, not on its seven heads. Horns being symbols of power, and ten being a symbol of completeness, the ten horns stand for a show of full, invincible power. The diadems are symbols of a usurper. The beast assumes, or arrogates, to himself the royal omnipotence of God. That is

[1] Our English Bible sometimes uses the same word for two different Greek words. The word "beast" is used in the KJV in Rev. 13; 4:6-9; 11:7. But the Greek word in Rev. 4:6-9 (lit., "living one") is different from that in the other passages. In Rev. 11:7 and Rev. 13 it was indeed a beast, "cruel, destructive, frightful, ravenous" (Lenski, p. 391), which John saw. See ch. 4, n. 15; ch. 11, n. 23.

[2] Rather, "diadems"; see the notes on Rev. 12:3.

blasphemy, an insult to God, plain also in the brazen display of "the name [3] of blasphemy" on the seven heads of the beast (cf. Rev. 17:3), "apparently arrogant titles insulting to God." [4] Blasphemy is speaking evil of God, or mocking Him. [5] We take the number *seven* as signifying God's dealings with man. What blasphemy for the dragon and the beast to have seven heads "as though all their plans and designs for men were holy and sacred as God's are!" [6]

This beast of the sea was "like unto a leopard, and his feet were as the feet of a bear, and his mouth as the mouth of a lion" (Rev. 13:2; cf. Dan. 7). The combined effect is one of such brute fierceness and strength as to fill the heart with fear and terror. Some have taken this beast to stand for the Roman Empire, which arose, it is were, out of the sea of nations. They draw parallels between its seven heads and the seven hills of Rome, its 10 horns and the 10 provinces of the empire, the names of blasphemy and Roman idolatry. Others regard the beast as standing specifically for the Roman Catholic papacy. Such interpretations are historical judgments, limited in their application. A stronger interpretation of this passage refers to "the whole anti-Christian power set in motion by Satan as the prince of this world." [7]

"The dragon [Satan] gave him [the beast] his power and his seat and great authority" (Rev. 13:2). The devil is the source of all anti-Christian power, rule, and authority. Yet in spite of all its terrifying advantages and supernatural power and strength, the beast was vulnerable. John saw "one of his heads, as it were, wounded to death" (Rev. 13:3). This was not a fatal wound for the beast as such, because its six other heads remained untouched. However, this one head was wounded in such a way that, humanly

[3] Rather, "names" (Rev. 13:1).

[4] Weidenschilling, "The Book of Revelation" in *The Bible Student* (St. Louis, April and July 1955), p. 59.

[5] Matt. 26:63-65; Rom. 2:23, 24.

[6] Lenski, p. 391.

[7] Lenski, p. 394.

speaking, it could not recover. It looked literally "slain to death." This indicates a partial, though apparently serious, setback for the anti-Christian world power. Some hold that Christ and His work of redemption are referred to here. However, He dealt a death stroke to more than one of the dragon's seven heads. We therefore rather understand this passage to speak of such merely apparent success as results from some of man's own efforts to overcome the Evil One.

Small wonder that when "his deadly wound was healed . . . all the world wondered after the beast" (Rev. 13:3), regarding it with great admiration. Visible power is so impressive that the world worships at its altar. Sometimes Christians are also tempted to think that the anti-Christian forces cannot be overthrown.

The devil once asked Christ to fall down and worship him (Matt. 4:9). But our Savior put him to flight with a reference to the Word of God (Deut. 6:13; 10:20). The devil is more successful with the children of the world. "They worshiped the dragon which gave [8] power unto the beast." [9]

"They worshiped the beast" (Rev. 13:4). Worship of the beast, a servant of the devil, is idolatry as much as worshiping the devil himself. All forms of idolatry are a type of submission to the devil, who works through his agents "with all power and signs and lying wonders" (2 Thess. 2:9), giving the false impression of incomparable greatness.

Encouraged by the power and the arrogance of the beast, its worshipers open their mouth in blasphemy, "saying, Who is like unto the beast?" (Rev. 13:4). Unmitigated insolence, taking the words which apply properly only to God (Ex. 15:11) and applying them to the devil's beast! It is a parody of the name "Michael." [10] Michael was seen to prevail against the dragon

[8] Rather, "for he had given."

[9] Rev. 13:4; cf. Lev. 17:7; Deut. 32:17; 2 Chron. 11:15; Ps. 106:37; 1 Cor. 10:20; Rev. 9:20.

[10] See the notes on Rev. 12:7.

(Rev. 12:7-9), whereas now the worshipers of the beast think that the tables are turned, so that they do not hesitate to ask: "Who is able to make war [do battle] with the beast?" completely inverting the thought of Mal. 3:2: "Who shall stand when He [the Lord] appeareth?" But God does as He pleases also with regard to this beast. (Ps. 135:5, 6)

"There was given unto him [the beast] a mouth" (Rev. 13:5). He who made man's mouth (Ex. 4:11) also gave this beast its mouth. The fact that the beast abused this gift of God, "speaking great [proud, arrogant] things and blasphemies" (Rev. 13:5; cf. Dan. 7:8, 11, 20), is not God's fault. It was done with His permission but without His sanction and approval. (Rom. 11: 7-36; 1 Cor. 2:7-16)

Without God's permission the beast could not have existed even for a moment. But "power [ability, permission] was given to him to continue forty and two months" (Rev. 13:5), that is, throughout the entire New Testament age.[11] At every point he is under divinely established limits. However, observing him in action, one would not easily suspect that this is the case. "He opened his mouth in blasphemy against God" (Rev. 13:6; see Dan. 7:25). Think of the atheists, who deny the existence of God; the Unitarians, who deny the Trinity; the rationalists, who deny the virgin birth of Christ and His deity; the Modernists, who deny His vicarious atonement.

God's name is blasphemed (Rev. 13:6), in direct violation of Ex. 20:7.[12] In the wider sense God's name includes every statement in which God tells us about Himself. God's Word is God's name. In this sense we pray in the First Petition of the Lord's Prayer: "Hallowed be Thy name!" Luther: "God's name is hallowed when the Word of God is taught in its truth and purity, and we, as the children of God, also lead a holy life according

11 See the notes on Rev. 11:2.
12 Also see Lev. 24:16; Deut. 5:11.

to it. . . . But he that teaches and lives otherwise than God's Word teaches, profanes the name of God among us." [13]

More, the beast blasphemes "God's tabernacle and them that dwell in heaven." [14] God spreads His tent, or tabernacle, over the saved in heaven so that they may dwell in safety and security under its cover and protection.[15] The saints above cannot be reached, or touched, or harmed by the beast. But that does not stop him from speaking against them.

The devil's agents open their arrogant mouth in loud blasphemy against God, against His Word, and against His church. For a time it seems as if they, symbolized by the beast of the sea, would be completely and forever successful. "It was given unto him [16] to make war [do battle] with the saints and to overcome them" (Rev. 13:7; Dan. 7:21). But this is not as hopeless for the saints as it first sounds, though it is true that because of the beast the way of the saints through this world often appears to be anything but a path to victory and glory.[17] Though the beast overcomes the saints,[18] that is not the last word on the subject. Here, as elsewhere in the Book of Revelation, "war" (KJV) means "battle." While the devil or his agents may win a battle, they lose the war.

"Power [authority] was given him [the beast] over all kindreds [tribes] and tongues and nations" (Rev. 13:7). The best manuscripts include also the words "and people" after "kindreds." [19] The realm of the beast, like the kingdom of God on earth, stretches from shore to shore. But while God rules in His

[13] Small Catechism, Explanation of the First Petition. Also see Rom. 2:23, 24; Is. 52:5; Ezek. 36:20; the notes on Rev. 15:4.

[14] Rev. 13:6; see the notes on Rev. 7:15.

[15] RSV, "His dwelling, that is, those who dwell in heaven."

[16] That is, the beast was allowed.

[17] See the notes on Rev. 11:7, where it is the beast of the bottomless pit that makes war against God's witnesses and overcomes them. Also see Rev. 12:11.

[18] Cf. Dan. 7:25: "wear out the saints of the Most High."

[19] On the four terms see the notes on Rev. 5:9.

own right, the beast has power only by God's permission. "The beast's worldwide authority goes back to the dragon's commission (v. 2), but ultimately to divine permission (so in v. 5)." [20]

It is interesting and important to note the similarities and differences between Rev. 5:9 and 7:9 on the one hand and Rev. 13:7 on the other. All mankind is referred to by the same four terms in all three passages. But while the former passages speak specifically of the saved, the latter speaks specifically of the lost. The saved are comparatively few,[21] while the lost are the large majority, so much so that the saved are not even taken into separate account when the beast is said to have power over all kindreds and people and tongues and nations.

This is the heyday of the devil's beast of the sea. Those who follow the crowd will have him for their leader and god. "All that dwell upon the earth [22] shall worship him" [23] — all, that is, "whose names are not written in the book of life [24] of the Lamb slain from the foundation of the world" (Rev. 13:8). The line of demarcation between the two divisions of all mankind is sharp, clear, and correct.[25] The statement that some names are not written in the book of life is parallel to Matt. 7:23: "I never knew you." But the figure must not be pressed beyond its intended meaning. It does not follow that those whose names are not written in the book of life are predestined to damnation. In His omniscience and prescience God knew from eternity who would be lost, but He did not predestinate them to their eternal fate. Because they would reject Christ, their names were not written in the book of life from the foundation of the world. They are

[20] James Moffatt, in the EGT, V, 431, on Rev. 13:7.

[21] "Redeemed . . . *out of* every kindred . . . *of* all nations" (Rev. 5:9; 7:9).

[22] See the notes on Rev. 3:10.

[23] See the notes on Rev. 13:4.

[24] See Rev. 17:8; cf. Rev. 3:5.

[25] Cf. Matt. 12:30; Mark 9:40; 16:16; Rev. 11:1, 2; also see the notes on Rev. 20:5.

lost by their own fault — not because God omitted their names from the book of life.

In the last part of Rev. 13:8 the KJV follows the order of the original Greek: "the Lamb slain from the foundation of the world." The RSV translates: "written before the foundation of the world in the book of life of the Lamb that was slain." Since there is no compelling reason to depart from the order in the original, we prefer the KJV in this passage and follow the old interpretation of it (1 Peter 1:19, 20). As predestination to salvation is so sure and certain that its final effect is spoken of as already past (Rom. 8:30), so was Christ's death so sure and certain in its foreordination that it is spoken of as having actually occurred "from [before] the foundation of the world." It is this certainty and assurance that lent validity to the Old Testament sacrifices and symbols pointing forward to the Savior who was to come. That is why and how the people of God in the Old Testament were saved — by the blood of the Lamb, though, historically speaking, that blood had not yet been shed. The saving power and effect of Christ's death extends backward to Adam as well as forward to the end of the world. (Matt. 8:11; Luke 13:28)

"If any man have an ear, let him hear." [26] When God speaks, as He does through St. John in this vision, it is for us to listen and learn.

The fate of the worshipers of the beast (Rev. 13:10) is a warning. The first part of Rev. 13:10 poses a problem for the translator. In the best manuscripts there is no verb in the first clause. Erasmus [27] added the Greek word for "leadeth." For the sake of good English a verb must be supplied. Since there is no good reason to choose a verb that is different from that in the second clause, we take the verb "go" also for the first clause. We also make the first clause conditional, as it is in the Greek:

[26] See the notes on Rev. 2:7.
[27] About 1466—1536.

"If anyone goes into captivity, he shall go into captivity." Those who give themselves to be captives of Satan in this world (Rev. 13:3-8) will be his captives also in the world to come.

"If anyone kills with a sword, he must be killed with a sword." [28] This is the old law of just retribution (Gen. 9:6), repeated by Christ (Matt. 26:52). In Rev. 13:10 it is applied to the followers of the beast who do not stop short of murder in persecuting the saints.[29] They will be killed with the sword of God's justice in hell. This passage does not prove that murderers must suffer capital punishment here on earth.

Under such circumstances the patience and the faith of the saints come into their own (Rev. 13:10), severely tried and tested, and strengthened as a result.[30] The inheritance of the Gospel promises in heaven is the final reward of the faithful (Heb. 6:12), because those who may kill their body are not able to kill the soul. (Also see Matt. 10:28; Luke 12:4)

Rev. 13:11-18: The Third Vision — The Beast of the Earth

The fact that the first beast rose up out of the sea and that the second one came up out of the earth may be taken to mean that the entire world is affected by their activity and influence. The two beasts have this in common, that they do not descend from heaven above, but come from below. To borrow the words of James 3:15, they are "earthly, sensual, devilish." They serve the dragon, who is their lord and master. He stands on the sand of the seashore.[31] On his one hand rises the beast of the sea (Rev. 13:1), and on his other the beast of the earth.[32] An imposing and impressive scene for those who are easily swayed by a display of power and show of strength!

[28] Rev. 13:10, literally.

[29] Rev. 13:7; 11:7; 12:11.

[30] See the notes on Rev. 1:9; 2:2, 3, 19; 3:10.

[31] Rev. 13:1, according to the best MSS.

[32] Rev. 13:11. The "false prophet" of Rev. 16:13; 19:20.

Because of the broad scope and sweep of the imagery in these visions, we hesitate to identify the beasts with any single individuals on the stage of the world's history or even with any groups or movements which are comparatively limited. They rather appear to be of worldwide significance. The suggestion is well taken that the two beasts stand for anti-Christian power and anti-Christian propaganda — both of them ruthless and both of them deadly for the unwary and unprepared.

The beast of the earth had "two horns like a lamb" (Rev. 13:11) Whoever had been frightened by the seven heads, ten horns, bear's feet, lion's mouth, and leopard's appearance of the first beast (Rev. 13:1, 2) would be tempted to say: "But *this* is *different!*" That is the purpose of such anti-Christian propaganda.

A lamb is a symbol of Christ. A false lamb may therefore be taken to represent a false Christ. Note the parallel descriptions of deception and seduction by great signs and wonders in Matt. 24:24; Mark 13:22, and Rev. 13:11-14. Therefore "if any man shall say unto you, Lo, here is Christ, or there, believe it not." [33] Appearances are deceiving. (2 Cor. 11:14)

This "lamb" is by no means weak and meek — not nearly as harmless as he appears to be at first sight. He "spake as a dragon" (Rev. 13:11). In the encounter between Christian and Apollyon in *Pilgrim's Progress,* John Bunyan writes of the dragon's "yelling and hideous roaring" and of the pride, haughtiness, arrogance, threats, craftiness, and seduction which he brought to bear against the pilgrim Christian.

The dragon suits his actions to his words. "He exerciseth all the power [authority] of the first beast before him" (Rev. 13:12), that is, in his sight. The second beast operates under the supervision and direction of the first.

It engages in all-out efforts to enslave men, knowing that in all it says and does it has the help and support of the dragon and the first beast. It does not hesitate to put shackles on the souls

[33] Matt. 24:23; also see Mark 13:21.

of men. Religion is its first target and victim: "He . . . causeth the earth and them which dwell therein to worship the first beast, whose deadly wound was healed" (13:12). "The earth and them which dwell therein" is a general reference to mankind with its large majority of unbelievers.[34] The "worship" of the beast is not merely civil respect, reverence, and honor, but means that people will "admire, adore, glorify this beast." [35] This is not something new. The second beast simply helps to continue what has already begun.[36] Anti-Christian propaganda closes the vicious circle begun by anti-Christian power. The recovery of the first beast from its mortal wound is successfully advanced as a reason for its supremacy. With this, the deception becomes complete, and men become captives not only of poor logic, but, what is far worse, also of false religion.

To hold them captive, the second beast "doeth great wonders, so that he maketh fire come down from heaven on the earth in the sight of men" (Rev. 13:13). Compare the "great signs and wonders" of false Christs and false prophets (Matt. 24:24; Mark 13:22) and the "power and signs and lying wonders" of the Antichrist. (2 Thess. 2:9)

It is not possible definitely to identify this sign of the beast with any single specific event that has actually taken place in the course of history. It is significant that the beast is spoken of as performing a supernatural work very similar to that of Elijah, the prophet of God (1 Kings 18:38). Occasionally there is some apparent similarity between the devil's displays and God's miracles. In our day this warning has special application to healing cults and various so-called miracles which lead the gullible masses astray. The mere fact that you cannot explain something, or even that it may be definitely supernatural, does not necessarily mean that it is of God. (2 Thess. 2:8-12; Matt. 24:24)

The beast "deceiveth them that dwell on the earth [37] by means

34 See the notes on Rev. 3:10.   36 See the notes on Rev. 13:3, 4, 8.

35 Lenski, p. 405.   37 See the notes on Rev. 3:10.

of those miracles." [38] The "signs" are not true miracles of God, and therefore they must be supported by lies and deceit; otherwise men would discover that they are not genuine and that they are not of God. Genuine miracles of God need no such support.

The fact that the beast "had power to do" (Rev. 13:14) these "miracles" is more accurately stated in the RSV: "the signs which it is allowed to work," literally, "the signs that were given it to do." Whatever the beast did was done only by permission of God.[39]

The last part of Rev. 13:14 speaks of idolatry in its coarsest form, the worship of an image, in open and flagrant violation of the clear word of God (Ex. 20:4, 5). The deception which leads men into this abyss of sin is accomplished through the age-old question: "Yea, hath God said . . . ?" (Gen. 3:1) or perhaps even the bold statement: "Yea, God hath not said . . . !" The god of this world still blinds the minds of those who do not believe (2 Cor. 4:4). It is the golden calf, Dagon, idols of silver and gold, the image that Nebuchadnezzar set up, and Diana of the Ephesians, all over again.[40] All idols are creatures that men make for themselves at the suggestion of the dragon and his beast. What a powerful attraction the suggestions of "the beast which had the wound by a sword, and did live," [41] have for the hearts and minds of men!

The beast suffered his deadly, mortal wound by a sword (Rev. 13:14). The only sword which could harm him is the sword of Christ,[42] the Word of God. (Eph. 6:17)

Ordinary man-made idols cannot speak.[43] But the beast of the

[38] Rather, "because of the signs" (Rev. 13:14). Also see Rev. 16:14.

[39] See the notes on Rev. 13:5.

[40] Ex. 32; Judg. 16:23, 24; 1 Sam. 5:2 ff.; Ps. 115:4; Dan. 3; Acts 19:24-35.

[41] Rev. 13:14. "Live" is the correct translation of the Greek. It should not be made to read "live *again*," neither here nor in Rev. 20:5. See also the notes on Rev. 13:3. Schonfield and the RSV translate the end of Rev. 13:14 "and yet lived."

[42] See the notes on Rev. 1:16.

[43] Ps. 115:5; 135:16; also see Jer. 10:3-5.

earth was allowed to give this image both life and speech (Rev. 13:15). Like the fire coming down from heaven in Rev. 13:13, this took place with God's permission.[44]

As soon as the image had received the gift of speech, it moved to secure the allegiance of men on pain of death (Rev. 13:15). A strong incentive to worship the image! Pliny the Younger (A. D. 62—113), governor of Bithynia, is said to have punished with death those Christians who would not worship the emperor's image with incense and wine (cf. Dan. 3:6). It is a pointed commentary on the blindness and perversity of human nature that men would rather worship an idol, and so embrace spiritual death, than die physically with the assured hope and promise of eternal life. They fail to see through the devil's greatest deception of all. The worship of an idol, tangible or intangible, leads to eternal death.

The Mark   "He (the beast) causeth all, both small and great,
of the Beast   rich and poor, free and bond, to receive a mark
              in their right hand or in their foreheads" (Rev. 13:16). The "mark" is also called the name of the beast and the number of his name.[45] The devil does not want to be outdone. God seals His servants, the 144,000 saints, in their foreheads (Rev. 7:9, 4). The devil marks those that are his "in the forehead by way of profession; in the hand with respect to work and service." [46] The "mark" is that by which it may be known to whom an individual belongs (John 8:44). Every human being has either the seal of Christ or the mark of the beast.[47] The mark of the beast can be removed and replaced with the seal of Christ, but those who are sealed by the Lord can never be lost.[48]

44 See the notes on Rev. 13:5.
45 Rev. 13:17; also see Rev. 14:9, 11; 15:2; 16:2; 19:20; 20:4.
46 Augustine, quoted in Jamieson, Fausset, and Brown, on Rev. 13:16.
47 Cf. Matt. 12:30; Mark 9:40; Luke 11:23; 9:50.
48 2 Tim. 2:19; John 10:27, 28; Rom. 8:29, 30.

The devil's agents and propaganda overlook no opportunities
to do their evil work in "small and great,[49] rich and poor, free
and bond" (Rev. 13:16). Whether or not a person is a child
of God cannot be determined by his station or position in life.
On earth, however, the balance of favor and good fortune often
appears to be on the side of those who have the mark of the beast.
"No man might buy or sell, save he that had the mark, or the
name of the beast, or the number of his name" (Rev. 13:17).
This is not to be taken literally but symbolically as referring to
the boycotts, hatred, ostracism, opposition, and antagonism which
the children of God are made to endure at the hands of anti-
Christian agents, power, and propaganda. The lines are drawn
as between Christians and unbelievers in this prophecy, which is
general rather than particular.

"Here is wisdom!" (Rev. 13:18). You are wise if you know
these things and are prepared to deal with them properly in your
life. There is a blessing for you also in this part of the Book of
Revelation (Rev. 1:3). Therefore, in the fear of the Lord, which
is the beginning of wisdom (Ps. 111:10) "let him that hath understanding count [reckon, compute] the number of the beast" (Rev.
13:18) so as to identify it. Wisdom and understanding have not
always been brought to bear on this passage, with the result that
especially Rev. 13:18 has been made the point of departure into
an almost unlimited and extremely fanciful world of speculation
and misinterpretation. It is not our purpose to follow again in the
fruitless, bootless paths of variant and even contradictory opinions.
Very little can be said with full assurance of being right in this
matter. The statement: "It is the number of a man" (Rev. 13:18)
may also be translated: "It is a human number" (RSV), that is,
it is counted as men generally count.[50] It is not divine: it does
not refer to God in any way. Beyond this we can say only that

[49] See the notes on Rev. 20:12.

[50] Cf. "the measure of a man" (Rev. 21:17), that is, the ordinary measure
used by man.

it is the number of the second beast in Rev. 13, which we have taken to signify worldwide anti-Christian propaganda.

Seven is a symbol of completeness, especially in its multiples of 10 (Matt. 18:21, 22). In contrast to this, six may be regarded as the number of incompleteness. Six, plus its multiple by 10 (60), plus its multiple by 10×10 (600), would then express intensified incompleteness, falling completely, finally, and conclusively short of God, of His glory, and of all His grace and salvation for man.[51]

Summary of Chapter 13

We take the first beast to represent worldwide ferocious anti-Christian power, and the second beast to represent worldwide deceptive anti-Christian propaganda, sometimes put forth under the guise of religion.

Note: Some take the first beast to represent secular power, and the second beast to represent spiritual power. Others take the first beast to represent the Roman Empire, continued in the kingdom of Antichrist as he showed himself mainly before the Reformation, and the second beast to represent him as he has appeared since that time. In addition to this, there are numerous other interpretations.

---

[51] Irenaeus, the most eminent teacher of the church in the second half of the second century, suggested the Greek word *Lateinos* as the probable key for the solution of the symbolism in the number 666. The numerical value of its letters: L 30, A 1, T 300, E 5, I 10, N 50, O 70, S 200. The sum: 666. Irenaeus: "It seems to me very probable; for this is a name of the last of Daniel's four kingdoms; they being *Latins* that now reign." (Barnes, on Rev. 13:18)

Revelation 14 describes the fourth, fifth, and sixth of the seven visions in Rev. 12:1 to 15:4: the Lamb and the 144,000 on Mount Zion (Rev. 14:1-5), the three angels (Rev. 14:6-13), and the harvest of mankind (Rev. 14:14-20). The first of these three visions supplements Rev. 7. The second supplements Rev. 13 and prepares for Rev. 18. The third brings the second "sign" or "wonder," begun in Rev. 12:3, to a close.

Rev. 14:1-5
The Fourth Vision — The Lamb and the 144,000 on Mount Zion

"The Lamb" (Rev. 14:1 RSV) which stood on Mount Zion had appeared to John in an earlier vision.[1] It was the Lamb of God, which another John, the Baptist, had once pointed out to the multitudes at the Jordan (John 1:29, 36). In Rev. 5:6 the Lamb "stood" ready for action; in Rev. 14:1 he stands in triumph "on Mount Zion" (14:1 RSV), that is, heaven.[2]

With Christ in heaven, in this vision, are the 144,000 of Rev. 7.[3] They cannot be identified as any one group or denomination in visible Christendom, but are all the saints in heaven, having "His [the Lamb's] name and His Father's name written

1 See the notes on Rev. 5:6.
2 Ps. 2:6; Is. 27:13; Heb. 12:22-24.
3 See the notes on that chapter.

on their foreheads." [4] It was clear, for all to see, to whom they belonged. Their mark was the counterpart of the mark of the beast (Rev. 13:16). They bore two names, that of the Father and of the Son (cf. John 14:6). The best commentary on the last part of Rev. 14:1 is in John 17. [5]

The "voice" which John heard at this point came out of heaven (Rev. 14:2; cf. Rev. 14:13), and was "like the sound of many waters" (Rev. 14:2), surging, restless, rising and falling, overwhelming and irresistible in its very persistence and power. [6]

It was also "like the sound of loud thunder" (Rev. 14:2 RSV), rumbling, rolling, and reverberating. The voice of God the Father sounded like thunder to some on one occasion (John 12:28, 29). In Rev. 6:1 one of the four "living ones" spoke "as with a voice of thunder" (RSV). In Rev. 19:6, as in Rev. 14:2, the voice of the great multitude of the saved in heaven is described as the voice of great, or mighty, thundering in its tremendous power.

But it was not simply a loud noise, like the mighty roar of a crowd in a stadium. The "voice," or sound, which John heard, was also "like the sound of harpers playing on their harps" (Rev. 14:2 RSV). This is the second specific mention of music in the Book of Revelation (Rev. 5:9; 15:3). The music of heaven, with its celestial melodies and harmonies, infinitely transcends the finest music of earth. Harps provide a wonderful background for the voice. Their sound is pleasant, lovely, uplifting, inspiring, thrilling. Surely it was no mere coincidence that God chose to include harps in John's visions of heaven. They are well suited to the "new song" mentioned Rev. 14:3. [7]

"They [the 144,000] sung as it were a new song" (Rev. 14:3). Its words are not set down here, but since only the

---

[4] Rev. 14:1 RSV. This follows the reading of the best MSS.

[5] Esp. John 17:6, 10, 24, 26; also see John 10:27-30; Rev. 3:12.

[6] See the notes on Rev. 1:15. Cf. Rev. 19:6.

[7] Also see the notes on Rev. 5:8. The KJV phrase "harpers harping with their harps" preserves the play on words which is in the Greek.

redeemed could learn it, it is safe to say that its theme was redemption accomplished by the Lamb of God. It was "new" in
distinction from the Old Testament song of a Redeemer who
was to come.[8]

The redeemed in heaven sing their new song "before the
throne, and before the four beasts [living ones], and the elders"
(Rev. 14:3), because the throne, a symbol of God's power and
authority, rule, and dominion;[9] the four living ones, symbols of
the living earthly agencies or instruments of God's providence;[10]
and the elders, symbols of the ministry of the Word,[11] were all
involved and concerned in the salvation of the 144,000.

The 144,000 are the elect, for only they finally reach heaven,
where the scene of this vision is laid. No other man can learn
their new song. It remains unknown to those who only "for
a while believe" (Luke 8:13), but are finally lost. In this respect
it is like the "new name" in Rev. 2:17. It can be known only
by those to whom it is given. They are "redeemed[12] from the
earth" (Rev. 14:3). Strangers and pilgrims on the earth (Heb.
11:13; 1 Peter 2:11), heaven is their home. Redeemed "from
the earth . . . to God" (Rev. 14:3; 5:9) is the key to a right
understanding of such other passages as: "These are in the world,
but . . . not of the world"; "Ye are not your own"; "Ye are
Christ's"; "Your body . . . and . . . your spirit . . . are God's";
"Whose I am."[13]

Rev. 14:4: "These are they which were not defiled with
women; for they are virgins [chaste]." This does not mean that
they were not married, or Peter would be excluded from them

8 Also see the notes on Rev. 5:9, 10.

9 See the notes on Rev. 4:2.

10 See the notes on Rev. 4:6.

11 See the notes on Rev. 4:4.

12 Lit., "bought." Cf. 1 Cor. 6:20; 7:23; 2 Peter 2:1. For the price see
Rev. 5:9, which also gives us the counterpart of the words "from the earth," namely,
"to God." Also see Rev. 14:4.

13 John 17:11, 16; 1 Cor. 6:19; 3:23; 6:20; Acts 27:23.

(Matt. 8:14; Luke 4:38). Rather "these" include all who go to heaven, both men and women, married and unmarried. "Marriage is honorable in all" (Heb. 13:4). Instituted by God Himself, the marriage relationship is not impure and dishonorable, but is chaste and pure, as Luther says: "We should fear and love God that we may lead a *chaste* and decent life in word and deed, and each love and honor his *spouse.*" [14] God's words to Adam and Eve "Be fruitful, and multiply, and replenish the earth" (Gen. 1:28) were spoken before the fall of man into sin. It is only illicit intercourse that defiles. "After the occurrences recorded in Gen. 6:4 physical defilement with pagan women came to be a symbol for defection from God." [15] The word "defiled" in Rev. 14:4 must be understood accordingly. On the other hand, virginity is a symbol of faithfulness to God (2 Cor. 11:2; Eph. 5:25, 27). It is in this sense that the expression "not defiled with women" and the word "virgins" ought to be understood in Rev. 14:4, in strong contrast to the lost, who engaged in spiritual fornication with the harlot Babylon. (Rev. 14:8; cf. Is. 1:21)

"These are they which follow the Lamb whithersoever He goeth" (Rev. 14:4). The sheep follow the Lamb (John 10: 4, 27). They do what a certain scribe, in the first flush of enthusiasm, once promised Jesus: "Master, I will follow thee whithersoever thou goest" (Matt. 8:19; Luke 9:57). That is what the Baptism and the confirmation vows mean: to renounce the devil and all his works and all his ways . . . and in faith, word, and deed to remain true to the Triune God, even unto death. The way He leads may not always be easy, but it leads to heaven, where He is. (Also see Rev. 2:10; 3:4)

"These were redeemed from among men" (Rev. 14:4), that is, out of the mass of lost mankind.[16] The saved in heaven are

14 Explanation of the Sixth Commandment.

15 Lenski, p. 424. See Ex. 34:15, 16; Lev. 17:7; 20:5, 6; Deut. 31:16; Judges 2:17.

16 Cf. Rev. 14:3, and see the notes on Rev. 5:9.

"first fruits for God and the Lamb" (Rev. 14:4 RSV; cf. James
1:18). These "first fruits" are all of those whom God has set
apart and sanctified for Himself by faith. The expression has its
Old Testament background in such passages as Ex. 23:19; Lev.
2:12. The first fruits were dedicated to God; the rest of the
harvest was, in the comparison drawn here, secular or profane.
Similarly, the 144,000 belong to God; the rest of mankind are
also harvested, but do not go to heaven.[17]

Of the saved in heaven John says further that "in their mouth
was found no guile."[18] "No guile," or "no lie," is not simply
a reference to deceit or untruth in the common sense. It is rather
all untruthfulness in contrast to the truth as it is in Christ Jesus
and His Word.[19] Whatever is out of harmony with, or in dis-
agreement with, or in contradiction to, God is "lie." Peter's
denial[20] was a "lie" in more than one sense. In the first place
what he said was not true, and secondly it was a specific rejection
of Christ. Yet include Peter in this vision. In fact, all the saints
were sinners on earth. How then can it be said that "in their
mouth was found no lie"? The answer is indicated in the words
"For they are without fault."[21] The church with Christ in heaven
has no spot, or wrinkle, or any such thing. It is holy and without
blemish, cleansed and purified from every "lie" by the water of
Baptism and the precious blood of Christ, Himself the perfect
Lamb of God, without blemish and without spot. (1 Peter 1:19)

17 There is a different comparison in 1 Cor. 15:20, 23, where Christ is the
"First Fruits," and the following harvest of believers also belongs to God.

18 Rather, "no lie." Cf. the contrast in Rev. 21:8; also see Rev. 14:5; cf. Zeph.
3:13; Ps. 32:2.

19 John 8:31, 32, 44; 14:6; 1 John 1:6-10; 2:22; 4:6; 2 Thess. 2:9-12;
Matt. 24:24; Rev. 13:14.

20 Matt. 26:69-74; Mark 14:66-71; Luke 22:54-60; John 18:17, 25-27.

21 RSV, "spotless." Eph. 5:26, 27; 1 John 1:7; 1 Cor. 1:8; Jude 24. The
words "before the throne of God" (Rev. 14:5 KJV) are not in any known ancient
Greek MS. They were added by Erasmus of Rotterdam (cf. C. E. Hammond, Outlines of Textual Criticism Applied to the New Testament [Oxford, 1890], p. 10)
and are corrcetly omitted in the RSV.

Rev. 14:6-13: The Fifth Vision — The Three Angels

Rev. 14:6, 7 is an Epistle for the festival of the Reformation, October 31. It speaks of the first of the three "angels," or messengers, in this vision. Among the interpretations which have been put forth is this, that the first angel is John Wycliffe, the second (Rev. 14:8) John Huss, and the third (Rev. 14:9) Martin Luther. However, it is best not to limit our understanding of these angels to such specific interpretations but to think rather of the Gospel messengers in the entire New Testament age after the Book of Revelation was written.

The angel [22] flew "in the midst of heaven," at its zenith (Rev. 8:13). The Gospel message of the angel is from above, from God. In his ministry he is high out of reach of any and all who may want and attempt to hurt or harm him and hamper, hinder, or halt his work.

His mission was: to preach the everlasting Gospel to those who dwell on earth (14:6). In the preceding vision all the saved were already in heaven. Now we hear of Gospel preaching on earth and, in Rev. 14:13, of those who die in the Lord. The visions which John saw are clearly not to be interpreted chronologically.

The angel's message was "the everlasting Gospel." [23] This "Gospel" is quoted verbatim in Rev. 14:7. It is "everlasting," or "eternal," because it never changes (Gal. 1:6-9); and it is to be preached to those who dwell on earth, that is, the inhabitants of the world. [24] The thought is that of worldwide missions. It is "Gospel" in the wider sense. [25] The angel was flying, to denote the rapidity with which the Gospel would spread through the

---

[22] The word "another" in Rev. 14:6 has no further reference or purpose than to distinguish the first angel from the two which were to follow (Rev. 14:8, 9).

[23] Rev. 14:6 RSV, "an eternal Gospel."

[24] The terminology is different from that in Rev. 3:10 and related passages.

[25] Matt. 24:14; 28:19; Mark 16:15; Acts 1:8; Rom. 10:18.

world." [26] He spoke "with a loud voice" (Rev. 14:7) for all to hear.[27]

There are three parts to the angel's eternal Gospel in Rev. 14:7.

First: "Fear God, and give glory to Him" (Deut. 6:2, 13; 10:20). The proper fear of God is true reverence. It is this of which Luther wrote in his explanations of the Ten Commandments: "We should *fear,* love, and trust in God above all things. . . . We should *fear* and love God that we may [resp., may not]. . . ." He who properly fears God will also give Him glory. This does not mean "add to His glory," for we cannot do that. It means to "make known His deeds among the people . . . talk . . . of all His wondrous works" [28] and sing and say, "All glory be to God alone!"

The second part of the angel's message gives the reason why we should fear God and give Him glory: "For the hour of His judgment is come" (Rev. 14:7). The "judgment," or "judging," which is spoken of here is not limited to any one point of time. It is rather like saying: "Now it's time for action!" The action which follows may extend over a long time. "Judgment" is not a single momentary act, but it includes all of God's individual judgments as they fall in time until they come to a final head in the Last Judgment. "The prince of this world is judged" (John 16:11). The woman's Child has been caught up to God's throne (Rev. 12:5). That was "the hour." Now the action follows in which God's "judgment" falls, continually and to all eternity, on the prince of this world and on his followers. (Rev. 14:9-11)

The last part of this angel's message is an echo of Matt. 4:10: "Thou shalt worship the Lord, thy God!" Worship is essentially an expression of the proper attitude of the heart toward God, in

[26] Barnes, on Rev. 14:6.

[27] On "every nation and kindred and tongue and people" (Rev. 14:6) see the notes on Rev. 5:9.

[28] Ps. 105:1, 2; also see Deut. 32:3; Is. 42:8; Jer. 13:16.

which He is regarded and approached as the pre-eminently Worthy One. The word "worship" was originally conceived as "worth-ship." Hence the essence of worship is expressed in the doxology of Rev. 5:9, 10 and especially also Rev. 5:12, 13.[29]

God, whom we are to worship, is specifically described and identified in Rev. 14:7 as the Creator of all: "heaven, and earth, and the sea, and the fountains of waters."[30] The references which the Book of Revelation makes to the Old Testament are allusions rather than quotations. Rev. 14:7 adds the phrase "and the fountains of waters," which is not found in the Old Testament passages referred to here. These words help us to understand and appreciate more fully Rev. 8:10 and 16:4, where the fountains of waters become instruments of vengeance and punishment under the direction of Him who made them.

The second of the three angels in this vision bears the message: "Babylon is fallen, is fallen, that great city, because she made all nations drink of the wine of the wrath of her fornication" (Rev. 14:8). This is the first time that "Babylon" is mentioned in the Book of Revelation.[31] It cannot mean ancient Babylon on the Euphrates, for that city had long ago disappeared from the face of the earth and was not rebuilt (Is. 13:19-22; 14:1-23). But the characteristics of that ancient city, and the part it played in the history of God's people, help us understand the use of its name in the Book of Revelation.

Babylon of old was a large, outstanding, and important city. At the height of its power it was the head of the heathen world, proud, haughty, insolent, and oppressive to the point of persecuting the people of God. With these features in mind, many commentators, both ancient and modern, have applied the "Babylon" passages in the Book of Revelation to "Babylon on the Tiber," that is, papal Rome. But a stronger interpretation regards

[29] See the notes on those verses. Cf. Ps. 33:8.

[30] Gen. 1:1; Neh. 9:6; Ps. 33:5-9; 124:8; 146:5, 6; Jer. 32:17; Acts 4:24; 14:15; 17:24; John 1:1-3; Heb. 1:1-3; Rev. 4:11.

[31] It occurs again in Rev. 16:19; 17:15; 18:2, 10, 21.

"Babylon" as the *entire* anti-Christian world city or empire built
up by the two beasts of Rev. 13. It is great [32] in the eyes of the
world, even as ancient Babylon was great in the sight of men.
(Dan. 4:30)

The complete overthrow and fall of ancient Babylon was
prophesied by Isaiah (Is. 21:9). How strange his words must
have sounded when the great city was still very strong and flour-
ishing — a hundred or more square miles in area, surrounded by
double walls at least 32 feet thick and 75 feet high or higher —
a well-nigh impregnable fortress at the height of its glory in the
6th century B. C. Yet in less than 200 years it became rubble
and ruin — in literal fulfillment of Jer. 51:31; 50:21-32. Heaps
and mounds are all that remain of it now. [33]

A similar fate is just as surely in store for the spiritual Babylon, with all that belongs to it. The church in the world may
seem small, and the people of God may appear to be in a powerless, helpless minority. But the message of the angel in Rev. 14:8
directs the eyes of those who will see to the complete and final
overthrow of every proud and haughty rival and insolent and
oppressive enemy persecutor.

The wickedness and successful deception of the spiritual
Babylon is described in the last part of Rev. 14:8: "She made
all nations drink of the wine of the wrath of her fornication." [34]
She "made all nations drink the wine of her impure passion"
(RSV). This latter is a good translation of a passage which is
practically unintelligible in the KJV. The thought is that
Babylon has given herself over to whoredom in her lewd, hot
passion, a symbol of spiritual unfaithfulness to the true God. [35]
She made the nations drunk with her seductiveness and the at-

[32] The best translation is: "Babylon the great" (RSV). The word "city" is not
in the attested reading.

[33] Davis, under "Babylon."

[34] "Because" (KJV) is not in the best MSS.

[35] See the notes on Rev. 14:4; also see Judg. 8:33-35; Is. 57:3-12; Rev. 13, esp.
vv. 7, 8, 16; 17:1-5; 18:3, 9; 19:2.

traction of temptations to spiritual whoredom. Moral restraints break down and give way under the intoxicating influence of strong wine. It beclouds the mind and the eye. So also the passion of spiritual fornication and adultery. It is heady and confusing. This passage is not directed primarily against literal drunkenness and sins of the flesh against the Sixth Commandment, although they are, of course, included; it rather speaks of everything that is unchristian and anti-Christian in religion.

The last of the three angels in this vision appears in Rev. 14:9-11. His message, like that of the first angel (Rev. 14:7), is proclaimed with a loud voice, for all to hear. It is a warning of the infinite punishment of God upon everyone who worships the beast and his image and receives his mark in his forehead or in his hand.[36]

There are not many other passages in the Bible which set the First Table of the Law, especially the First Commandment, into such sharp and clear focus and perspective as Rev. 13—14. Idolatry, lying and deceiving under the guise of religion, and departing from the Word of God, are drawn in diametric opposition and contrast to the worship of the one and only true God — with all that it implies and involves.

"Fear God . . . give glory to Him . . . and worship Him" is like a hub around which this entire passage revolves. The devil and his henchmen make their demands and threats. He who dared to say to the Son of God, "Fall down and worship me" (Matt. 4:9), will not stop short of asking you to do the same, saying: "If you will not worship the beast and his image, you will be killed; if you will not receive the mark of the beast in your hand or in your forehead, you will not be able to buy or sell" (Rev. 13:15-17). God's stern and final answer to that is the point-blank warning: "If any man worship the beast and his image, and receive his mark in his forehead, or in his hand, the same shall drink of the wine of the wrath of God, which is poured

[36] Cf. Rev. 14:9 with Rev. 13, esp. vv. 4, 12, 14-16.

out without mixture into the cup of His indignation; and he shall be tormented with fire and brimstone in the presence of the holy angels and in the presence of the Lamb. And the smoke of their torment ascendeth up forever and ever; and they have no rest day nor night, who worship the beast and his image and whosoever receiveth the mark of his name." (Rev. 14:9-11)

So the lines are drawn and the tension is established from which there is no escape in this world until God Himself provides release for a child of God in a blessed death. When all is said and done, putting Rev. 13:15-17 side by side with Rev. 14:9-11, there can be only one proper course of action to follow. It is that which is so beautifully pointed out by our Savior Himself: "Fear not them which kill the body, but are not able to kill the soul; but rather fear Him which is able to destroy both soul and body in hell!" (Matt. 10:28). Jesus Christ, our Savior, drained the cup of sorrow and suffering for us (Matt. 26:39, 42; John 18:11; 19:30), in order that we might not taste the wrath of God in eternity. Those who will not believe this, nor receive Him into their hearts in saving faith, shall drink the cup of infinite and eternal suffering themselves. (Mark 16:16; John 3:18b)

An interesting play on words is carried over from the Greek into the KJV, but partly lost in the RSV, in Rev. 14:8 and 10: "the wine of the wrath of. . . ." In its reference to God the picture is amplified: the wine of God's wrath is pure, unmixed. There will be no mercy in the final condemnation and punishment, but the hot anger of God is "poured out," released, set free unmitigated, in its full strength, in all its fury. But it is not unreasonable: it is poured "into the cup of His indignation," that is, the *righteous* anger of God. He is entirely within His right and the bounds of justice in meting out the fearful punishment described in Rev. 14:10, 11. (Also see Rev. 15:1, 7; 16:1 ff.)

"Fire and brimstone" are associated with the infinite torments of hell.[37] "In the presence of [before] the holy angels and in

---

[37] See Rev. 19:20 and the notes on Rev. 20:10.

the presence of the Lamb" (Rev. 14:10) means that the angels and the Lamb agree in the fearful judgment which is both necessary and appropriate because of the justice of God. It is altogether true and righteous. This verse should not lead us to think that heaven and hell are located geographically, in space, in such a way that from heaven you can see what is going on in hell. Rather than taking the words "in the presence of" as a reason to ask, "Where is hell?" we shall be much wiser and do far better to ask: "How can we keep from going there?" The answer to that question is in Rev. 14:12, 13 and in many other passages.

As the saints on earth consider the just punishment of the lost in hell, they become the more ready themselves to endure affliction and to be faithful unto death.[38] "The commandments of God" (Rev. 14:12) are not only the Ten Commandments but also "precepts" in the wider sense: the entire Word of God to man. To "keep" the Word of God means to hold fast to it and not let it go or give it up (Rev. 12:17). To "keep the faith of Jesus" means not only to believe in Him but also to hold on to faith securely and successfully, under fire and trial (Rev. 12:17; 2 Tim. 4:7), as to a precious trust, gift, or deposit.

In one of Paul's most beautiful and comforting passages he writes: "Patience [worketh] experience; and experience, hope; and hope maketh not ashamed!" (Rom. 5:4, 5). The same truth is put before us in Rev. 14:12, 13. In their patience the saints have faith and a hope that does not disappoint them. The end of their faith, the salvation of their souls (1 Peter 1:9), is assured for them in the promise that is solemnly sealed by the Holy Spirit of God Himself.

"I heard a voice from heaven saying unto me," says John, "Write: Blessed are the dead which die in the Lord from hence-

---

[38] See the notes on Rev. 13:10. The RSV phrase "Here is *a call for* the endurance of the saints" (Rev. 14:12) says more than the text. The KJV's "Here is the patience of the saints" is accurate. The verse continues in the best readings simply: "who keep the commandments of God and the faith of Jesus." See the notes on Rev. 12:17.

forth. Yea, saith the Spirit, that they may rest from their labors, and their works do follow them" (Rev. 14:13). This is one of the best-known passages in the Bible. It is often used in Christian burial services. St. Piran ("the apostle to Cornwall," A. D. 352 to 430) used it as a preparation for his death. When he lay dying, he ordered his assistants to dig his grave and repeated this verse.[39] Countless others have also found divine comfort in it.

The "voice from heaven," which directed John to write the specific words in this verse, is not described or identified. It came from heaven and must have in God its ultimate, if not immediate, source. All Scripture is verbally inspired by God. The holy men of God who wrote the various books of the Bible used exactly those words which God wanted them to use. In Rev. 14:13 we see one way in which the specific words were given to the holy writer.

The beatitude in this verse is the second of seven in the Book of Revelation.[40] Some connect the words "from henceforth" with the word "die": blessed are those who from now on die in the Lord. While that can be correctly understood, it leaves unanswered the question: What about those who died in the Lord previously? We hold it best and most meaningful to connect "blessed" with "from henceforth"; the one derives emphasis from its position at the beginning of the verse, the other from its position at the end. In more idiomatic English we would group the two in combined emphasis at the beginning: "Blessed from henceforth are those who die in the Lord!" They are blessed from the moment of their death and to all eternity. This also rules out any fanciful intermediate state, such as purgatory, or soul sleep.[41] Those who "die in the Lord," that is, with saving faith in Jesus Christ, know where they will go the moment they leave this world. The grave holds no terrors for them, for it receives only the body.

[39] F. R. Webber, *History of Preaching* (Milwaukee, 1952—57), I, 62, 63.
[40] See Rev. 1:3; 16:15; 19:9; 20:6; 22:7, 14.
[41] Also see Heb. 9:27; 2 Cor. 5:8; Phil. 1:23; Luke 16:22.

To this the Holy Spirit adds His solemn "Yea," it is so! The saints in heaven are blessed in that they "rest from their labors, and [42] their works do follow them" (Rev. 14:13). There is literally no rest for the wicked (Rev. 14:11), but "there remaineth . . . a rest to the people of God" (Heb. 4:9, 10; also see 2 Thess. 1:7; Rev. 6:11). It is a rest "from their labors," that is, from the fatiguing demands of being Christians on earth. This is an indirect reminder that the life of a child of God, as it should be lived, is not easygoing, but is "labor."

Those who give themselves to it will find at the last that when they enter eternal rest "their works do follow them." No more weariness, toil, and fatigue! The saints in heaven are forever through with all of that, forever out of it. The things which they accomplished in their life on earth, their good works, literally "follow along with them" as proof of their saving faith. The good works of Christians are "worth more than heaven and earth in that, while heaven and earth will pass away, the good works of Christians abide. All the earthly possessions of men — of Christians, too — will be consumed by the fire of Judgment Day, but the good works of Christians, also those performed by means of their perishable possessions, will not be consumed, but will follow them into eternity, and will be crowned with an eternal reward of grace (Matt. 5:12; 19:29; 10:42; Gal. 6:9)." [43]

Rev. 14:14-20; The Sixth Vision — The Harvest of Mankind

This vision sets before us the gathering of the harvest of mankind at the end of the world. The harvest includes both the living and the dead, and both the saved and the lost will be reaped simultaneously in the fulfillment of the prophecy of this vision (in harmony with Matt. 25:31-46). The fact that "another angel" reaps part of the harvest (Rev. 14:17 ff.) does not point

[42] Rather, "for."

[43] Pieper, III, 61; cf. Matt. 25:34-40.

to a sequence in time, as if there were two separate resurrections from the dead and two judgments.[44]

As the vision began, John saw a white cloud with a man sitting on it as upon a throne.[45] White is a symbol of holiness, righteousness, and justice.[46] The cloud connects this vision with other passages.[47] In view of the fact that the One who sat on the cloud was "like unto the Son of man,"[48] there can be no doubt as to who He was. It was Jesus Christ, the Son of God Himself. (Also see Matt. 8:20; 16:13; 25:31 ff.; Acts 7:55, 56)

On His head was a golden crown, here at once a symbol of victory and royalty as well as glory and honor.[49] In His hand was a sharp sickle (Rev. 14:14), a symbol of reaping. The Son of man holds and wields the sickle to reap that harvest which is His, that is, to take the elect to heaven. The other sickle (Rev. 14:17-19) is held and wielded by an angel to reap that harvest[50] which is to be dealt with in hell according to the consuming wrath of God. Both sickles are "sharp," cutting swiftly, surely, cleanly, and completely. They do not symbolize death, for not all shall die (1 Thess. 4:17). The picture of death as the "grim reaper" is not properly based on this passage.

As the action in this vision began, "another angel"[51] came out of the temple.[52] This angel cried "with a loud voice to Him

44 Cf. Mark 4:29. Also see Matt. 3:12, where the separation of the chaff from the wheat, and their final disposal, is part of one harvest. Similarly Matt. 13:30. See Ps. 1.

45 Cf. the "great white throne" in Rev. 20:11 and the "white horse" in Rev. 6:2.

46 Is. 1:18; Rev. 19:11; also Ps. 19:9; Rev. 16:7; 19:2.

47 For example, Rev. 1:7; Matt. 24:30; Luke 21:27; Dan. 7:13.

48 Rather, "like a son of man." See Rev. 1:13; Dan. 7:13.

49 Heb. 2:7; Rev. 17:14; 1 Tim. 6:15. Victory and royalty are also combined in the scene described in Rev. 19:11-21. Also see Rev. 6:2.

50 The tares in Matt. 13:30.

51 In distinction from those in Rev. 14:6, 8, 9, 17, 18.

52 Or "sanctuary," last mentioned in Rev. 11:19. Also see the notes on Rev. 3:12.

that sat on the cloud" (Rev. 14:15). It was not an uncertain sound. The angel acted with clear knowledge of the contents of his message and in full assurance that this was the precise moment to speak.

"Thrust in thy sickle, and reap, for the time is come [53] to reap" (Rev. 14:15). This verse has raised considerable discussion. Some commentators hold that the One on the cloud was not the Son of God but an angel, because, so they argue, an angel would not give orders and directions to the Son of God. However, they do not give proper consideration to the fact that the angel was not speaking by his own authority. The fact that he came out of the temple indicates that his message was from God the Father, in whose hand and power are the times and the seasons (Acts 1:7). Without a special revelation from God neither this angel nor any other could know God's appointed day and hour for the final harvest of mankind (Matt. 24:36; Mark 13:32). Even the Son of God did not know it in His state of humiliation, according to His human nature (Mark 13:32). In this vision this angel merely carries a message from the Father to the Son and announces it so loudly that also John could hear it clearly and distinctly. The message was simply: Reap, for the time has come, because the harvest of the earth is "ripe." [54] The hour appointed by God had struck.

There was not a single moment's further delay. "He that sat on the cloud thrust in his sickle on the earth; and the earth was reaped" (Rev. 14:16). How much can be put into so few and simple words! They paint at a single stroke the "moment, the twinkling of an eye" of 1 Cor. 15:52. (1 Thess. 4:13-17)

How deliberately God proceeds and operates in all of this! Unhurried, yet right on schedule! Not so much as a single sheaf, or ear, or kernel, intended for the granary of heaven, drops unnoticed by the wayside or is lost. All are safely gathered in.

[53] "For thee" (KJV) is not in the best MSS.
[54] Or, "dried." RSV, "fully ripe."

The entire act is pictured and described in the past tense, as having already taken place.[55] Here is the highest comfort and assurance of Christian, saving faith.

The other part of the great harvest of mankind is described in Rev. 14:17-20.

"Another angel came out of the temple which is in heaven,[56] he also having a sharp sickle.[57] And another angel[58] came out from the altar, which [angel] had power over fire" (Rev. 14:18), literally "over the fire," that is, the fire on this altar. The direct reference apparently is to Rev. 8:3-5, and the indirect reference is to Rev. 6:9. Inasmuch as he came from the altar, this angel, like the one in Rev. 14:15, is a messenger of God. The altar is the altar of incense. The angel's "power over the fire" may be taken to signify "the authority that is given by God to declare when, according to God's will, the judgment is finally to come upon the wicked in answer to the prayers of the saints." [59] The prayers of the saints are heard and answered in due time and in God's way.

The angel from the altar brought his message from God "with a loud voice [RSV] to him [the other angel] that had the sharp sickle, saying, Thrust in thy sharp sickle." [60] The harvest is a harvest of the grapes of wrath and of the vine of the earth, symbolizing the wicked (Deut. 32:32; Jer. 2:21). It is "fully ripe" (Rev. 14:15; Matt. 23:32; 1 Thess. 2:16). God's patience is not eternal. It has an end, and when it is reached, there is no more delay, no more time of grace, no "second chance." When the word was given, "the angel thrust in his sickle into the earth." (2 Cor. 6:2; Heb. 3:7-11)

55 Cf. "glorified" at the end of Rom. 8:30 and "hath" in John 3:36.

56 See the notes on Rev. 14:15; 3:12.

57 Rev. 14:17; see the notes on Rev. 14:14.

58 See the notes on Rev. 14:15.

59 Lenski, p. 448.

60 Rev. 14:18; see the notes on Rev. 14:15.

The vine ["vintage," RSV] of the earth was gathered and cast into the great winepress of the wrath of God (Rev. 14:19). The entire vine was completely stripped bare of its clusters, which were cast into a winepress, to be crushed with such a vengeance as only the great and righteous anger of God could mete out (Is. 63:1-6). The winepress in which these grapes were trodden was "without the city" (Rev. 14:20), that is, outside of it. The city is the New Jerusalem, heaven (Heb. 11:10; 12:22; Rev. 21:2). Outside this city there is no salvation (Rev. 22:15). When the winepress was trodden, its product was not wine but blood, as a vivid symbol of the gruesome fate which overtakes the wicked in everlasting living death. The picture presented here seems incongruous only if we fail to consider and remember that it is a highly concentrated figure, such as is not unusual in the Book of Revelation.[61]

The last part of Rev. 14:20 is admittedly difficult to explain. It is cast in highly symbolical language, with its extreme imagery related to the modern term "blood bath." "Up to the bridles of the horses[62] refers to depth. "By the space of a thousand and six hundred furlongs" ["stadia," RSV] refers to distance, or extent. It does not help much to translate furlongs, or stadia, into miles, because the symbolism seems to lie rather in the very figure 1,600. If four is taken as the number of the world,[63] we arrive at 1,600 by multiplying 4 by itself and by 100 (10×10) as a symbol of completeness. Universal judgment will overtake the wicked.

[61] Cf. Rev. 7:14: robes made *white* in *blood*.

[62] Rev. 14:20, in Lenski's translation.

[63] See the notes on Rev. 1:4.

Revelation 15 divides evenly into two parts. The first four verses set before us seven angels with the seven last plagues in the final vision of the seven which begin at Rev. 12:1. In the last four verses of Rev. 15 the seven angels receive seven golden "vials" (KJV), or "bowls" (RSV), full of the wrath of God, in preparation for the pouring out of these vials in the seven scenes pictured in Rev. 16. Rev. 15 and 16 belong together, while at the same time Rev. 15 is a complete unit in itself and forms a smooth link and transition between the preceding and the following.

Rev. 15: The Seventh Vision —
The Seven Angels with the Seven Last Plagues

John "saw another sign [wonder] in heaven" (Rev. 15:1). This was not only the seventh, and last, in this entire series of visions,[1] but it was also the last in a special series of three which John describes as "signs in heaven." [2] Rev. 15:2-4 presents an interlude between vv. 1 and 5, which are connected in thought.

The "sign" in heaven in Rev. 15:1-4 was "great and marvelous" in its nature, appearance, and significance, causing amazement and terror. There were "seven angels having the seven last plagues, for in them is filled up [ended, RSV] the wrath of God"

1 See the notes at the beginning of the chapter on Rev. 12.
2 For the first two see Rev. 12:1, 3.

(Rev. 15:1). We may regard these plagues, poured out of the seven vials upon the earth (Rev. 16), as the last warnings God gives the unbelievers.

The seven angels are good angels, strong servants of God. The figure *seven* is a symbol of God's dealings with man.[3] We do not take the figure *seven* literally here, as if these last plagues (judgments, punishments) were exactly seven in number. Nor do we identify the seven plagues with seven events or periods in the history of the world. They are the sum total of the remaining expressions of the wrath of God as seen in His righteous judgments,[4] dramatized in some detail before the eyes of John as the vision unfolds. (Rev. 16)

First John describes the preliminary, or preparatory, vision. He saw "as it were a sea of glass," which some regard as a type of God's providence.[5] But whereas in Rev. 4:6 it was simply glassy, or transparent, "like unto crystal," it appears in Rev. 15:2 as "mingled with fire" and is a symbol of the punishment that God deals out in His overruling providence. It emphasizes the fact that God's wrath is "filled up." [6]

The fiery punishment of God does not strike, or hurt, or harm the children of God, those who "had gotten the victory over the beast, and over his image, and over his mark, and over the number of his name." [7] This victory is gained "through our Lord Jesus Christ" (1 Cor. 15:57) by those who believe in Him (1 John 5:4). The beast with his image and mark, which is the number of his name,[8] has no power over them. They "stand on [at, beside] the sea of glass" (Rev. 15:2). God's providence supports and sustains them. Far from being consumed by the fire of His

[3] See the notes on Rev. 1:4.

[4] See also the notes on Rev. 8:5, 7.

[5] See the notes on Rev. 4:6.

[6] Rev. 15:1; cf. Matt. 3:10-12 and similar passages.

[7] Rev. 15:2; see Rev. 13:11-18; 2 Tim. 4:7, 8; Rev. 2:7, 11, 17, 26; 3:5, 12, 21; 12:11; 21:7.

[8] See the notes on Rev. 13:16.

anger, they are safe — so much so that they can occupy themselves with "the harps of God" (Rev. 5:8; 14:2). These instruments are "of God" because God gave them and because they are used to His glory.

The Song of   The song of the conquerors is "the song of
the Conquerors   Moses, the servant of God, and the song of
                   the Lamb," [9] that is, it deals with the things
God did through His servant Moses and through the Lamb, His Son, Jesus Christ. Moses, the leader of the Children of Israel in their deliverance out of bondage in Egypt, was a type of Christ, who delivered us from the bondage of sin, death, and the devil. Moses and Christ are linked together also in Heb. 3:5, 6.

In its form the song is a perfect example of beauty in variety of expression and balance, following the pattern of the Psalms. It is addressed to God, who is called Lord (Rev. 15:4), Lord God Almighty, and King of saints (Rev. 15:3 KJV); the latter title, however, should rather read "King of the nations" (Jer. 10:7) or "King of the ages." [10] He is the supreme Ruler over all at all times. [11]

God is great and marvelous not only in this vision (Rev. 15:1) but also in all His works. [12] All His ways are righteous, just and true, [13] though we on earth may not be able fully to grasp and understand them. For us here in time His judgments are unsearchable, and His ways past finding out (Rom. 11:33). But in the final Judgment and through all eternity it will be and remain abundantly clear that God is always right. The saints in heaven will raise and join their voices in song to praise and glorify Him for it.

[9] Rev. 15:3. On music in heaven see Rev. 5:9; 14:2, 3.

[10] Cf. the RSV text and footnote.

[11] Rev. 1:8; 4:8; 11:17; 16:7; 21:22; Ps. 86:9.

[12] Amos 4:13; Ps. 111:2; 139:14.

[13] Rev. 16:7; 19:2; Hos. 14:9; Ps. 145:17.

"Who shall not fear [Thee], O Lord, and glorify Thy name?" [14] The obvious answer to this rhetorical question is: No one (Phil. 2:9-11). All will fear Him and glorify His name, though not all will do it willingly. The perfect holiness of Him who alone is holy demands it and will not take no for an answer.

The name of God is not simply "God," or some other divine name, but it "includes everything we know of Him from the Bible — His essence, His attributes, His works, His commandments, and His promises. The name of God is God Himself as He has revealed Himself to us. In the Bible God has recorded His name (Ex. 20:24)." [15] God's name is God's Word. [16]

To "fear" the name of God means to have a proper reverence and respect both for Him in His holiness and for His holy Word, the Bible. Is. 66:2b combines the two thoughts: before the holy God sinful man ought to be properly "poor and of a contrite spirit," having every reason to "tremble" at His Word. [17] To "glorify" the name of God means so to regard and publicly acknowledge Him for what He is and does that He and His Word and judgments are recognized and acclaimed to be true and righteous altogether.

"All nations," without exception, "shall come." [18] They shall "worship" before God. [19] This is not necessarily in "worship" as we understand the word today. The unbelievers will also fall down before God, being brought to their knees by Him because of their unbelief, which refuses to worship Him in spirit and in truth.

[14] Rev. 15:4. Some MSS omit "Thee."

[15] E. W. A. Koehler, *Luther's Small Catechism Annotated* (River Forest, Ill., 1946), pp. 53, 54.

[16] See the notes on Rev. 13:6.

[17] Cf. Ex. 15:14-16 in the song of Moses after the Children of Israel passed through the Red Sea.

[18] Rev. 15:4; see 2 Cor. 5:10.

[19] KJV. RSV: "worship Thee." The Greek words literally mean "bow before Thee." The explanation is in Phil. 2:10: "Every knee shall bow."

In all of this, the "judgments," that is, the righteous verdicts and acts of God, "are made manifest," or public (Rev. 15:4). "In the end the whole universe shall acknowledge the righteousness of all God's acts and verdicts." [20]

"After that," that is, after the interlude described in Rev. 15: 2-4, the vision begun in Rev. 15:1 continues and introduces a new series of seven: the seven angels with seven golden vials. This series is described in this section, ending with Rev. 16.

"The temple of the tabernacle of the testimony [21] in heaven was opened" (Rev. 15:5). This is the same holy of holies which John had seen open in the vision described in Rev. 11:19.[22] It is a symbol of the presence of God, who sends out the seven angels with the seven last plagues (Rev. 15:6). "It is called the 'tabernacle of testimony,' because it was a testimony or witness of the presence of God among the people — that is, it served to keep up the remembrance of Him." [23]

The angels were "clothed in pure white [bright] linen" (Rev. 15:6), a symbol of holiness.[24] The golden girdles their breasts were girded with may be regarded as symbols of royalty (Rev. 1:13). The angels are the holy servants of the King of kings. (Rev. 17:14; 19:16; 1 Tim. 6:15)

"One of the four beasts [living ones] gave unto the seven angels seven golden vials [bowls] full of the wrath of God" (Rev. 15:7). It is idle to speculate which one of the four "living ones" enters into the action here. We regard all four of them as symbols of the earthly agents of God's providence.[25] The one who gives the bowls to the angels apparently acts also for the other three. These earthly agents have finished their work so

20 Lenski, p. 459.

21 RSV, "the temple of the tent of witness."

22 Also see the notes on Rev. 7:15. Cf. Ex. 40:34; Acts 7:44.

23 Barnes, on Rev. 15:5.

24 Rev. 3:4, 5; 4:4; 7:13, 14; Dan. 7:9; Matt. 17:2; Luke 9:29; Mark 16:5; Acts 1:10; 10:30.

25 See the notes on Rev. 4:6.

far as their part in the visions is concerned. They appear only once more (Rev. 19:4), in an attitude of worship. What still remains to be done, represented by the seven golden bowls and their contents, now passes out of their hands into the hands of the seven angels, heavenly agents of God's providence.

We will not endeavor to explain how the angels could have the seven plagues as they came out of the temple (Rev. 15:6) before the "living one" gave them the seven bowls (Rev. 15:7), or how the plagues were represented or symbolized in Rev. 15:6 so that John could recognize them as such. These are some of the many curious questions put by the inquisitive mind of man to which we do not need to know the answers. God lives not only now but "forever and ever." [26] As God's eternity is cause for boundless joy on the part of the saved (Ps. 16:11; 23:6), so also does it leave the lost in endless misery. (Mark 9:42-48)

When God appeared to Moses on Mount Sinai, the mountain smoked (Ex. 19:18; 20:18). When the prophet Isaiah received the vision of heaven described in Is. 6:1-4, "the house [that is, the temple] was filled with smoke." In John's vision "the temple was filled with smoke" (Rev. 15:8). In describing it he helps us understand the Old Testament passages, for he adds that the smoke was "from the glory of God and from His power." Similarly, the cloud that covered the tent of the congregation (Ex. 40:34) was a symbol of the glory of the Lord, which filled the tabernacle (also see 1 Kings 8:10, 11). It served, moreover, as a screen to shield human eyes from the glory of the Lord. (Ex. 33:18-20)

Not only the glory of God but also His power gave rise to the smoke which filled the temple. His glory is His power in action. [27] In this particular case His almighty power was manifested in the seven last plagues that were to overtake the unbelievers. In this also He is glorified. "The salvation of the

26 Rev. 15:7; see Rev. 1:6, 18; 4:9; 10:6.
27 James Moffatt, in the EGT, V, 445, on Rev. 15:8; cf. 2 Thess. 1:9; Is. 2:19.

righteous and the destruction of the wicked both glorify God. One is a display of His grace, the other of His justice, and in both He is glorious and worthy of everlasting confidence, affection, and praise." [28]

So firmly has His purpose of punishment been formed, and so surely will it be carried out that "no man was able to enter into the temple till the seven plagues of the seven angels were fulfilled" (Rev. 15:8; cf. Ex. 40:35; 1 Kings 8:10, 11). God's patience has an end, which is reached in this vision before the end of the world. When God has irrevocably determined upon a course of action, there is no appeal. Abraham interceded for the inhabitants of Sodom and Gomorrah because of the righteous who might be among them (Gen. 18:16-33). The plea was not successful, because there were not even ten righteous there. In Rev. 15:8 it is not even possible for any man to come before the mercy seat of God, in the holy of holies, for prayer to avert the determined judgment of God.

[28] *Concordia New Testament with Notes* (St. Louis, 1942), on Rev. 15:4.

Rev. 16:1: Introduction to the Seven Last Plagues

As the vision begun in Rev. 15 continues in Rev. 16, John hears "a great [loud] voice out of the temple" speaking to the seven angels. Some regard it as the voice of God, perhaps because of Rev. 1:10, 11 and because it came out of the temple, that is, from the presence of God.[1] However, if God were speaking, we might well expect Him to say, "Pour out the vials of *My* wrath," instead of "the vials of the wrath of God." We therefore leave the voice unidentified.

Each angel in turn is to go his own way and carry out his task. "To pour out the vials of wrath on" means "to visit vengeance or anger on."[2] As the seven successive strokes of God's righteous wrath fall on the wicked inhabitants of the earth in Rev. 16, the seven angels, God's willing and obedient servants, obey His command and act as His agents of justice in pouring out their "vials."

Before we look at the seven plagues in detail, we note in a general way: (1) that none of them strike the children of God, even as the Children of Israel were not affected by the plagues which struck the Egyptians (Ex. 7—12; also see Ps. 91:10). (2) that they take place here on earth before the end of the world; the Last Judgment is not included in them. (3) John's description of them must be understood figuratively, not literally.

---

[1] See the notes on Rev. 15:5.

[2] Webster's New Collegiate Dictionary, under "vial."

This follows the rule of interpretation that, except for compelling reasons, a passage is either literal throughout (which is not possible in Rev. 16), or it is figurative throughout. (4) The seven plagues follow in rapid succession, emphasizing their cumulative effect (Rev. 8:7 ff.). (5) It is not possible definitely to identify any or all of the seven plagues with events which have already taken place in world history or to say to what extent they have occurred. The reason for this lies largely in the difficulty of establishing the meaning of the various points of the symbolism employed here.

Rev. 16:2: The First Plague

As the first angel went in immediate obedience to the command to pour out his bowl of the wrath of God on the earth, "there fell a noisome [foul] and grievous [evil] sore [boil, ulcer] upon the men [people] which had the mark of the beast (Rev. 13:16-18), and upon them which worshiped his image" (16:2; see 13:14, 15). Some identify the "sore" with the French Revolution, but that is, in historical perspective, too limited an application. A more helpful suggestion is that which speaks of "virulent sores in the whole social, economic, educational, [and] political world where the anti-Christian power rules . . . involving a thousand aches and pains in all the departments of life." [3]

Rev. 16:3: The Second Plague

In view of the entire series of affected areas, it appears that "earth" in Rev. 16:2 means the land in distinction from the rivers and the sea, etc. One after another the doors of escape to health and life are closed to the wicked. It will not help them to "take the wings of the morning and dwell in the uttermost parts of the sea" (Ps. 139:9). For the sea becomes "as the blood of a dead man" (Rev. 16:3). The plague envelops the world with a stench of death and decay. It extends the effects of the

[3] Lenski, p. 466. Also see Rev. 13:17; 1 Tim. 6:9, 10; James 4:1-4; 5:1-6.

first plague not only geographically but also in intensity. The first plague brought painful ulcers; the second involves death. "Every living soul [thing] died in the sea." (Rev. 16:3)

Some have identified this plague with the world's great naval engagements and the carnage which accompanied them. But we believe that we are here dealing with figurative language which pictures the complete rottenness of all anti-Christianity everywhere. There is no real life in it, but only the foul seeds of death and corruption.

Rev. 16:4-7: The Third Plague

The third plague is even more drastic than the second. It is pictured as turning "the rivers and fountains of waters" (Rev. 16:4), streams and springs, into blood. Man cannot live without fresh water to drink (Rev. 16:6). Similarly, the streams of life and thought, good common sense, knowledge, and a proper philosophy need to flow free and clear. To the extent that they are corrupted, beclouded, adulterated, and impure, human life suffers. When political science fails, national strength and good international relations deteriorate and break down. All of human society begins to crumble at its foundations when marriages fail for lack of knowledge or application of sound principles and practice, and when the young are not properly trained. In this sense the wicked are subject to a very special kind of death by thirst for lack of a cup of this necessary clear water of sound understanding. There will be no one to cry: "Ho, everyone that thirsteth, come ye to the waters!" (Is. 55:1). God will give them over to their vaunted human wisdom, which is as blood to drink.

Perhaps the question: "Is God justified in this?" occurred to John as he saw this fearful judgment unfold in the vision. If so, he had the answer immediately. "The angel of the waters" [4] said: "Thou art righteous . . . because Thou hast judged thus" (Ps. 119:

4 Rev. 16:5; the "third angel" of Rev. 16:4.

137; 145:17; Rev. 15:3, 4). The judgments themselves establish His righteousness, even as the verdict of Solomon in dealing with two women proved and established his wisdom. (1 Kings 3: 16-28)

God is not only righteous in these judgments but also holy. The words "and shalt be" (Rev. 16:5 KJV) are not in the best manuscripts, but rather the words "the Holy One!" (Phillips). "The Lord is now no longer He that *shall* come, for He *is come* in vengeance." [5] Note the inner relationship: (1) Wicked men cannot stand before the Holy One; they fall under His righteous judgments. (2) Death could not hold the Holy One; He not only was — He also *is!*

The justice of God is clearly shown by the specific proof which the angel presents. These wicked ones who are given blood to drink "are worthy" (Rev. 16:6 KJV), that is, they deserve it. They have it coming to them, because they "have shed the blood of saints and prophets." [6] Are they bloodthirsty? Let them have blood to drink!

As in Rev. 11:3; 22:6, 16, the testimony not only of one but of two witnesses is put on record. The first is the "angel of the waters." [7] The second is "the altar"; [8] we take this to mean the angel which "came out from the altar" (Rev. 14:18). His testimony underscores that of the other angel. "Even so," [9] he says; that is: Yes, indeed! "True and righteous are Thy judgments!" [10] There is no miscarriage of justice here. Not a single unbeliever suffers unjustly. God makes no mistakes.

[5] Jamieson, Fausset, and Brown, on Rev. 16:5. Also see Ps. 16:10; Acts 2:27; 13:35; Rev. 15:4.

[6] Rev. 16:6; see Rev. 6:9; 11:8, 18; 18:24; Ps. 79:1-3; Is. 49:26; Matt. 23:37; 22:6; Acts 7:59; 1 Thess. 2:15; Heb. 11:37.

[7] Rev. 16:5; the "third angel" of Rev. 16:4.

[8] Rev. 16:7; the best MSS read: "I heard the altar say."

[9] On "Lord God Almighty" see the notes on Rev. 4:8.

[10] Rev. 16:7; see Ps. 19:9; 92:15; 119:137; Rev. 15:3; 16:5; 19:2.

Rev. 16:8, 9: The Fourth Plague

The fourth plague compounds the severe torture of the first three. Sick with ulcers, the stench of death in their nostrils, and parched with thirst, the wicked find to their utter dismay that they are not yet at the end of their suffering. The fourth angel pours his bowl of God's wrath on the sun, which is not darkened as a result, as in Rev. 8:12, but which is intensified in its heat so as to "scorch men with fire." (Rev. 16:8)

In its promise to the child of God, Ps. 121:5 ff. gives us a key to this vision: "The Lord is thy Shade upon thy right hand. The sun shall not smite thee by day. . . . The Lord shall preserve thee from all evil." With His blessing the sun normally provides comfortable, life-sustaining, cheerful light and warmth.[11] But when the Lord turns against those who turn against Him, the Sun of righteousness becomes a fearful, consuming fire of destruction.

God's purpose in such judgments is to bring men to repentance. But in this case it failed of its accomplishment. Instead, when men were scorched with the great heat, they insulted God by blaspheming His name. The reason is that they recognized Him as the One by whose authority and direction these plagues came upon them. In spite of better knowledge they did not repent so as to give Him glory.[12] However, by their violent reaction against God, their impenitence, and their refusal to glorify Him they accomplished nothing in their favor, but only showed all the more clearly the complete justice and righteousness of God's continued judgments on them.

Rev. 16:10, 11: The Fifth Plague

The first four plagues fell on the men who bore the mark of the beast and worshiped its image. The fifth strikes "the seat of the beast" itself (Rev. 16:10), that is, his throne, a symbol of

[11] Compare the symbolism in Ps. 84:11; Mal. 4:2.

[12] Rev. 16:9; see Rev. 2:5, 16, 21; 9:20, 21; 16:11, 21.

his power, rule, and dominion (Rev. 13:2). The kingdom of the
beast was darkened permanently, never to be lighted up again.

"God is Light" (1 John 1:5). Whatever is not of God is not
light but darkness.[13] "The anti-Christian empire is itself darkness. . . . Now this empire is struck with the darkness of God's
anger."[14] There is no greater darkness than that. (Rom. 1:21;
Eph. 4:18; Acts 26:18)

This added darkness which enveloped the kingdom of darkness is not further described by John, except as to its effects.
In its own way it added to the most exquisite pain in the citizens
of the kingdom of darkness, so keen and so intense that because
of it "they gnawed their tongues" (Rev. 16:10). This is one of
the most graphic notes in the entire Book of Revelation. Only
one who has experienced such sharp pangs that he actually bit
his tongue because of it can begin to appreciate its full force. The
jaws and tongue will at times move involuntarily under stimulus
of excruciating pain in some part of the body. In this vision the
wicked literally "kept biting" their tongues. It was not simply
a single sharp pain that shot through them, but rather a sustained condition of extreme anguish and suffering.

Yet they did not repent, but "blasphemed the God of heaven
because of their pains and their sores (Rev. 16:2), and repented
not of their deeds."[15] Here the God of heaven and the followers
of the beast stand in sharply detailed contrast. God is not called
"their God" but "the God of heaven" — and they are not in
heaven. Stopped short of it, they stop short of nothing in their
ranting and raving. Some Lutheran theologians correctly refer
Rev. 16:11 to the conduct of the wicked while on earth.[16] The
end of the world has not yet come in this series of visions. Two
more angels have their bowls to pour out.

13 Prov. 4:18, 19; Is. 60:1-3; Matt. 8:12; Luke 22:53; Eph. 5:11; 6:12; 1 Peter
2:9; Jude 6, 13.

14 Lenski, p. 474.

15 Rev. 16:11; see the notes on Rev. 11:13; 16:9.

16 Pieper, III, 547.

Rev. 16:12-16: The Sixth Plague

Not many passages of the Bible have been so much discussed, misinterpreted, and misunderstood as Rev. 16:12-16. These verses tell of the sixth angel pouring out his bowl of the wrath of God "upon the great river Euphrates" (Rev. 16:12), and of the events which followed in the vision which John saw.

The historical school of interpretation attempts to trace parallels between the visions and events in world history. It identifies the fifth plague with the diminishing of the power of the Roman papacy about the middle of the 19th century and looks for the fulfillment of the symbolism of the sixth plague in the further unfolding of world history, perhaps in contemporary events. But we do not believe that the name "Euphrates" or, for that matter, any other part of this prophetic vision, is to be understood literally. It should be perfectly obvious, especially in view of the following verse, that its language is figurative. As in Rev. 9:14, we understand "Euphrates" here to be a general reference to heathen world domination. It is not to be taken in a specific historical or geographical sense, but includes *all* opposition to God.

Geographically the Euphrates is a natural water barrier. In its drying up in the vision this barrier is removed, and a way is opened and prepared for forces which it had previously held back. These forces are called "the kings of the East" (Rev. 16:12), symbols of some of the anti-Christian powers. With the river dried up and thus the way prepared for them, it seemed so easy for them to come and join forces with other kindred powers and so to proceed together to the kill, the last battle against God and His people. It seemed as if the hour of their victory had come (Luke 22:53). It seemed so easy — fools that they are! It was actually a cursed, fatal delusion. "He that sitteth in the heavens shall laugh; the Lord shall have them in derision." (Ps. 2:4; also see Rev. 20:9)

For a time the plans of the anti-Christian powers seem to be successful both in word and in deed (Rev. 16:13, 14). John saw

"three unclean [foul] spirits like frogs come out of the mouth
of the dragon, and out of the mouth of the beast, and out of the
mouth of the false prophet" (Rev. 16:13). The dragon is the
devil (Rev. 12:9). The beast is the first beast in Rev. 13:1 ff.,
anti-Christian power (19:20). The false prophet is the second
beast, Rev. 13:11 ff., anti-Christian propaganda. "The mouth" is
mentioned in connection with all three as the evil source out of
which the foul spirits come (1 John 4:1-6). They are "spirits of
devils" ["demons," Rev. 16:14]. They deceive and mislead not
only in their preaching and teaching but also through their deeds,
for they work "miracles" (Rev. 16:14). These "miracles" are
lying signs and wonders,[17] which impress and convince the followers of the beast (2 Thess. 2:9-11). Not only the common
people, gullible as many of them are in their ignorance and superstition, but also some in palaces and other high places fall victim
to anti-Christian agents, who do not hesitate to approach even
the kings of the whole world.

A tremendous responsibility is here placed on the leaders of
the people. It is on their conscience if they take their citizens
into the camp of those who are hostile to God and His church
(Ps. 2:10-12). Many, however, will not listen to such a word
of God as this, preferring instead the bewitchingly attractive prospect of alliance with strength as the world reckons power. There
is a comfortable feeling in being on the side of the apparent majority, especially when it comes to a battle. It is just that which
seems to be in the making in this vision: "the battle of that
great day of God Almighty." (Rev. 16:14)

The battle promises to be between God Almighty and all
who are His, on the one hand, and the devil and all that are his,
on the other. It will be a "great day," not only because of the
prospective engagement but also because of its outcome. This will
be the Last Day. No more war, no more conflict for the Church
Militant after this! It is God's day; there will not even be a real
battle. (Rev. 19:11-21; 20:9; Ps. 46)

17 See the notes on Rev. 13:14. Also see 2 Cor. 11:13-15.

That great day of the Lord — the day of His final coming, in power and great glory, for judgment — will come as a thief in the night.[18] The end will come suddenly, unexpectedly, at an hour which is not known even to those who are the Lord's, but only to God Himself (Matt. 24:36, 42-51). Preparedness must be our constant watchword.[19] "Blessed is he that watcheth!"[20] To "watch" here means to be vigilant (1 Peter 5:8), alert, awake and aware, keeping your eyes open, as it were, looking for the coming of Christ.

"Keepeth his garments" (Rev. 16:15) is a reference to Rev. 3:18; 7:14. The "garments" are the garments of salvation, the robe of Christ's righteousness — ours by faith (Is. 61:10; Gal. 3:27). What a blessing it is that the sinner can come to the Savior for such a dress! "Lest he walk naked and they see his shame"[21] — a warning added to the blessing (2 Cor. 5:3; 1 John 2:28). "Shame" is a very strong word and here means "most disgraceful sin." Cf. Rom. 1:27: "that which is unseemly." (RSV: "shameless acts")

Rev. 16:16 takes up the description of the vision broken off at the end of Rev. 16:14. "He[22] gathered them together into a place called in the Hebrew tongue Armageddon," for the proposed battle spoken of in Rev. 16:14. For God's side of the "battle" and its outcome see Rev. 19:11-21; 20:9. The name "Armageddon" may be taken as a transliteration of the Hebrew *Har-Magedon,* which means "mountain of Megiddo" (the city was built on an elevation[23]), or of a combination of *Harmah,* which means "a place marked for destruction" (Num. 21:3; Judg.

[18] Rev. 16:15; see 1 Thess. 5:2; 2 Peter 3:10; and the notes on Rev. 3:3.

[19] Amos 4:12. Also see the notes on Rev. 22:20.

[20] Rev. 16:15. The third of the seven beatitudes in the Book of Revelation. Cf. Rev. 1:3; 14:13; 19:9; 20:6; 22:7, 14.

[21] Or impersonally: his shame be seen (Rev. 16:15).

[22] Some translate "they." The subject is variously taken to be either God, or Christ, or the sixth angel, or the dragon, or the beast, or the unclean spirits. The important thing is not who gathered the worldwide anti-Christian powers but that they were gathered.

[23] Tell el-Mutesellim. Cf. Finegan, p. 169.

1:17), and *Megiddo.* Perhaps there is a clue [24] for the interpretation of Rev. 16:16 in Judg. 5, where Deborah and Barak sing of
the overthrow of the Canaanite kings "by the waters of Megiddo"
(Judg. 5:19) and add (v. 31): "So let all Thine enemies perish,
O Lord." Rev. 16:16 is in a figurative context and must not be
taken literally. Megiddo, resp. Armageddon, is a symbol of the
complete and eternal defeat and destruction of all the forces
and powers of evil.

Rev. 16:17-21: The Seventh Plague

With the seventh, and last, plague comes the fall of Babylon
the great, a symbol of all that is anti-Christian (Rev. 14:8). It
began when the seventh angel poured out his vial into the air
(Rev. 16:17), from which the final blow was to be heralded and
initiated by lightnings, thunders, a great shaking and upheaval,
and hail. (Rev. 16:18-21)

As in Rev. 16:1, John heard "a great voice out of the temple." [25] The temple is associated with "the throne" (Rev. 7:15).
We may regard the voice as the voice of God. In a single Greek
word with the definite note of finality the voice said: "It is done!"
that is: Now we're past the point of no return. Actually the
plague had not yet occurred in the vision, but it was inevitable
from the moment in which the angel poured out his bowl. It is
like the strokes of a clock at the 11th hour: The hour itself ar-
rives with the first stroke; the remaining strokes follow inevitably.
"It is finished," said our Savior on the cross (John 19:30). His
death and burial, which were also a part of His humiliation, had
not yet occurred, but would follow in short order as a matter of
course. What followed in John's vision after the words "It is
done!" is described in Rev. 16:18-21. (Cf. Rev. 11:19b)

There were "voices" [loud noises] and thunders and light-

---

[24] As suggested by Bengel, in the German translation by C. F. Werner (Basel,
n. d.).

[25] Rev. 16:17. Also see Is. 66:6. The words "of heaven" are not in the best
MSS.

nings, in demonstration of God's almighty power moving into
action on a large scale.[26] "And there was a great earthquake,"
literally: a great shaking, or upheaval, not necessarily in the
limited sense of an earthquake.[27] In this case it definitely included
the earth (Rev. 16:19, 20). It was greater and mightier than any
other quake which had ever occurred. Its destruction of Babylon,
symbolizing the sudden, violent breaking up of the anti-Christian
world power, is graphically described in Rev. 16:19: "The great
city was divided into three parts," broken to pieces beyond repair
(cf. German, *entzwei*). Lenski explains this expression as an
idiom: "The whole city and every structure in it fell in a heap in
utter ruin. Every structure collapsed, one wall falling to the right,
another to the left, the roof and the floors falling down between
them. 'Three parts' indicates this form of disintegration"
(p. 484). "And the cities of the nations [28] fell" (Rev. 16:19) —
today we would call them the satellites of Babylon. They could
not long survive after their capital had been destroyed.

God does not forget. These things came to pass because "great
Babylon came in remembrance before God, to give unto her the
cup of the wine of the fierceness of His wrath" (Rev. 16:19.
Also see Hos. 7:2). The thought that God forgets the sins of
the wicked even if they do not repent is only one of many strong
delusions with which the god of this world completely deceives
and blinds the hearts and minds of those who do not believe.
"God is Love" (1 John 4:8). But He is also just (Rev. 22:12;
2:23). Babylon received not one drop more than she deserved
when God made her drain the cup of the wine of the fierceness
of His wrath to the very dregs (Rev. 16:19; cf. 14:10). When
this judgment overtakes the wicked, they have no place of refuge
and safety, for "every island fled away, and the mountains were
not found" (Rev. 16:20; 6:14). They are "men without God
in the hour of peril":

[26] See the notes on Rev. 4:5.
[27] See the notes on Rev. 6:12.
[28] That is, the heathen (Rev. 11:18).

Islands are places of refuge and safety when the oceans are dis-
turbed by great storms. If the mariner can guide his boat into
the shelter of an island, he can be safe. When great hurricanes
arise, he always seeks to do so. Mountains are also places of refuge.
When floods come upon the earth, men seek the mountaintops.
When the rivers rise, people flee to the hills. . . . Men seek to
provide many refuges for themselves, but they are all insufficient.
God brings each to naught. Some have sought to build mountains
and islands with their wealth. But in a moment wealth can be dis-
solved. Some have sought security in positions of influence and
power. But history reveals the utter vanity of such hopes. The
meaning is clear. In God's testing time no refuge which any man
outside the kingdom of God may throw about himself will avail.
The unbeliever cannot escape the penalty of his failure to accept
the grace of God in Christ Jesus and to embrace the love and
security which God freely offers in the Gospel.[29]

No other hailstorm has ever equaled that of Rev. 16:21 in
its intensity and fury: "Great hailstones, heavy as a hundred-
weight,[30] dropped on men from heaven (Rev. 16:21 RSV).
Think of this vision in terms of the ancient world. In those days
few buildings, least of all those already reduced to ruins by an
earthquake (Rev. 16:18, 19), could have provided safe shelter in
such a hailstorm. Nor was it possible to dodge the hailstones. By
reason of their weight it could be crippling and even instantly
fatal to be struck by one of them. This, if nothing else, should
have served to put the fear of God into the hearts of men. But
this plague did not move them to repent (Rev. 16:9, 11). Instead, they "blasphemed God because of the plague of the hail,
for the plague thereof was exceeding great." (Rev. 16:21)

The Last Day has not yet come. The wicked are still alive on
earth and still rage violently in their cursing and blasphemy
against God. What God will do to them when the last hour
strikes remains to be seen. Some of the following sections in the
Book of Revelation deal with that.

[29] L. Frerking, in *Portals of Prayer* for April 26, 1956.
[30] Lit., a "talent," 60 to 100 pounds.

Rev. 17: The Great Whore

In her faithfulness to Christ the holy Christian church is called the bride and wife of the Lamb.[1] Because of their faithlessness, all others are described as associated with "the great whore" (Rev. 17, etc.). God uses such language in speaking to us of these things in order to make as plain as possible the issues which are involved. Forty-five verses (Rev. 17:1—19:3) deal with this matter. Not one of them is improper or objectionable in its language.

The vision John saw concerning the great whore may be divided into three scenes: (1) Rev. 17 describes her in her appearance, activity, and following, and indicates her downfall. (2) Rev. 18 tells of her destruction, recalls memories of what she had been, and records the mourning and lament of her followers. (3) Rev. 19:1-10: doxology and transition.

While many Lutheran commentators take the great whore and her followers to be specifically the Roman papacy, others understand this vision as referring in a larger sense to the entire anti-Christian empire and all of its forces.

Perhaps because of its nature, showing the woman in all her seductive charms, this vision is not presented to John without a preliminary warning. "One of the seven angels which had the seven vials" came to him and said, Come here, and I will show you the judgment of the great whore who sits on many waters

[1] Rev. 21:9 etc.; also see the Song of Solomon.

(Rev. 17:1; 15:7). From the very outset she is called a great whore and is marked for "judgment," or a verdict, further described in its execution in Rev. 17:14-17. The "many waters" on which she sits are explained in Rev. 17:15. That she was sitting, the position of an established ruler (Rev. 4:2) indicates the firm control she exercised over her followers.

Her charms have been brought into play effectively in high places. "The kings of the earth," influential leaders in various areas of life (politics, education, art, science, amusements, etc.), "have committed fornication" with her, and "the inhabitants of the earth," those "whose whole heart and life are attached only to the earth," [2] have become drunk with the wine of her fornication (Rev. 17:2). Any and all unfaithfulness to God is like strong, heady wine. It intoxicates with a feeling of newly found freedom from restraint, while at the same time it confuses the heart and mind and beclouds the sense of judgment. Those who drink deeply of it will let no one, not even God, tell them what to do, what not to do, and how they are to be. At no point are they inclined to admit that they have gone too far and to retract, retrace, and make amends accordingly. They set themselves up as a law to themselves, do not hesitate to go to war against the Son of God (Rev. 17:14), and finally turn in deadly, gory revenge on their mistress (Rev. 17:16). In all of this the reference is not merely to sexual sins, but included is all unfaithfulness to God, spiritual adultery, on the part of those who reject Him in favor of loyalty to another. [3]

Having told John what to expect in the vision, the angel carried him away in spirit [4] into a wilderness, [5] a place separate

2 Lenski, p. 491. Also see the notes on Rev. 3:10.

3 See the notes on Rev. 14:8. For an Old Testament parallel in which a prophet of God played a very dramatic part see Hos. 1:2-9. Also see Rev. 21:8; 22:11 ("unjust" and "filthy"), 15; Prov. 20:1; 23:31-35; 1 Cor. 6:9, 10; Is. 23:15-18; Nahum 3:4; Ezek. 16:15-59; 23:1-49; Is. 1:21; Jer. 2:20; 3:6-9; Hos. 2:1-13.

4 Rev. 17:3. Not: "in the Spirit"; see the notes on Rev. 1:10; 4:2.

5 Rev. 17:3. Not: "the wilderness" (KJV); the reference is not to Rev. 12: 6, 14.

and apart, where John and the angel could see her but remain untouched by her moral and spiritual corruption. John saw her in proper perspective, and he describes her in Rev. 17:3b-6.

He "saw a woman sit upon a scarlet colored beast" (Rev. 17:3). This is obviously not the woman of Rev. 12 who represents the faithful church. But we have met the beast before (Rev. 13:1 ff.). Its color is scarlet, or crimson red, the color of sin (Is. 1:18). The woman sits on the beast, ruling over it, guiding and directing it, but at the same time she is dependent on it for success because it carries her. Here, then, is a picture of the essential interdependence between the anti-Christian world powers. When the house of Satan becomes a house divided against itself, it falls. (Matt. 12:25, 26; Rev. 17:16 ff.)

The beast is "full of names of blasphemy," KJV, or "blasphemous names," RSV (Rev. 17:3). In Rev. 13:1 we were told that the names are on the seven heads of the beast. In Rev. 17:3 they are spread all over its body, indicating its intensified arrogance and lack of regard and respect for God. The seven heads and ten horns complete the identification of this beast with that in Rev. 13:1.

More about the woman: She was "arrayed in purple and scarlet" (Rev. 17:4), rich, beautiful, royal colors, with their attraction for the eye skillfully woven into her overall seductive appeal to the "kings" of the earth. She certainly knows her business well, how to make herself appear desirable! A woman in her profession often commands the finest jewelry, usually as gifts from her lovers. The woman on the beast is adorned with gold and precious stones and pearls, enhancing her allurements. Her personal, physical beauty of face or form is not mentioned. Her power to entice is pictured as lying in outward finery designed to capture the eye, the heart, the mind, and the imagination of men.

In her hand she holds a golden cup, the glint of its precious metal adding a final touch to the scene. It is her crowning deception. As in the case of the hypocritical scribes and Pharisees (Matt. 23:25, 26), the outside of the cup is clean, but the inside

is full of abomination to God, everything connected with idolatry
(Deut. 29:17), including specifically "the impurities of her fornication" (Rev. 17:4 RSV). No brazen hussy was ever more
shameless, bold, or impudent. According to an old custom of
well-known Roman prostitutes, she also lets her name be publicly
known, wearing it on her forehead. (Rev. 17:5)

There is a difference of opinion as to whether or not the word
"Mystery" is part of the name written on her forehead (Rev.
17:5 KJV). The RSV translates this part of the verse: "On her
forehead was written a name of mystery, 'Babylon the great.'"
Luther's translation does not include the word in the name either.
The oldest MSS were written in capital letters and without spaces
between the words. Therefore the question regarding this word
is one which the Bible as such does not answer. But the meaning
of the word in question is not difficult to determine. It refers to
something hidden which is about to be revealed (Rev. 17:7 ff.).
It also seems to echo 2 Thess. 2:7: "the mystery of iniquity doth
already work."

The name identifies the woman as "Babylon the great,[6] the
mother of harlots and abominations of the earth" (Rev. 17:5).
She is the source of all her evil brood. No good can ever come of
the father of liars (John 8:44) and the mother of harlots, but
only a scurrilous spawn of earthbound abominations, that is,
everything and everyone associated with idolatry and unbelief —
a family and household that is the exact opposite and counterpart
of the holy Christian church, the household of God. (Eph. 2:19;
3:14, 15)

Not many sights are so revolting and disgusting as that of
a drunken whore. The extreme is reached when the drunkenness
of the mother of harlots is compounded with the bloodthirsty
murder of the saints and [7] of the martyrs of Jesus.[8] John does not
give us a complete record of all that he saw and heard. He does

---

6 See the notes on Rev. 14:8; 16:19.

7 Rather "even"; the "saints" and the "martyrs" are the same persons.

8 Rev. 17:6; cf. 16:6; 18:24.

not tell us how he knew that the woman was drunken with blood (and not with wine) and that it was the blood of the martyrs. But what John does tell us is sufficient for God's purposes here. One of these purposes was accomplished in John's reaction to what he saw. He "wondered with great admiration" (Rev. 17:6). Here the KJV is a bit misleading. John did not "admire" the whore. "I marveled greatly" (RSV) is better. Literally: "I wondered with great wonder; I was astonished."

This led to an explanation by the angel (Rev. 17:7-18), who begins with a question: "Wherefore didst thou marvel?" He recognizes the natural amazement of John and uses some of the questions he must have had in his heart and mind as points of departure in the interpretation which follows. He does not wait for an answer, but continues immediately: "I will tell you the mystery of the woman and of the beast with seven heads and ten horns that carries her." (Rev. 17:7 RSV)

The first part of the explanation (Rev. 17:8) is closely related to Rev. 13:1-8. "The beast, which you saw, was," it existed before it came up out of the sea. Then, it "is not," it received a fatal blow, the "deadly wound" of Rev. 13:3, at the exaltation of Christ. After that, it "shall ascend out of the bottomless pit," its "deadly wound was healed" (Rev. 13:3), and the beast becomes active again. Though consigned to "the bottomless pit," [9] the devil and his agents are able to carry on their evil work in the world to the present day. 1 Peter 5:8 is still true: "The devil, as a roaring lion, walketh about." But just as surely as he once received a fatal blow, so surely are he and his going to their place of reward. The beast literally "is going [present tense] into perdition" (Rev. 17:8). He is on his way to his final end.[10]

Meanwhile, before the final end, the beast will have a large and admiring following. "They that dwell on the earth [11] shall wonder [marvel] . . . when they behold the beast" (Rev. 17:8).

[9] Rev. 17:8; cf. Rev. 9:1, 2, 11; 11:7; 20:1, 3.
[10] See Rev. 19:20; 20:10; Rev. 17:11.
[11] See the notes on Rev. 3:10.

Their wonder is described in greater detail in Rev. 13:4-8. Their "names were not written in the book of life [12] from the foundation [beginning] of the world." [13]

In the KJV the end of Rev. 17:8 reads: "the beast . . . is not and yet is." In copying the old Greek MSS a copyist made a mistake. A change of only two letters changed the meaning from "and is to come" (*kai parestai*) to "yet is" (*kaiper esti*), and this error was carried over in the KJV. The RSV has the better reading: "the beast . . . is not and is to come." [14]

The first part of Rev. 17:9 is similar to Rev. 13:18. But the word "is" is not in the Greek in Rev. 17:9; it was supplied by the translators. Other translators have chosen other words. For example, "This calls for a mind with wisdom" (RSV), and "Now for the interpretation of the discerning mind!" (Moffatt). The section which follows is easily one of the most difficult in the Book of Revelation.

There were seven heads on the dragon of Rev. 12:3 ff. and on the beast of Rev. 13:1 ff. Neither of those two passages includes an explanation or interpretation of the seven heads. But of the beast in Rev. 17:3 ff. the angel says that its "seven heads are seven mountains, on which the woman sitteth" (Rev. 17:9). At first glance this seems to give us something definite, and we begin to think about groups of seven mountains. Ancient Rome, for example, was built on seven hills. Partly for this reason the traditional Protestant interpretation of Rev. 17 ff. has pointed to Catholic Rome. But Jerusalem was also built on seven hills. So was Constantinople. It is therefore best not to regard either the "seven" or the "mountains" in a literal sense. Rather, mountains suggest proud and durable strength. Here we see them drawn into the service of the great whore, symbol of all that is anti-Christian and ungodly. The sacred number *seven* is blasphemously

12 See the notes on Rev. 3:5.

13 The names of the elect were written in the book of life from the foundation of the world. See Eph. 1:4; 2 Thess. 2:13; 2 Tim. 1:9; Rev. 3:5.

14 On the meaning of those words see the notes on the first part of Rev. 17:8.

adopted by these forces as their own, and they boast of their strength as that of the "everlasting hills," as though it were invincible.

"There are [15] seven kings" (Rev. 17:10). We regard them also as symbolical, like the woman and the seven mountains. Heads represent the realm of thoughts, plans, and designs. In its seven heads the beast "usurps the place of God's holy thoughts," [16] and as seven kings it endeavors to rule over and dominate the mind and intellect of man. The powers of man's reason are prostituted to the purposes of the great whore and are drawn into her service in such a way as to take away the intellectual liberty and freedom of thought that properly belongs to a Christian man.

But in the case of these "kings" more is included in the figure "seven" than an arrogant usurping of the things of God. There is also a historical significance. To the extent of five kings the symbolism has already been fulfilled, for "five are fallen" (Rev. 17:10). We regard the entire figure *seven* as symbolical, and do not endeavor to list or identify seven specific kings or rulers in the history of the world as corresponding to this prophecy. "All that the five which have fallen included we may gather from the old historians, when they are read with spiritual eyes, when by means of the beast Satan 'deceived the nations' (Rev. 20:3) during the time before Christ." [17]

"One [king] is" (Rev. 17:10). This refers to the claim the beast fastened on the mind of men at the time of St. John the Divine, and the intellectual subservience he still demands today (2 Cor. 4:4a). The subjects of the "seven kings" of Rev. 17:10 do not dedicate to the glory of God their ability to think.

The symbolic number *seven* is completed in the passing of the present (sixth) king and the appearance of the seventh and last one, who "when he cometh . . . must continue a short

[15] Rather, "And they [the seven heads] are."

[16] Lenski, p. 505.

[17] Lenski, p. 506.

space."[18] This points to the last times immediately preceding the end of the world.[19] The time will come when the entire phenomenon of the "seven kings" will forever be a thing of the past. Every endeavor, no matter how zealous or persistent, to defeat the eternal counsels of God will come to an unsuccessful and ignominious end.

In blind devotion to a lost cause the beast personally resorts to his last desperate measures. He "was and is not."[20] All his seven kings have failed and fallen, and he cannot save the day for himself by stepping into the breach as the eighth. His fate, previously announced (Rev. 17:8), is confirmed: "He . . . goeth into perdition" (Rev. 17:11). These words of God, spoken by the angel, we see fulfilled in Rev. 19:20; 20:10; cf. 17:17b.

The words "he . . . is of the seven" (Rev. 17:11) are difficult to understand and explain. Some speak of seven stages occurring in the development of the Roman Empire and culminating in the papacy. Others list the various kingdoms that successively rose to power in the ancient world and regard the papacy as the eighth. Neither interpretation can be definitely established as the only correct one. We regard them both as too narrow. Let us rather take the seven heads, as well as the ten horns (Rev. 17: 12), of the beast as symbolizing various phases, or aspects, of universal anti-Christianity, with the beast itself (Rev. 17:11) representing their final concentration, embodiment, and consummation.

In addition to the seven "head kings" there are also ten "horn kings" (Rev. 17:12-14). Ten may be regarded as a symbol of totality (cf. Matt. 18:22). Horns are symbols of power and strength. They remind us of a rhinoceros, or unicorn, bull, etc.[21] We may not be far wrong in regarding the "head kings" as sym-

18 Rev. 17:10. RSV, "must remain only a little while."

19 Rev. 20:3, "a little season."

20 Rev. 17:11; see the notes on Rev. 17:8.

21 Also see Deut. 33:17; Dan. 7:7, 8; 8:21; Ps. 148:14; Luke 1:69; and the notes on Rev. 5:6; 12:3; 13:1.

bols of mental and intellectual forces and the "horn kings" as symbols of physical forces, all co-ordinated in a death struggle with Christ and His church.

None of these ten powerful kings had as yet come into his own at the time of St. John the Divine. Their part on the stage of the world was to be played for "one hour" (Rev. 17:12), that is, a definitely limited and comparatively short period, during the last times of the beast. This indicates not a succession of kings or kingdoms in this series but a combination or co-ordination of all ten at one time in their alignment with the beast. Some have attempted to identify these kings and their kingdoms with ten specific nations or world powers. But we hold that this prophecy does not lend itself to such literal interpretation.

Not to be overlooked is the fact that these "kings" will "receive" their kingdom and power as kings. They would have no authority or dominion unless it is given them. The text does not say from whom the kings would receive their kingdom and power. But what was true of Pilate (John 19:11) is true also of all who imagine themselves to be lords over the Lord and over His church. They exist and act only by divine permission and within the limits which God sets.

They "have one mind" (Rev. 17:13). Whatever other differences they may have between themselves, they agree in their opposition to Christ and in their allegiance to the beast, into whose service they place themselves and their power and strength also in their last hour. (Rev. 16:13, 14)

"These shall make war with the Lamb" (Rev. 17:14). How foolish can a man be? (Ps. 2). Those who are against God shall be overcome. The final result isn't even in doubt for a single moment. He "shall overcome them, for He is Lord of lords and King of kings!" (Rev. 17:14). These "lords" and "kings" are not secular rulers but are the believers.[22]

"They that are with Him are called and chosen and faithful"

[22] Deut. 10:17; 1 Tim. 6:15; 1 Peter 2:9; Rev. 1:6; 2:26, 27; 3:21; 5:10; 11: 15; 19:16; 20:4-6.

(Rev. 17:14). They are "with Him," not helping Him but rather
"associated with Him and sharing in His royal victory." [23] They
are with Him, not by their own choice but by God's grace. He
called them by the Gospel.[24] They are His "chosen," elect, people.
The Greek word for "chosen" is used in 22 passages in the New
Testament. Perhaps the most important is Rom. 8:33, where it
embodies what the apostle describes in Rom. 8:28-30. It refers
to election, predestination, salvation. "The decree of predestination is that essential internal act of the Triune God by which He
from eternity, moved only by His grace and the redemption of
Jesus Christ, purposed to sanctify and save by faith, through the
means of grace, all saints who finally enter into life eternal." [25]

Those who are with the Lamb in the victory over the beast
and its "kings" are also "faithful" (Rev. 17:14), continuing steadfast in the saving faith through time into eternity.[26] This also is
God's work in and for us.

Rev. 17:15 refers back to Rev. 17:1. John saw the "many
waters" on which the whore sat, though he does not mention
them in his description of the vision. They represent "people and
multitudes and nations and tongues." [27] "Multitudes" is a word
used only in Rev. 17:15 in the series of seven lists; it means large
numbers of people in a mixed and motley crowd, without any particular grouping. The emphasis is on large numbers: as many as
could be attracted and seduced by the whore into misbelief, despair, and other great shame and vice (Ezek. 16:15-34). She is
successful on a worldwide scale.

But there will be a reaction against her which will be fatal
for her. Rev. 17:16: The "ten horns" which John saw "upon [28]

23 Little, p. 179.

24 2 Thess. 2:14; 2 Tim. 1:9; Luke 14:16, 17; Matt. 22:1-10.

25 J. T. Mueller, *Christian Dogmatics* (St. Louis, 1954), p. 177.

26 Rev. 2:10; Matt. 10:22; 1 Peter 5:9a.

27 Rev. 17:15. See Jer. 51:12, 13 and the notes on Rev. 5:9.

28 Rev. 17:16 (KJV). Rather "the ten horns *and* the beast." Also see Rev.
17:3, 7, 12-14.

the beast shall (1) hate the whore, and (2) shall make her desolate and naked, and (3) shall eat her flesh, and (4) burn her with fire." Revulsion and loathing grow out of excessive indulgence in sensuousness. Many a one who has abandoned herself to sensual enjoyments has paid for it with her life at the hands of her lovers, who turned murderously against her. This part of the vision is not altogether unnatural. Besides, the revolt of the horn kings and the beast against the whore is fanned into a strong, consuming flame by the knowledge that they are inescapably trapped and confronted by overwhelming odds in the conflict into which she led them (Rev. 17:14). Going down in final and complete defeat, they move quickly and pitilessly to carry their mistress down with them, desolate (no more lovers!) and naked — stripped bare of every attractive adornment, unveiled and revealed for every eye to see her sin and shame and filth.[29] Like dogs and wild beasts they rend and tear her and eat her flesh [30] — a gory, gruesome scene! What is left of her after this cannibal feast is consigned by the hot fire of hatred to a consuming fire of destruction. This, with a built-in vengeance, is the fall of the house of Satan, a house divided against itself.[31]

"They shall burn her [burn her up] with fire" (Rev. 17:16) suggests the fearful thought that in hell those who were misled will torture those who misled them. For this is neither a temporal fire nor a fire which annihilates, but it is an eternal fire.[32]

Majestically and unfailingly overruling the plots and plans of the beast and its kings is the will of God. "For God hath put in their hearts to fulfill His will" (Rev. 17:17). They do not want to follow the will of God, but under His providence their designs

[29] Cf. Ezek. 16:37; Lam. 1:8, and note the contrast to the picture drawn in Rev. 18:16.

[30] Lit., "her fleshy parts."

[31] On this entire scene compare the remarkable parallels of thought and graphic symbolism in Ezek. 23.

[32] Cf. Rev. 17:16 with 18:8, 9, 15, 18; and 19:3; also see Is. 66:24; Mark 9: 42-48.

and actions serve His purposes.[33] It is as when in war the strategy adopted by one side plays right into the hands of the other. So also the wicked become instruments in the hands of the righteous God, who punishes sin with sin and its consequences. In the agreement they strike among themselves, consenting together in their evil ways and joining hands and forces with all that is opposed to God, they bear testimony, unwitting and unwilling though it be, to the truth of God's Word. Everything will come to pass exactly as He said. Note the specific reference to the individual *"words* of God." [34]

Rev. 17:18 completes the angel's explanation of the vision: "The woman . . . is that great city, which reigneth over the kings of the earth." The name of the city is Babylon,[35] a symbol of the entire anti-Christian world city or empire and its seductive influence and power in ruling over the kings of the earth. (Ps. 2:2)

[33] Cf. Gen. 50:20; Acts 4:27, 28; Ps. 110:2b
[34] Rev. 17:17; also see Matt. 5:18; Rev. 10:7; 19:9.
[35] Cf. Rev. 14:8 with 16:19; 17:5; 18:10.

Rev. 18 may be divided into six parts: (1) An angel's announcement of Babylon's fall, vv. 1-3. (2) A warning to God's people to separate themselves from Babylon, vv. 4, 5. (3) God's judgment on Babylon confirmed and sealed, vv. 6-8. (4) Lament over the fall of Babylon, vv. 9-19. (5) An exhortation to rejoice over God's judgment on Babylon, v. 20. (6) An angel's action symbolizing Babylon's sudden, violent, and complete disappearance, vv. 21-24.

Rev. 18:1-3:
An Angel's Announcement of Babylon's Fall

After the vision of the great whore (Rev. 17) John saw "another angel come down from heaven" (Rev. 18:1), a "minister of the Lord" (Ps. 103:21), with a message for man. It must have been an extremely impressive sight, for John is moved to describe the angel in terms of "great power" [1] and great "glory." "The earth was lightened [made bright, RSV] with his glory." [2]

The angel's voice suited both his character and his message. He cried out mightily as he proclaimed the appalling destruction and complete overthrow of proud Babylon: "Fallen, fallen, is Babylon the great!" [3] Actually, the end of the city had not yet

---

[1] Or "authority," lending added weight to his mission.

[2] Rev. 18:1. Cf. Ezek. 43:2.

[3] Rev. 18:2 RSV; Is. 21:9; Jer. 51:8.

come, as we see from Rev. 18:4 ff. But the solemn repetition
"fallen, fallen," emphasizes the inevitable fact, which could be
spoken of as already past.[4] For a child of God this statement,
that godless Babylon (everything that is anti-Christian and ungodly) is even now already as good as gone forever, is a rich
source of strength, comfort, and hope. For he can put next to it
another verb in the past tense, "glorified" (Rom. 8:30), which
emphasizes the certainty of the salvation of the elect.[5]

The angel in John's vision gives us a thumbnail sketch of
Babylon lying in ruins: "the habitation of devils [demons] and
the hold [haunt] of every foul spirit and a cage [haunt] of
every unclean and hateful bird." [6] The picture is one of complete
desolation, an eerie place, where unclean spirits and foul birds
live undisturbed — the exact opposite of a large metropolis, busy
and bustling with industry and commerce.

The first part of Rev. 18:3 is very similar to Rev. 17:2. "All
nations" are "the inhabitants of the earth" around the world.
Babylon has a universal following. Inexorably the charges against
her are stated, repeated, and multiplied:[7] (1) "All nations have
drunk of the wine of the wrath of her fornication." [8] (2) "The
kings of the earth have committed fornication with her." [9]
(3) "The merchants of the earth are waxed rich through the
abundance of her delicacies." These "merchants of the earth"
are all who deal in any way in any of the devil's wares. They
"wax [grow] rich" (Rev. 18:3) in this trade — not in true riches
but in such things as the world counts gain, wealth, or profit
(Luke 12:15; Matt. 6:20, 21). Their heart belongs to Babylon,
and their affections are set on "the abundance [power] of her

4 Also see the notes on Rev. 14:8; 19:20.

5 Also see the notes on Rev. 14:16.

6 Rev. 18:2. For similar prophetic language in the Old Testament see Is. 13:
19-22; 34:11-15; Jer. 50:39; 51:37; Zeph. 2:15.

7 Rev. 18:3; see Rev. 14:8; 17:2.

8 Rather, "the wine of her impure passion." See the notes on Rev. 14:8; 17:2.

9 See the notes on Rev. 17:2.

delicacies" (Rev. 18:3). "Delicacies" here means such excessive luxury as is incompatible with Christian stewardship; sinful self-indulgence in the lusts and desires of the flesh, whatever they may be; in short, the whole fertile soil which fosters the growth of wantonness, extravagance, and arrogance. These are the grounds on which the anti-Christian Babylon of this world stands irretrievably condemned. Therefore let God's people come out of her!

Rev. 18:4, 5: A Warning to God's People
to Separate Themselves from Babylon

John does not identify or describe the "voice from heaven" (Rev. 18:4) which brings this warning. We may regard it as the voice of God or even specifically as the voice of Christ.[10]

The warning begins: "Come out of her, My people." [11] Luther felt that the prophecy of Babylon was fulfilled in papal Rome. But the meaning is broader than that. It calls for a practical cleavage all down the line between the things that are of God and those that are of men (Matt. 16:23). It is not a call to monasticism or holy orders, but simply bids the children of God remember that though they are in the world, they are not of the world (John 17:11, 16) and are not to be partakers of other men's sins (1 Tim. 5:22; 2 John 10, 11). "Come out of" has the same practical meaning and application as "avoid" in Rom. 16:17, namely, to have no fellowship that is inconsistent with the Word and will of God.[12]

Those who will not listen, learn, and heed the warning will fall under the same condemnation as Babylon and will "receive of her plagues." [13] "Her sins have reached unto heaven" (Rev.

10 See the notes on Rev. 18:14, 20.

11 Rev. 18:4. See Is. 48:20; 52:11; Jer. 50:8; 51:6, 9, 45.

12 There is a remarkable parallel, both in words and in thought, between Rev. 18:4 and 2 Cor. 6:14-18 ("My people . . . come out!"). Also see Eph. 5:11; 1 John 1:3ff.; Prov. 29:24.

13 Rev. 18:4 RSV: "share in her plagues." See the seven plagues in Rev. 16, and compare expecially Rev. 16:19b with 18:5.

18:5). They are multiplied, added, and heaped upon one another until their sheer mass extends, as it were, from earth to heaven (Gen. 18:20, 21). They fairly clamor for God's attention and challenge Him to deal with them. Nor is He unmindful or forgetful of them. He is patient. But His patience with the wicked is not infinite. It comes to an end, and His justice finally prevails.[14]

Rev. 18:6-8: God's Judgment on Babylon Confirmed and Sealed

As the "voice from heaven" (Rev. 18:4) continues to speak, it addresses those who are to execute vengeance on Babylon: "Reward her even as she rewarded (you)";[15] render to her as she rendered to others. We are not told who the agents of vengeance are, but we may think of the ten horn kings.[16] The important point is the evenhanded justice which is to be observed in dealing with Babylon. Justice is not violated, but rather confirmed, by the command: "Double unto her double according to her works" (Rev. 18:6). This does not mean that she is to suffer twice as much as she deserved, but rather notes the fact that in her own dealings Babylon was extremely generous in what she had to offer — a double portion, as it were, of evil. Now in return, "according to her works," she is to receive "double," measure for measure.[17] The same thought lies in the words "In the cup which she hath filled, fill to her double." [18]

Inexorably the sentence of just punishment continues: "How much she hath glorified herself," being proud and boastful, "and lived deliciously [played the wanton, RSV], so much torment and sorrow give her" (Rev. 18:7). "Torment," or torture, is the

14 See the notes on Rev. 16:19.

15 Rev. 18:6. "You" is not in the best MSS.

16 See the notes on Rev. 17:12-17.

17 Ps. 137:8; Jer. 16:18; 17:18; 50:15, 29.

18 Rev. 18:6. On her "cup" see the notes on Rev. 14:8; 17:2, 4. On the cup of the indignation and wine of the fierceness of the wrath of God given to Babylon see the notes on Rev. 14:10; 16:19.

pain she is to endure commensurate with her former arrogant indulgence in sinful pleasures. "Sorrow," or mourning, for her lovers now taken from her points forward to the last part of the verse.

God knows what is in the heart of Babylon, and how she says within herself: "I sit a queen," a law unto myself and ruling over all who do my bidding, "and am no widow" (Rev. 18:7) — an insolent indirect reference to the fact that she never had a husband. Nor does she ever expect to see any sorrow or mourning; why should she, when the kings of the earth and all nations are at her service? She is a perfect example of pride going before destruction and a haughty spirit before a fall (Prov. 16:18). The mills of God may often seem to grind slowly, but they grind extremely fine, and sometimes their work is done quickly. Everything for which Babylon stands in the Book of Revelation will pass through them. Anti-Christian power with its seductive appeals and attractions, invincible though it may appear at any given time, is riding high for a sudden and inevitable fall.

"Therefore" (Rev. 18:8), because Babylon is what she is — proud, smug, and shameless — her whole world will come tumbling down about her like a house of cards. She says: "I shall *never* see sorrow" (Rev. 18:7, literally), or mourning. But God says: *"In one day,"* [19] suddenly and unexpectedly, "shall her plagues come: death, and mourning, and famine" (18:8), the latter in contrast to her former abundance.[20] "We may say that death is placed first, and then 'mourning and famine' follow, because the picture is that of a city which 'death' invades but strikes down gradually, part after part, 'mourning and famine' occurring in the parts before 'death' reaches them in its progress." [21] "She shall be utterly burned with fire," the eternal fire

[19] Rev. 18:8. Cf. "in one hour," Rev. 18:10, 17, 19; also see Is. 47:9; Jer. 50: 31; 1 Thess. 5:3.

[20] The RSV uses the word "pestilence" here instead of "death," as in Rev. 6: 8b. But also see Rev. 2:23: RSV, "I will strike her children dead."

[21] Lenski, p. 522.

of hell.[22] "For strong is the Lord God, who judgeth her" (Rev. 18:8). Babylon is called "strong" ["mighty," KJV] in Rev. 18:10. But God is also "strong," equal to the challenge which she presents — yes, more than equal, for in the final issue and upshot judgment rests and remains in His hands. Babylon must submit to it without appeal.

Rev. 18:9-19: Lament over the Fall of Babylon

Those who turned viciously on the whore (Rev. 17:16) weep and wail over her violent and fearful end. There is no rhyme or reason in any departure from the Word and will of God. It is not reasonable to doubt the Word of God, or call Him a liar, or test His patience, or challenge His power and justice, by deliberate sin. "The lover of a whore strangles her and then weeps like a fool." [23] This is the paradox which the "kings of the earth . . . and the merchants of the earth . . ." (Rev. 18:9, 11, etc.) present in the drama which continues to unfold in the visions which John saw.

"The kings of the earth, who have committed fornication and lived deliciously with her,[24] shall bewail her [25] and lament for her,[26] when they shall see the smoke of her burning" (Rev. 18:9). Other plagues, death, mourning, and famine will also be her lot (Rev. 18:8), but punishment by fire is significantly the chief feature in these prophecies,[27] as it is in other prophecies which speak of the end of this world and all its treasures and of those whose heart was set on them and who took pleasure in them.[28]

[22] See Rev. 19:3 and the notes on Rev. 17:16.

[23] Lenski, p. 522.

[24] See the notes on Rev. 17:2; 18:3.

[25] Lit., "will sob," or "weep."

[26] Same word as "wail" in Rev. 1:7; lit., to beat one's breast for grief.

[27] Rev. 17:16; 18:8, 18; 19:3.

[28] 2 Peter 3:10; Matt. 25:41; Is. 66:24; Mark 9:43-48; Luke 16:24; Rev. 14:10; 20:10.

So great is her torment [29] that the kings of the earth stand afar off for fear of it.[30] When a raging fire spreads out of hand and leaps from building to building, racing with the wind through the streets of a city which it destroys, it is an awe-inspiring sight which can be safely seen only from a great distance. This does not mean that all the "kings of the earth . . . and the merchants of the earth . . ." (Rev. 18:9, 11, etc.) escape the punishment which overtakes their mistress. They shall also likewise perish.[31]

Rev. 18:9-19 emphasizes the intensive and extensive judgment of God on those who are guilty of enticing and seducing men to commit spiritual whoredom. But we hear from them not a word of repentance or of faith in the Lamb of God. They mourn only over the loss of Babylon and its splendor, wealth, and pleasure. In general the people of the earth lament only over the losses, pain, and sorrow which sin causes. They give little or no thought to the fact that, above all, sin is a transgression of God's Law and calls for heart-rending contrition and a return to the Lord in saving faith. (Joel 2:13)

The lament of the kings of the earth over Babylon is dramatic: "Alas, alas, great city Babylon! Mighty city! For in one hour has your judgment come!" [32] "Mighty" is the same word that is translated "strong" in Rev. 18:8, and it suggests that Babylon claimed for itself the attributes of God.[33] But Babylon was not strong in the Lord and in the power of His might and therefore could not stand before Him.[34] It was built on sand; therefore it fell, and great was the fall of it. (Matt. 7:26, 27)

The kings of the earth are joined in their lament over Babylon by "the merchants [35] of the earth" (Rev. 18:11, 15-17), who also

[29] See the notes on Rev. 18:7.
[30] Rev. 18:10; see Ezek. 28:18.
[31] Rev. 19:11-21; 20:7-9; 21:8.
[32] Lit., Rev. 18:10.
[33] See the notes on Rev. 12:3.
[34] Ps. 33:16-18; 147:10, 11; 1 Sam. 17:45-47; Eph. 6:10.
[35] See the notes on Rev. 18:3. Compare the description in Rev. 18:11 ff. with Ezek. 27.

"shall weep and mourn over her." Paradoxically, the merchants, with a large supply of goods on hand, and desolate Babylon have something in common. They both "mourn" (Rev. 18:8, 11): Babylon for lack of merchandise, and the merchants because of their superabundance of it, for which there is no longer any demand.

The merchandise itself is itemized as in an inventory in Rev. 18:12, 13.[36] There is little point in trying to make each of the items mean something specific. In their sum total they represent the things which the world regards as most precious and desirable. All this merchandise is not to be understood literally, but as representing the traffic connected with anti-Christian seduction and indulgence in its almost endless variety. Lenski (pp. 524 f.) suggests that in the interpretation we think of such things as godless politicians, graft in government, lawyers without conscience, skeptics in the field of literature and education, anti-Christian religious leaders, etc. It includes everything that comes into play against the Christian faith; all this should remind us impressively that we ought never take our Christian faith for granted. The archenemy of our souls is cunning and crafty in drawing everything into his service in an effort to accomplish his purpose (Matt. 4:8, 9; Luke 4:5, 6). He will not overlook any appeal that he can make to us; he will not rest in his attempts to make us also (body and soul) his own — like so much chattel and merchandise.[37]

Babylon's treasure was not in heaven but on earth, in "the fruits that her soul lusted after [38] . . . and all things which were dainty and goodly." [39] Dramatically God speaks directly to Babylon: "All these things are departed from thee, and thou shalt find them no more at all." [40]

[36] The RSV follows a better reading than the KJV in including "spice" in Rev. 18:13 after "cinnamon."

[37] Rev. 18:13b; see Mark 4:19; Luke 21:34; Matt. 6:21.

[38] Lenski, "the flush season of the lust of thy life," pp. 525—526.

[39] Rev. 18:14, the phrase summarizes the entire preceding list.

[40] Rev. 18:14; cf. Luke 12:16-21; Is. 3:16-26.

Like the kings of the earth,[41] the merchants of the earth show no signs of repentance. They weep and wail and mourn only over the loss of their trade, which made them rich, and over the loss of the great treasure which perished with Babylon.[42]

Next, the kings and merchants of the earth are joined by "every shipmaster, and all the company in ships, and sailors, and as many as trade by sea," in standing afar off, weeping, and lamenting the fall of Babylon.[43] Navigation linked the various parts of the earth in commerce and trade. It also played its prosperous role in spreading the rule and influence of anti-Christian power and seduction to the ends of the earth. All who profited by their connection with it mourned when they saw the market which was the hub of their activity go up in smoke.[44]

"What city is like unto this great city!" (Rev. 18:18). It has been argued whether this refers to the city in its greatness (Rev. 13:4) or in its destruction (Ezek. 27:32). It refers to both: the greatest city lies waste in unequaled devastation before the eyes of her former patrons.

"And they cast dust on their heads," in token of grief and sorrow,[45] "and cried, weeping and wailing."[46] Their deep regret extends only to the loss of their profits, "wherein were made rich all that had ships in the sea by reason of her costliness," and the sudden and complete loss of the great wealth which perished with Babylon, "for in one hour is she made desolate."[47] In due time God's judgment overwhelms all who will not walk in His ways. (Luke 13:3, 5)

41 See the notes on Rev. 17:2; 18:9, 10.

42 Rev. 18:15-17; cf. 1 Tim. 6:10.

43 Rev. 18:17-19; see Ezek. 27, esp. vv. 29-36.

44 See the notes on Rev. 18:9.

45 Ezek. 27:30; Josh. 7:6.

46 Rev. 18:19. See Rev. 18:11, 15.

47 Rev. 18:19; cf. Rev. 18:9 ff.

Rev. 18:20: An Exhortation
to Rejoice over God's Judgment on Babylon

The children of the devil and of the world bewail and lament the fate of Babylon, but the children of God in heaven have every reason to rejoice. God [48] speaks to them in a striking apostrophe: "Rejoice over her, thou heaven" (Rev. 18:20). "Heaven" is used by metonymy for "the inhabitants of heaven" (Rev. 12:12). The angels are not included in Rev. 18:20, because the vengeance which God wrought on Babylon was not for anything that they suffered but for the saints (Rev. 6:10, 11). The words "and ye holy apostles and prophets" (KJV) are better rendered: "even ye saints, apostles, and prophets," that is, all the saints in heaven in general, and the apostles and prophets in particular, both of the Old and of the New Testament.[49] This is the day and hour of their triumph and of the song of rejoicing over fallen Babylon and of praise to Him, whose right hand and whose holy arm has gotten Him and them the victory! (Ps. 2, 46, 98; Rev. 19:1-9)

Rev. 18:21-24: An Angel's Action
Symbolizes Babylon's Sudden, Violent,
and Complete Disappearance

As an angel with a "strong" voice announced the fall of Babylon (Rev. 18:2), the "strong" city (Rev. 18:10), so now a "strong" ("mighty," KJV) angel performs a symbolical act emphasizing certain features of Babylon's final end.[50] Babylon in all her vaunted strength is helpless in the hand of God and His angels. The Greek text speaks clearly of "one" angel and so reminds us that the angels of God are indeed very strong

48 The "voice from heaven" (Rev. 18:4).

49 See Heb. 11; Rev. 17:6; 18:24; Matt. 14:10; 21:33-41; 23:37; Acts 7:51-60; 12:2.

50 For similar symbolical acts see Acts 21:11; Jer. 51:63, 64. Also see Rev. 14:8; 16:19.

(Ps. 103:20). This one "took up a stone like a great millstone," very large and heavy, "and cast it into the sea." (Rev. 18:21) The angel's action was obviously not carried out hastily, on the spur of the moment. It called for clear decision and deliberate action. But the action suddenly took on the nature of violence when the large stone struck the water. Quickly the waters closed over the stone, and it sank forever from view, to the bottom of the sea. Violence, suddenness, and permanence combine in the overthrow and disappearance of Babylon (Rev. 18:21). The beast of Rev. 13:1 ff. came out of the sea; Babylon is, as it were, engulfed in the sea, never again to raise its proud head to deceive the nations with its sorceries (Rev. 18:23), seduce kings, or entice the great men who traded with her on land or by sea. "It shall be found no more at all!" (Rev. 18:21)

Vv. 22, 23a of Rev. 18 are like waves sealing Babylon in the deathly silence, stillness, and darkness of a watery grave — from which there is no return or recall. The recurring words "no more at all" have about them the doleful sound of a dirge and of the somber tolling of a death knell. No more music, no more crafts, no more mills, no more light, no more weddings — all progress, action, life, and activity stopped dead in its tracks.

Lest there be any who still do not understand the reasons for this, Rev. 18:23b-24 puts them all together in three simple statements: (1) "Because thy merchants were the great men of the earth," that is, her evil traffic was worldwide and reached into high places (Rev. 17:2; 18:3, 9; 19:19); (2) "Because by thy sorceries were all nations deceived (Rev. 12:9; 13:14); these "sorceries" are the potions which she mixed in her cup and by which she made the inhabitants of the earth drunk (Rev. 17:2); (3) "In her was found the blood of prophets, and of saints, and of all that were slain upon the earth" (Jer. 51:49; Rev. 17:6), both Testaments combining against her in the accusations and testimony of those whose blood cries to heaven for vengeance (Gen. 4:10; Rev. 6:10). Her enormous guilt called for such great punishment (Rev. 18:5-7a). God's justice is vindicated.

There are several passages in the Book of Revelation which are both conclusions to the sections which precede them and transitions to that which follows (e. g., Rev. 8:1-6; 16:17-21). Rev. 19:1-10 is one of them. For the sake of convenience in outlining the book we take these verses as the third and last section dealing with the great whore.[1] But these verses also point forward. They may be divided into three parts:

Rev. 19:1-6 is the New Testament Hallelujah Chorus (Rev. 19:1, 3, 4, 6). The word "Hallelujah" occurs nowhere else in the New Testament. The reference to God's judgment on the great whore (Rev. 19:2, 3) makes this the conclusion of the section which begins with Rev. 17:1. The reference to God's almighty rule (Rev. 19:6b) is a preview of the victory of the Word of God. (Rev. 19:11-21, esp. 15, 16)

Rev. 19:7-9 speaks of the marriage of the Lamb. These verses are joined to the preceding by the pronoun "Him" (Rev. 19:7), and they point forward to Rev. 21:2, 9 ff.

Rev. 19:10 is joined to the preceding by the pronouns "his," "him," and "he," while the last part of the verse points specifically and clearly to our God and Lord, who holds the center of attention to the end of the book.

1 See the notes on Rev. 17:1.

Rev. 19:1-6: The New Testament Hallelujah Chorus in Praise of God for His Judgment on the Great Whore

Like the Gloria in Excelsis in the liturgy of the Christian church, the Hallelujah Chorus in Rev. 19:1-6 was begun in heaven with the church on earth joining in its conclusion. The Gloria celebrates and commemorates the birth of our Savior; the Hallelujah sings the praises of His final and complete victory over His enemies.[2] The former was intoned by a multitude of angels (Luke 2:13, 14), the latter by the multitude of the saints in heaven (Rev. 19:1), the Church Triumphant.[3]

The first part of the song of praise in Rev. 19:1-6 is sung by the redeemed in heaven in response to Rev. 18:20 and begins and ends with the word "Hallelujah" (Rev. 19:1-3), a Hebrew word which means "Praise ye the Lord!" We may say that those who sang this chant in this vision were not only New Testament saints (Jews who had died in the Christian faith, and Gentiles who had embraced the Jewish faith in the Christian spirit) but also the Old Testament saints who for many centuries had chanted their Hallelujahs on earth. (Ps. 104:35; 105:45)

"Salvation and glory [and honor] and power unto[4] [the Lord] our God."[5] He is our only and all-sufficient Savior (Acts 4:12). Therefore praise Him for the salvation which He so gloriously wrought and so graciously bestowed! Praise Him also for His power, evident in the destruction of Babylon! There are echoes of the conclusion of the Lord's Prayer in this chant of the redeemed: "Thine is the kingdom and the power [the Lord God Omnipotent reigneth, Rev. 19:6] and the glory [Rev. 19:1]." Even the words "forever and ever" have a counterpart in Rev. 19:3: God's enemies are forever overcome.

---

[2] "After these things" (Rev. 19:1), i.e., after the things described in Rev. 17, 18 and closely connected with them.

[3] See the notes on Rev. 7:9; 11:15.

[4] RSV, "belong to our God."

[5] Rev. 19:1; the best MSS do not have "and honor" and "the Lord." Cf. Rev. 7:10, 12; 12:10.

God is to be praised because His judgments are true and righteous.[6] "Hallelujah" first occurs in the Bible (Ps. 104:35) in connection with the thought that sinners are to be consumed out of the earth and that the wicked are to be no more (cf. Ps. 1:5). The justice of God is clearly evident in His dealing with the great whore. He judged her for what she was and what she did. She corrupted the earth with her fornication. By false doctrine and the attractions of a sinful life she deceived, seduced, and enticed most of mankind away from God and led them in the way of sin and shame, destruction and perdition (Rev. 11:18). Not content with that, she did violence to those who refused to follow her and remained steadfast in their service to God. They sealed their loyalty to Him with their blood.[7] Now, at last, the cry of the martyrs (Rev. 6:10) is answered in the chant of the saints in heaven: "(God) hath avenged the blood of His servants at her hand."[8] There is no escape from His just and proper vengeance on those who turn against Him. Sometimes it overtakes them here on earth (2 Kings 9:7). In all cases it is as sure and certain as if it were already a thing of the past. God is praised for all of this by the "Hallelujah!" of the saints in heaven (Rev. 19:1, 3), as the great whore receives her eternal due.

"Her smoke rose up forever and ever,"[9] a picture of final and complete ruin.[10] There is no appeal from the judgment of God.[11] He is always justified when He speaks, and clear, or blameless, when He judges. (Ps. 51:4)

"The four and twenty elders and the four beasts[12] fell down

6 Rev. 19:2. Cf. Rev. 15:3; 16:7.

7 See the notes on Rev. 16:6; 6:9; 18:24.

8 Rev. 19:2. Also see Gen. 9:5; Deut. 32:43; 1 Chron. 16:22; Ps. 50:22; 105:15; Is. 34:8; Rev. 18:20; Luke 18:7, 8.

9 Rev. 19:3. See the notes on Rev. 14:11; 17:16; 18:9.

10 Cf. the fate of Sodom and Gomorrah (Gen. 19:28); also see Is. 34:10.

11 Is. 66:24; Mark 9:43-48; 16:16b; John 12:48.

12 Rather, "living ones"; see the notes on Rev. 4:4, 6.

and worshiped God [13] that sat on the throne, [14] saying, Amen! Hallelujah!" (Rev. 19:4). Far from arguing with God, contradicting Him, denying His righteousness, or questioning His justice in dealing with the great whore, the representatives of the ministry of God's Word and the earthly agents of His providence agree to His ways. Their "Amen," a Hebrew word, means: "Yea, it shall be so!" To this they add a "Hallelujah!" in praise of God.

Rev. 19:4 is the hinge, or pivot, on which this entire passage turns. "Amen! Hallelujah!" marks the end of the story of the great whore. [15] This is emphasized by the worship of the elders, which in a similar way helps to mark the end of a major passage in Rev. 11:16 ff. Rev. 19:5, 6 is also a part of the Hallelujah Chorus, but its main purpose and function is to point forward.

"A voice," unidentified but authoritative, "came out of the throne" (Rev. 19:5). The words "our God" (Rev. 19:5) show that it is not the voice of God. Perhaps it was the voice of one of the saints in glory, who sit with Christ on His throne (Rev. 3:21). It speaks for "the company of heaven," as it is called in the Lutheran Communion liturgy, and calls on all the servants of God, (and) [16] those who fear Him, both small and great, to join in praising God. [17]

The entire holy Christian church, the communion of saints, rises and responds to the call. [18] The majestic and triumphant sweep of this vision refuses to be bound by any considerations of space and time. We must think here not only of the church on earth as singing in antiphony with the church in heaven, but

[13] See the notes on Rev. 11:16.

[14] See the notes on Rev. 4:2 ff.

[15] Cf. Ps. 106:48, closing the fourth main division of Psalms.

[16] This "and" is not in the best MSS of Rev. 19:5.

[17] See the notes on Rev. 11:18; 20:12.

[18] "Servants" echoes Ps. 2:11; 100:2; 134:1; 135:1; Rev. 1:1; Rom. 1:1; Acts 4:29; Judg. 2:7; "those who fear Him, small and great," echoes Ps. 115:13; 8:2; Matt. 11:25; Joel 2:16.

of the entire host, the grand total of all the saved, both of the Old and of the New Testament, past, present, and future, joining to sing as with one voice the resounding praises of Almighty God! Were it not for the inspiration of God, who told John what to write, we might say that words almost fail the divine seer in his attempt to describe what he heard: "as it were the voice of a great multitude, and as the voice of many waters, and as the voice of mighty thunderings,"[19] innumerable individuals, inconceivable volume, immeasurable reverberations. Small wonder that Handel was fairly overcome by the grandeur of the vision as he endeavored to recapture it in the Hallelujah Chorus of his oratorio *Messiah*.[20]

"Hallelujah![21] For the Lord God Omnipotent reigneth!"[22]

Rev. 19:7-9: The Marriage of the Lamb

In one of the loveliest of all pictures Christ appears as Bridegroom and the church as His bride.[23] In terms of prophecy and fulfillment as applied to time, the marriage takes place at the final coming of Christ. However, we must not rigidly superimpose the limitations of time on the sequence of the visions which John saw, as though there will be a gap, or span of time, between the destruction of Babylon and the preparations for the marriage of the Lamb. Here, as in the first verses of this chapter, the holy writer simply describes one part of the larger picture that will unfold simultaneously at the end of time. In Rev.19:7-9 the marriage itself does not take place, but only the preparation of the bride and the blessedness of the guests are mentioned.

[19] Rev. 19:6. See the notes on Rev. 14:2; 19:1. Cf. Rev. 1:15.

[20] See the notes on Rev. 11:15.

[21] See the notes on Rev. 19:1.

[22] Compare Ps. 2; 93; 110; 115, esp. v. 3; 145; 146.

[23] Song of Solomon; Rev. 21:2, 9; 22:17; Ps. 45:13, 14; Eph. 5:22-32. The KJV uses the word "wife" (Rev. 19:7). Cf. Matt. 1:18-24.

The bride of Christ, the church, gives expression to over-flowing happiness. "Let us be glad and rejoice and give honor [glory] to Him!" (Rev. 19:7). The children of God are the happiest people on earth. You see it in the light which is in the eyes of the bride and hear it in the note of a song which is in her voice. There is only one wonderful man in her life — the Man Christ Jesus (1 Tim. 2:5). She lives for Him, speaks most highly of Him, and does all to His glory (1 Cor. 10:31) — the more so when her marriage day has come.[24] She is not afraid, because she has made herself ready. Everything is prepared, including her wedding dress.

John describes the bride as decked out in a beautiful glorious dress, "arrayed in fine linen, clean and white" (Rev. 19:8). He does not say that it symbolizes the righteousness of Christ, but "the fine linen is the righteousness [righteousnesses] of saints" (Rev. 19:8), that is, their righteous deeds, or acts, good works. When Paul (Phil. 3:9) distinguishes between his "own right-eousness, which is of the Law," and the righteousness "which is through the faith of Christ, the righteousness which is of God by faith," he uses a different word and means something else (Is. 64:6; Dan. 9:18). When John says that the righteousness of saints is as fine linen, clean and white (Rev. 19:8), he does not contradict Is. 64:6, which says that "all our righteousnesses are as filthy rags." The two passages speak of different things, of two different kinds of "righteousnesses." While Isaiah speaks of "the deeds which *men* might consider righteous and laud-able," [25] John speaks of works which are good and acceptable in the sight of *God*.[26] The latter ought never to be despised or disparaged but encouraged (Heb. 10:24). A voice from heaven (Rev. 14:13) told John that the good works of those who die in the Lord follow them. Our Savior also commends them most

24 Heb. 10:25; 2 Peter 3:11, 12; Ps. 126:5, 6.

25 P. E. Kretzmann, Old Testament, II, 393.

26 John 15:5; Mark 12:41-44; 14:3-9; Luke 10:38-42.

highly in His own descriptive prophecy of the Last Judgment.
(Matt. 25:34-40)

This does not mean that we are saved either entirely or in
part by good works. John says: "To her was granted" (Rev.
19:8), that is, it was *given* her, the church, the bride of Christ,
to be adorned with good works. John does not say here how
she became His bride, but only that her wedding dress is altogether lovely and that it is a gift from the Bridegroom.[27]

Rev. 19:9 speaks of the wedding guests. We learn who they
are from the parable of the marriage of the king's son (Matt.
22:1-14) and the parable of the great supper (Luke 14:15-24).
The Gospel does not bless those who reject it. Only those who
accept the invitation derive any benefit from it. "Blessed are
they which are called unto the marriage supper of the Lamb"
(Rev. 19:9) is therefore equivalent to "Blessed are they that
hear the Word of God and keep it" (Luke 11:28; cf. 8:8, 15).
The reference is not merely to the invitation, which many decline,
but to the effective call and its results in making a person a believer and an heir of heaven (2 Thess. 2:14). So rich is this call
in its reward to those who accept it that they are called blessed
in this (the fourth) beatitude in the Book of Revelation.[28]

Twice in Rev. 19:9 John says, "He [29] saith unto me." The
first time John receives the simple direction "Write." Specifically,
he is to write the beatitude which then follows. But John was
told to write, and in one case (Rev. 10:4), not to write, at
various times during the course of the visions recorded in the
Book of Revelation.[30] This, we believe, points to the fact that
the book was written at the time when John saw the visions
and not at a later date.

The second time John is addressed in Rev. 19:9 he is assured:
"These are the true [genuine] sayings [words, cf. Rev. 17:17]

27 John 15:5; Heb. 11:6; Phil. 2:13; Gal. 2:20.

28 Rev. 1:3; 14:13; 16:15; 20:6; 22:7, 14.

29 That is, as we take it, the one whose voice spoke in Rev. 19:5.

30 Rev. 1:11, 19; 2:1, 8, 12, 18; 3:1, 7, 14; 14:13; 21:5.

of God." That refers specifically and directly to the beatitude in the light of the entire vision and impresses on us the assurance, comfort, and hope which lie in it. God cannot lie (Titus 1:1, 2; Heb. 6:17-20). In a wider application, "These are the true sayings of God" can be properly inscribed on the title page of the entire Bible, which is the Word — specifically the "words" (Jer. 1:9; 1 Cor. 2:13) — of God. His Word is truth! (John 17:17)

Rev. 19:10: Worship God!

Because John thought it was God who spoke to him, he "fell at his feet to worship him" (Rev. 19:10; cf. 22:8, 9). Several angels and an elder had spoken to him in previous visions, but he did not fall down to worship them. But it is easy to see why he thought God was speaking to him now. The voice came "out of the throne" (Rev. 19:5), and it commanded him to write (Rev. 1:11, 19; 2:1; etc.). For a moment the implication of the word "our" seems to have escaped him, but the speaker reminded him of it.

John was sincere but wrong. "You must not do that," said the one who spoke to him, adding, by way of explanation: "I am a fellow servant with you and your brethren who hold the testimony of Jesus." [31] Though he was in heaven, he was not so high as to be worshiped. He put himself on a level with John and all other Christians in the work of the Lord and in their faith in the Word of God. To make the point completely clear, he adds, "Worship God." [32] All acts of worship (prayer, adoration, etc.) are to be directed only to the true God.

"For the testimony of Jesus is the spirit of prophecy" (Rev. 19:10). This is one of the more difficult and obscure statements in the Book of Revelation, not so much in itself, as in its connection with the preceding context, with which it is connected by the word "for," or "because." That word points to the reason

[31] Rev. 19:10 RSV; see Rev. 19:5; 1:9; 6:11; 12:17.
[32] Rev. 19:10; see Matt. 4:10; Luke 4:8; Ex. 20:3; Deut. 5:7.

why the speaker said, "Worship God." He had already identified himself as a fellow laborer with John and as "holding the testimony of Jesus," that is, believing the Gospel, with him. Now he says that this testimony of Jesus, which both hold and which has given direction to their entire lifework, is the inner content, the heart and core, of all true prophecy. The Word which the prophet John preached would give him the reason why he was not to worship one of his fellow servants but only God. Rev. 19:10, then, is an application of the truth set forth in Rev. 5: 11-14. (John 1:1; Heb. 1:6)

Rev. 19:11-21: The Lord and His Armies
Overcome the Beast and His Armies

If someone could accurately and infallibly predict the tides of battle in civil and international war, the world would beat a path to his door. There is one conflict, however, of which we can say with complete assurance what the outcome will be. That is the warfare between God and all that are God's, on the one hand, and Satan and all that are Satan's, on the other. The Book of Revelation removes every question or shadow of doubt in this matter. Again and again it carries us forward to the end of time and shows how God rules supreme, also in the unfolding of the last things, governing the world in the interest of the church on earth, which He protects as the apple of His eye and which He takes to Himself in heaven. This repeated assurance is one of the greatest of all the blessings that are ours through the last book in the Bible (Rev. 1:3). In Rev. 19:11-21 we see the Lord and His armies deal specifically and effectively with the beast and its forces.

Majestically, and as in answer to the prophet's prayer (Is. 64:1), Rev. 19:11 marks the beginning of the end of history.[33] Rev. 19:11-16 describes the Lord and His armies.

John mentions the white horse at the head of the heavenly

[33] On the "opening of heaven" also see Ezek. 1:1; Matt. 3:16; Mark 1:10; Luke 3:21; Acts 7:56; Rev. 4:1.

hosts before he mentions its rider. Perhaps it first caught his eye and attention because in an earlier vision he had seen another white horse.[34] The entire scene suggests that it must have been a magnificent steed, surely one befitting its rider, the Son of God going forth to war.

Several names of God are used in this passage. The first two are "Faithful" and "True" (Rev. 19:11). He is altogether trustworthy and dependable. This is of vital importance in anyone who heads an army, for only then can his followers safely have full confidence in him. He has promised us the victory (Rom. 8:31-39), and "He is faithful that promised." [35]

"In righteousness He doth judge and make war" (Rev. 19:11). His righteous judgment marks it as a just war (Is. 11: 3-5; 41:1). It is a war against the beast, the false prophet, the kings of the earth, and their armies (Rev. 19:19, 20), and so continues the story of Rev. 16:14-16. We must not think of it in terms of war among men. It is not long, its outcome is never in doubt, and there are no losses on the Lord's side.

"His eyes were as a flame of fire" (Rev. 19:12), symbolic evidences of His penetrating omniscience and His burning, consuming zeal against all that is unholy and impure.[36] "And on His head were many crowns," symbols of royalty.[37] There were many of them, because He is King over all (Phil. 2:10, 11; Rev. 19:16). They were not crowns in our common sense of the word, or wreaths, but "diadems" in the shape and form of bands, or ribbons, or narrow fillets, bound round about the brow.

With regard to the name which He had written, "that no man knew but He Himself" (Rev. 19:12), it is obviously useless to speculate what it was.[38] Perhaps it was incomprehensible and

[34] See the notes on Rev. 6:2.

[35] Heb. 10:23. Also see Is. 25:1; Rev. 1:5; 3:7, 14; Heb. 11:11; 1 John 5:20; Is. 65:16.

[36] See the notes on Rev. 1:14.

[37] Cf. Rev. 1:13-16, where the royalty of the Son of man is symbolized by a golden girdle.

[38] Prov. 30:4; Ps. 139:6; Phil. 2:9. See also the notes on Rev. 2:17b.

inexpressible, or perhaps John, under divine, verbal inspiration, wrote here not only what he saw but also mentioned the name at the direction of the Holy Ghost, even though he did not see it. Be that as it may, John no doubt saw that the rider on the white horse was "clothed with a vesture dipped in ["sprinkled with"] blood" (Rev. 19:13), a visual representation of Is. 63:1-3 (cf. Rev. 14:20). The blood on His garment is that of His enemies.

"His name is called the Word of God" (Rev. 19:13). This name of Christ is used only by John (John 1:1, 14; 1 John 1:1). Lenski (p. 554) suggests that its significance is this, that the Son of God is in His very person "the final saving revelation of God" (cf. John 1:18; 14:9). But the name "Word of God" is especially appropriate here also because of the sharp sword which goes out of His mouth.[39]

The armies which follow the Lord, as He comes to wreak final vengeance on His enemies, are described in Rev. 19:14. The plural ("armies") refers not only to the legions of angels[40] but also to the multitude of the saints, who ride on white horses.[41] White is a symbol of holiness, emphasized in this case also by the garments of "fine linen, white and clean" (Rev. 19:14), in which the armies of the Lord were clothed.[42]

Note the contrast between the "vesture dipped in blood" (Rev. 19:13) and the "fine linen, white and clean" (Rev. 19:14). It is not the armies of the Lord which conquer the enemy; they merely accompany Him and glorify Him (2 Thess. 1:10; John 17:10). The victory itself is accomplished single-handedly by the Captain of our salvation. He has trodden the wine press alone.[43]

As the conquering Hero rides forth to His final victory at

[39] Rev. 19:15; see Rev. 1:16, and cf. Heb. 4:12; Eph. 6:17.

[40] Matt. 26:53; 13:41; 24:31; 25:31; Mark 8:38; Luke 9:26.

[41] See the notes on Rev. 6:2.

[42] Rev. 3:4, 5; 19:8; Matt. 28:3; Mark 16:5.

[43] Is. 63:3. Also see the notes on Rev. 17:14.

the head of His armies, a sharp sword goes out of His mouth.[44] Its purpose is to "smite the nations" (Rev. 19:15). The incarnate Word uses the inspired Word.[45] The sword of the Word is the only weapon of this Warrior, even as rejection of the Word in unbelief is the only sin which damns.[46]

"He shall rule them with a rod of iron" (Rev. 19:15). Under His hand they will lie completely broken and shattered.[47] The same thought is repeated in another picturesque way: "He treadeth the wine press of the fierceness and wrath of Almighty God" (Rev. 19:15). As grapes are trodden, so God's enemies are crushed. This is another reference to Is. 63:1-3,[48] where the word "alone" is included, to emphasize the fact that He Himself, personally, overcame all enemies. Rev. 19:15 expresses the same thought by its emphasis on "He": *"He* shall rule. . . . *He* treadeth the wine press." Our salvation is all *His* work.

"He hath on His vesture and on His thigh a name written" (Rev. 19:16). Riding forth as the great Captain of our salvation, He makes His name known to His adversaries, that the nations might tremble at His presence (Is. 64:2). The name was "King of kings and Lord of lords" (Rev. 19:16). He is the Head of the church, every member of which is a king and a lord.[49]

The outcome of the battle between the Lord and the Lord's armies and the "beast" and the beast's armies is predetermined. As God in His holy Word prophesied many other events, so here does He appoint a messenger, an angel, to announce the coming victory. John saw the angel "standing in the sun" (Rev. 19:17). Perhaps the angel appeared in heavenly light and sublime grandeur at a point which commanded universal atten-

[44] Rev. 19:15. See Eph. 6:17; Heb. 4:12; Rev. 1:16; 2:12; 19:21; and the notes on Rev. 19:13.

[45] John 12:48; Deut. 18:18, 19; Acts 3:22, 23.

[46] Mark 16:16b; Hos. 4:6; John 8:47; Matt. 25:41.

[47] See the notes on Rev. 2:27; 12:5; also see Ps. 2:9.

[48] See the notes on Rev. 19:13; 14:19, 20.

[49] See the notes on Rev. 11:15; 17:14.

tion, possibly in such a way that the rays of the sun formed a halo around him.[50] This surely must have been another "mighty" angel (Rev. 10:1; 18:21), as is evident in this, that "he cried with a loud voice" (cf. Rev. 10:3) and that in his message he addressed "all the fowls [birds] that fly in the midst of heaven" (v. 17). His message rings out for all to hear and tells of a fearful carnage about to take place. (Cf. Deut. 28:26; Jer. 7:33; 16:4; Ezek. 39:4, 17-20)

"Come and gather yourselves together unto the supper of the great God,"[51] a gruesome counterpart of "the marriage supper of the Lamb" (Rev. 19:9). God prepares them both, and to both apply the words "Come, for all things are now ready" (Luke 14:17). But the one is an occasion of life, light, and joy; the other is a desolate scene of death and destruction. (John 5:29)

The fivefold repetition of "flesh" in Rev. 19:18 helps emphasize the wide extent of the slaughter in the battle. Kings, captains, mighty men, horses, riders, all men, free and bond, small and great — there is an unmistakable note of completeness and finality in the itemized list. Everyone and everything connected with the entire anti-Christian power would be overthrown and killed. Vultures, buzzards, etc., would add their eerie touch in swooping down to feast on the carrion. (Rev. 19:21)

But first, as the Son of God moves forward on His white horse at the head of His armies (Rev. 19:11 ff.), "the beast, and the kings of the earth, and their armies"[52] gather together to make war against Him and His armies (Rev. 19:19). Little: "The beast symbolizes the whole anti-Christian power; the kings of the earth, the anti-Christian forces; and their armies, all the lesser forces under their management and control" (p. 199). The anti-Christian power involves persons, things, and influences which aim at

[50] Cf. the "woman clothed with the sun" (Rev. 12:1).

[51] RSV: "the great supper of God" (Rev. 19:17), according to the best MSS.

[52] On the "beast" see the notes on Rev. 13:1-8; on the "kings of the earth" see the notes on Rev. 16:12-16; also Rev. 17:2, where "the inhabitants of the earth" are in effect the "armies" of Rev. 19:19.

the destruction of the soul. The angel of God announces their overwhelming failure, death, doom, and destruction (Rev. 19: 17, 18). Yet they gather and gird themselves as though they could win. Sometimes they are easily recognized for what they are, and sometimes not. Satan himself, the dragon, is a real, personal being (1 Peter 5:8), who can transform himself into "an angel of light" (2 Cor. 11:14). Sometimes he adopts the disguise of religion (Matt. 4:6). But his object always remains the same: "to make war against Him that sat on the horse and against His army." (Rev. 19:19)

John does not describe the war itself. We have no reason to believe that in his vision he saw the opposing forces come to grips "with confused noise and garments rolled in blood" (Is. 9:5). It was all over but the shouting, even before it began.[53] The beast and the false prophet were "taken," or captured. "Both were cast alive into a lake of fire burning with brimstone."[54] "Alive" stands in sharp contrast to the scene of death in Rev. 19:18, 21, indicating a greater degree of punishment and suffering (Luke 12:47, 48). The "lake of fire burning with brimstone"[55] is eternal damnation. The followers of the beast and of the false prophet are not annihilated when they are "slain" (Rev. 19:21), but they go into everlasting torments. (Rev. 14:10; 20:15)

"The remnant," the followers of the beast and of the false prophet, "were slain with the sword of Him that sat upon the horse, which sword proceeded out of His mouth."[56] The only weapon that comes into play is the sword of the Lord (Rev. 19:11-15). His armies do not help in any way at any time to achieve this victory. The victories they win are against a foe whom their Lord has already defeated (1 Cor. 15:25), and they

[53] See the notes on Rev. 17:8; 20:9, 10; 18:2.

[54] Rev. 19:20. On the beast see the notes on Rev. 13:1-8; 19:19; on the false prophet and his activities see the notes on Rev. 13: 11-18; 16:13.

[55] Cf. Rev. 9:17, 18; 20:10, 14, 15; 21:8.

[56] Rev. 19:21. On the "sword" see the notes on Rev. 19:15. Also see Rev. 1:16; 2 Thess. 2:8; Is. 40:5; Heb. 4:12; Eph. 6:17; John 12:48.

triumph over them only through faith in him [57] and by the power of His Word (Eph. 6:10-17). All other weapons are ineffective, blunted, and broken lances.

"All the fowls [birds] were filled with their flesh." [58] In Rev. 11:7-11 the bodies of God's two witnesses also lie unburied, but their flesh is not consumed, and they return to life. Those who will not hear and heed the testimony of God's witnesses, however, come to a most miserable end, becoming food for the unclean birds (Lev. 11:13 ff.; Prov. 30:17). While the saved pass from life to life (John 3:36a; 2 Tim. 1:10), the lost pass from death to death.[59]

[57] 1 Cor. 15:57; 1 Tim. 6:12; 1 Peter 5:8, 9.

[58] Rev. 19:21; direct fulfillment of Rev. 19:17, 18. Cf. the fate of the great whore (Rev. 17:16).

[59] See the notes on Rev. 20:4-6, 13-15.

CHAPTER

20

Revelation 20 is without doubt, and in a certain sense, one of the best-known chapters in the Bible. Its references to, and description of, the "thousand years" are practically household terms to many.

Some who look for the millennium [1] think of it as a time of worldwide peace and prosperity during which there will be a universal conversion of the Jews to the Christian religion, while the believers rule over all nations. But is that how the Bible speaks of the "thousand years"? In the first three gospels there are passages which speak of wars and rumors of wars, various great upheavals in creation, the falling away of many from the Christian faith, the love of many growing cold, and enmity and bloody strife on every hand just before the end (Matt. 24:Mark 13; Luke 21). Where and how do these texts fit into the picture?

When and where do the "thousand years" fit into the unfolding picture of time? In the past, the present, or the future? On this question also there is a very wide divergence of opinion. It is said that some regard the 1,000 years as having begun at the time of the resurrection of Christ (or at Pentecost). Others are said to believe that the millennium began with the reign of Constantine the Great, who became Roman Emperor A. D. 306.

[1] "Millennium" (lit., 1,000 years) comes from the Latin *mille* (1,000) and *annus* (year). Another word with a related meaning, *chiliasm* (belief in the millennium), comes from the Greek *chilioi*, meaning "a thousand."

Others hold that it began at the time of the Protestant Reformation. Again, according to missionary Fjelstedt, the Jews in the East expected the millennium to begin in 1810. When it did not arrive then, they argued that the present Hebrew Bible must contain some chronological errors. The Western Jews looked for the 1,000 years to begin in 1466. Whiston placed the date in 1776, Jurieu in 1785, Bengel in 1836, Miller in 1843, Sander in 1847, Schmucker in 1848, and others variously in 1866, 1879—87, 1880, etc. Some set 1914 as the year that the millennium was to begin, only to find that it brought World War I.[2] Louis Adamic, in *My America,* speaks of a cult which expected the millennium in 1933 (p. 281). The end of date setting is not in sight.

Some say that Christ will come again at the beginning of the millennium, while others says that He will not come again till the end of the millennium. Still others remove the millennium entirely out of time, as it were, and say that it refers to the blessed state of the souls in heaven.

Who can help us find the way out of such a maze as this? No one but God, in whose hand are our times (Ps. 31:15). Only as we turn to Him and continue in His Word shall we know the truth. (John 8:31, 32)

It is possible for the "thousand years" of Rev. 20 to be longer than 1,000 calendar years. The Bible sometimes uses definite numbers to denote indefinite numbers. It uses the figure 1,000 that way in Ps. 50:10. Besides, the rest of Rev. 20 is largely figurative; for example, the devil is a spirit and therefore cannot be bound with a literal chain; and all literal pits have bottoms.

All things considered, including, above all, the light which other plain passages of the Bible throw on such figurative language as found in Rev. 20, the most satisfactory explanation of the 1,000 years is that they are figurative and stand for the New Testament age. The "little season" of Rev. 20:3 follows the "thousand years" and immediately precedes the end of the world.

[2] Th. Graebner, *War in the Light of Prophecy* (St. Louis, 1941), pp. 59, 60, 8.

Rev. 20:1-3: What Happened at the Beginning of the Thousand Years

Verse 1: The Angel and His Equipment

Verse 2: The Angel in Action

Verse 3: The Angel's Mission Accomplished

Verse 1   Some hold that the "angel" at the beginning of this vision is Christ. But there is no compelling reason for adopting this view. We take this "angel" to be a literal angel.[3]

John "saw" the angel. This does not prove that angels as such are visible. It was only for the purpose of the vision that the angel took on a visible form. The same applies to the key, chain, bottomless pit, etc.

It was a good angel, because he came down from heaven and, in the unfolding of the vision, was in opposition to the devil. The angel was in human form, because John saw his hand.

In the angel's hand were two things: a key and a chain. As to the key, we may perhaps safely assume that it fitted a lock, although a lock is not specifically mentioned. The key controlled the entrance to "the bottomless pit." Both the key and the pit came into John's vision already in Rev. 9:1, 2. We take the key in both passages to refer to the power to open the pit and to close it securely. The chain represents the power to restrict and restrain effectively. Rev. 20:2 indicates that it was used to bind the devil. Because he is powerful, it had to be "great."

Verse 2   The angel moves to action and lays hold on the devil with the grasp of divine authority and power, from which there is no escape. There is no word of a struggle. The devil must submit and give himself up into the hands of God's angel, and he soon finds what is in store for him. The angel binds him.[4]

---

3 As in Rev. 1:1.

4 The same word as in Matt. 22:13: *"Bind* him hand and foot."

The devil is strong, but good angels are stronger.[5] Most powerful of all is the supreme Lord. He does not need personally to move to action in order to take the devil captive, bind him, and shut him up, sealed, in his place. He simply sends one of His angels, and it is done. (Matt. 26:53; Eph. 1:20-22)

Four Names   "Dragon," a name given also to a fabulous dreadful sea monster which inspired fear and terror;[6] "old serpent," a reference to Gen. 3; "devil," slanderer, false accuser; "Satan," adversary, opponent.[7]

1,000 Years   A thousand years is a long time in more ways than one. In this case it is specifically the New Testament age from the incarnation and enthronement of the Son of God (Rev. 12:5) to the "little season" and the final casting of Satan into hell (Rev. 20:7-10). We are living in the "thousand years."

Verse 3   Having bound the devil, the angel "cast him into the bottomless pit, and shut him up, and set a seal upon him, that he should deceive the nations no more till the thousand years should be fulfilled." The "bottomless pit" is not a comfortable and pleasant place (Rev. 9:2ff.). In Rev. 20:3, however, the emphasis is not on the devil's suffering there, but on the restrictions which God imposed on him. In Rev. 20:7 the pit is spoken of as a "prison." The final punishment of hell, on the other hand, is more definitely symbolized by the lake of fire and brimstone (Rev. 20:10; 21:8). The pit is "bottomless"; the devil never strikes bottom. He has never a moment's rest or respite in his captivity.

5 Ps. 103:20; Dan. 6; 2 Kings 19:35.

6 See the LXX in Jer. 51:34; Ezek. 29:3; 32:2; Ps. 74:13; etc. In the N. T. it occurs only in the Book of Revelation.

7 These four names are used together also in Rev. 12:9, and they occur elsewhere in the book. "Dragon" is first used in Rev. 12:3; "serpent," in 12:9; "devil," in 2:10; "Satan," in 2:9.

Satan's work, indeed, still goes on, but his activities are hedged in by the limits and bounds which God has set. He is like a vicious dog on a strong leash securely anchored, or like the angry sea, to which God said: "Hitherto shalt thou come but no further, and here shall thy proud waves be stayed." [8] He can no longer successfully accuse us, and we can overcome his temptations. Though he is like a roaring lion walking about and seeking whom he may devour (1 Peter 5:8), he cannot do altogether as he pleases. (James 4:7)

There is a certain definite finality about the heaping of expressions: "Bound . . . cast . . . shut up . . . sealed." So far as God is concerned, the devil is well in hand and must wait "a thousand years" until God is ready to break the seal at the entrance to the pit.

"He should deceive the nations no more till the thousand years should be fulfilled." John does not say: "The nations should no more *be deceived,*" but "he [the devil] should deceive the nations no more," that is, personally and directly, as he once came to Eve in the voice of the serpent (Gen. 3:1 ff.) and to Christ (Matt. 4:1-11). He is reduced to working through others.

When a fierce, wild lion has been caged and barred, you are safe from him, unless you put your hand into his cage or in some other way expose yourself to his vicious teeth and claws. Some people, cocksure of their "faith," think that they can safely play patty-cake with the devil. They tempt God. He does not promise them protection under such circumstances (1 Cor. 10:12). "Satan is chained for believers only through faith in the Gospel." [9]

The end of the 1,000 years is referred to in Rev. 20:3 in the words "Till the thousand years should be fulfilled." We have no way of determining when that will be. But when the time comes, God will do what needs to be done. The devil "must be loosed a little season." God is not forced to release him. A different kind

[8] Job 38:11; also see the notes on Rev. 12:12.
[9] Pieper, III, 524.

of necessity is involved here. The devil "must" be loosed because that is a part of God's plan and overruling providence.[10] The devil will not be released in order to harm the church but only to gather all his servants and agencies together for their combined and final overthrow and everlasting damnation (Rev. 20:9, 10). Only a "little season," a short time, is necessary for that.

Rev. 20:4-6: What Happens During the Thousand Years

1. Thrones of Judgment, v. 4
2. The Souls of Martyrs and Other Saints, v. 4
3. The "First Resurrection," vv. 4-6
4. A Beatitude, v. 6

1. Thrones of Judgment (Rev. 20:4)

"I saw thrones." With a single stroke of the pen the apostle John sets before us a contrast which is sharp and strong in the extreme. There is Satan, bound and cast into the noisome depths of the bottomless pit, shut up and sealed securely for a thousand years — and here are the thrones of those who sit in judgment!

A throne is a symbol of principality, power, might, dominion, rule, authority, and judgment. Judgment is specifically mentioned here as being given to those who sat on the thrones in this vision. Ruling, or reigning — with power, authority, might, and dominion implied — is mentioned in the context (Rev. 20:4, 6). Every member of the church is a king.[11] Perhaps for this reason neither heaven nor earth is mentioned as the scene of the thrones in this vision. Their symbolism has application to both, inasmuch as some of the kings are still on earth, some are already in heaven, and some may be as yet unborn.

We are not told how many thrones there were in this vision.[12]

10 Cf. "must" in Rev. 1:1; 22:6.

11 See the notes on Rev. 1:6.

12 There is no exact parallel between Matt. 19:28 and Rev. 20:4.

If we take the thrones as symbols of the royalty of the children of God, with a throne for each, there must be thrones without number. (Rev. 7:9)

"They sat upon them." Sitting on a throne symbolizes the exercise of ruling power and judgment. We take those who sat on the thrones as being all the children of God in heaven and on earth.

"Judgment was given unto them." How easy it is for us to think here immediately of Judgment Day! But these words do not speak of the Last Judgment at the end of the world. Here the reference is to the office, power, and business of judging during the "thousand years" before the end (Dan. 7:22). God, of course, is and remains the final judge of all the earth (Gen. 18:25), and we must all appear before His judgment seat (2 Cor. 5:10), saints and sinners alike. But in another sense it is also true that even before their death the saints have already "passed from death unto life" and do not come into "judgment" (John 5:24 RSV). Instead, they themselves sit in judgment.

The office of the keys is involved here. This helps us to see and understand the part the saints in heaven play in this "judgment." Whatever the church binds on earth shall be bound in heaven, and whatever the church shall loose on earth shall be loosed in heaven. (Matt. 18:18)

An important and significant part of the function of the church in the world, then, is to speak up and speak out fearlessly against sin whenever and wherever it may be found or of whatever nature it may be — be it among the high and mighty, whose favor we are tempted to curry, or be it at the grass roots, among the masses, where the foundations of society and civilization begin to crumble. Sin is sin, and those to whom judgment is committed have the solemn responsibility to call it by its right name and to drive home the stubborn twin truths that "righteousness exalteth a nation; but sin is a reproach to any people." (Prov. 14:34)

2. The Souls of Martyrs and Other Saints (Rev. 20:4)

When the church in the world carries out its function of judgment, some of its members literally lose their heads for it. According to tradition, Paul was beheaded. James, the brother of John, was also killed with the sword (Acts 12:2), perhaps beheaded. Clement of Alexandria, Christian theologian and church father, says that "as James was led to the place of martyrdom, his accuser was brought to repent of his conduct by the apostle's extraordinary courage and undauntedness and fell down at his feet to request his pardon, professing himself a Christian and resolving that James should not receive the crown of martyrdom alone. Hence they were both beheaded at the same time." [13] Matthias (Acts 1:26) is said to have been stoned at Jerusalem and then beheaded.[14] No doubt others, whose names are not preserved in recorded history, also lost their lives in this way for the sake of the Gospel of Christ. But, losing their temporal life, they found eternal life. John saw their souls alive with Christ. (Rev. 6:9-11)

The martyrs lost their lives "for the witness of Jesus and for the Word of God," that is, because they were steadfast in His Word and faith to their end (Rev. 6:9). Like all the other saints they "had not worshiped the beast, neither his image, neither had received his mark upon their foreheads, or in their hands." These expressions derive their meaning from the vision of the beast in Rev. 13 and point up the steadfast faithfulness of all the saints in the face of strong temptation to deny their God and Savior and His Word.[15] The mark in the forehead or in the hand is a symbol of identification with the kingdom of Satan. To refuse this mark means to make practical application of 2 Cor. 6:14-18: "Be ye not unequally yoked together with unbelievers. . . . Come out from among them, and be ye separate, saith the Lord."

The first part of Rev. 20:4 speaks of all the elect. The second

13 Foxe, p. 2.

14 Foxe, p. 3.

15 Ex. 20:3; Deut. 6:13, 14; 10:20; Matt. 4:10; Heb. 11.

part speaks of the church in heaven, with special mention of the beheaded martyrs. The last part of the verse, as a summary, again speaks of the entire communion of saints. "They lived and reigned with Christ a thousand years."

The Easter story and its Gospel promise are woven into this verse. Christ is spoken of as being alive, and the martyrs and other saints have found true His words "Because I live, ye shall live also" (John 14:19), and "Where I am, there shall also My servant be." (John 12:26)

3. The "First Resurrection" (Rev. 20:4-6)

We take the words "they lived" (or "came to life") as referring to the beginning of spiritual life at the moment when the elect come to faith here on earth (John 5:24, 25; Eph. 2:5, 6). That is the real beginning of life in the fullest sense of the word.[16]

They (the elect) "reigned" with Christ. This is true of the *church on earth* in the sense of Rev. 5:10: "We shall reign on the earth," not in a kingdom of this world but in a spiritual kingdom.[17] As kings the children of God on earth reign, conquer, and triumph over all (2 Cor. 2:14; 10:4; 1 John 5:4). We are more than conquerors (Rom. 8:31-39), because our victory and rule is assured forever. The *saints in heaven* are reigning "with Christ" in the kingdom of glory. By His grace we too shall reign there with Him and them. He is their King of kings and ours.[18]

The expression "the rest of the dead" (Rev. 20:5) refers to those who remain dead in trespasses and sins, as opposed to those who were thus dead, but were made alive (Eph. 2:1, 5, 6; Col. 2:13). They "lived not[19] until[20] the thousand years were finished." (Rev. 20:5)

[16] John 10:10; 11:25, 26; 13:36.

[17] John 17:11-16; 18:36; Luke 17:21. (See the notes on Rev. 1:6.)

[18] 1 Tim. 6:15; Rev. 17:14; 19:16.

[19] The word "again" (KJV) is not in the best MSS and says too much. The sense of the words is simply this: "They did not come to life during the 1,000 years." We are not told here what happened to them after the 1,000 years.

This is a striking commentary on the words of Jesus "He that is not with Me is against Me."[21] He that is not spiritually alive is spiritually dead. There is no middle ground.

What is more, those who are spiritually dead and die physically in that state of unbelief remain dead. They have fallen victim to "the second death" (Rev. 20:14). They do not have a "second chance" for eternal life after they leave this world. When unbelievers die, their souls leave their bodies. Far from living and reigning with Christ, their souls continue to exist in a state of spiritual death (a "living death"), with the infinite misery that this involves.[22] Their souls remain in this state of death till the final Judgment on the Last Day. Nor will the lost have another chance for heaven then, but they will be cast, body and soul, into everlasting damnation. (Rev. 20:12-15)

Summary: The "first resurrection" (Rev. 20:5) takes place on earth, in time. It is spiritual, not physical. It occurs whenever the Holy Ghost brings a chosen person to saving faith in Jesus Christ. We are living in the millennium. The first resurrection is taking place now. (John 5:24, 25; Eph. 2:1, 5, 6)

4. A Beatitude (Rev. 20:6)

Rev. 20:6 contains the fifth beatitude in the Book of Revelation.[23] It speaks of those who have part in the first resurrection, that is, they share in it as the elect, who pass from death to life by faith (John 5:24), who are quickened with Christ, raised up, and made to sit in heavenly places in Him (Eph. 2:1, 5, 6). He who has part in the first resurrection is "blessed," that is, happy

Among the translations which do not have the word "again" here are the ASV, Moffatt, Douay, the 1941 Catholic Confraternity New Testament, Schonfield, and the latest printing of the RSV.

[20] "Until" does not imply that they came to life at the end of the thousand years. Compare the use of "until" in 1 Sam. 15:35.

[21] Matt. 12:30. Cf. Mark 9:40; Luke 9:50; 11:23.

[22] Ps. 49:14; 1 Peter 3:19; Is. 66:24; Mark 9:43-48; Luke 16:22-28.

[23] The other six: Rev. 1:3; 14:13; 16:15; 19:9; 22:7, 14.

in the highest sense and degree. And he is "holy" (Rom. 1:7; Col. 3:12). This does not mean that a child of God on earth does not commit sin, but that his sins are forgiven, that he is made holy by faith in Christ, and that he serves God with holy works.

To remove any and every possible doubt, the beatitude deals also with the world to come. "On such the second death [24] hath no power." [25] Far from falling victim to it, they shall live (Rev. 20:4) and "shall be priests of God and of Christ and shall reign with Him a thousand years."

"Priests of God and of Christ" must be understood in the light of 1 Peter 2:5,9 (Heb. 4:16; 13:15,16). Christians are priests who commune intimately, directly, and personally with God. There is no room here for an intermediary estate through which, as through a channel or means of communication, they must approach God. Our spiritual sacrifices on earth are prayer and the worship of God in general; witnessing to Christ; Christian stewardship of our time, our money and possessions, our abilities and blessings; Christian charity. In heaven the priesthood of believers continues in the everlasting song of praise of the redeemed. (Rev. 7:9,10; 19:1ff.; 5:8ff.)

Rev. 20:7-15: What Will Happen at the End of the Thousand Years

1. The Final Doom of the Devil and His Forces, vv. 7-10

The end of the world is commonly, and properly, thought of by Bible readers in terms of such passages as Matt. 25:31-46; 2 Peter 3:10,12. But those passages do not draw the whole picture. A few more lines in the closing scenes of time and the transition into eternity are filled in by Rev. 20:7ff. Some of these details picture the last acts of Satan. In Rev. 20:2,3 he was

---

[24] Eternal damnation in the lake of fire (Rev. 20:14). The first death is temporal death, the separation of body and soul. See Rev. 2:10,11.

[25] Rev. 20:6. See John 10:28; 3:16; 11:26; Rev. 14:13.

bound, cast into the bottomless pit, shut up, and sealed securely for 1,000 years. Now, "when the thousand years are expired," at the end of the world, when the Gospel of the kingdom will have been preached in all the world for a witness to all nations (Matt. 24:14), and when the last of the elect will have been born and brought to saving faith, then Satan "shall be loosed out of his prison." [26]

This is part of God's plan and overruling providence. Satan does not make a successful prison break. He is released only with God's permission. He was bound at the beginning of the New Testament age. Since that time the Book of Revelation pictures him as active on earth only in an indirect way, through anti-Christian power,[27] propaganda,[28] and seduction.[29] The end of the two beasts [30] and of the whore has been described (Rev. 16:12 to 19:21). Now it is Satan's turn. He "shall be loosed" (Rev. 20:7), but not to hurt or harm the church, which is safe in the hands of God (John 10:27-29). Satan is simply to gather all his followers, and he and they are to be completely and finally overthrown together. In this he is like a defeated general who rallies his forces for a final attack. He cannot inflict any damage, but for a short time, just before the end, God permits him to think that he can and to act accordingly.

Completely deluded himself, Satan will "go out to deceive the nations" (Rev. 20:8). Not as though they had not yet been deceived by him (Rev. 13:14; 19:20), but this will be their last and greatest deception. Deception is the devil's ace. He scored with it in the Garden of Eden (Gen. 3). He is using it now (2 Thess. 2:1-12). And he will play it again at the end of the world.[31]

26 On "prison" cf. 1 Peter 3:19.

27 The first beast (Rev. 13:1-10).

28 The second beast (Rev. 13:11-18); also called the false prophet (Rev. 16:13; 19:20).

29 Babylon, the whore (Rev. 17:1 to Rev. 19:3).

30 Resp., including the false prophet.

31 Matt. 24:24; 1 Tim. 4:1-3; 2 Peter 3:3, 4.

The "nations" that will be deceived so completely and with such tragic results are "in the four quarters [corners] of the earth" (Rev. 20:8; 7:1). In every part of the world there are some who are blinded and misled by Satan in this final, fatal delusion.

These "nations" are called Gog and Magog.[32] To determine the significance of these names in Rev. 20:8 we must note how they are used in the grammatical structure of the sentence. They do not stand for two of the "nations," but they stand in apposition to "the nations which are in the four quarters of the earth." "Gog and Magog" are all these "nations." The RSV translates correctly: "the nations which are at the four corners of the earth, that is, Gog and Magog."

Attempts to associate these names with any one specific nation have given rise to theories according to which Gog and Magog are Russia, or England, or India, etc. In view of the particularly vicious anti-Christian character of the Turks, Luther called them Gog and Magog. But the fact that the names stand in apposition to "the nations," and that these "nations" are "in the four quarters of the earth," eliminates the thought of any one nation alone, or any two nations together, being "Gog and Magog." To the extent of their anti-Christian character the Turks, for example, would indeed be included, and so would all other nations and individuals of the same stripe.

In Rev. 20:8 the names "Gog and Magog" apply to all enemies of the spiritual Israel (Rom. 9:8; 2:28, 29), to all who set themselves up in opposition to those who are the children of God by faith in Christ Jesus.[33] Their number "is as the sand of the sea" (Rev. 20:8), innumerable. They gather for battle. At least they seem to realize that they will have a fight on their hands. They also hope to engage in a successful battle. Perhaps they en-

---

[32] Rev. 20:8. See Gen. 10:2 and 1 Chron. 1:5 (Magog was one of the sons of Japheth); 1 Chron. 5:4 (Gog was a son of Joel, but not of the prophet by that name); Ezek. 38 and 39 (where the names are given to enemies of the people of Israel).

[33] Gal. 3:26; 2 Thess. 2:3-12; 1 John 2:18.

courage one another with the thought that "in numbers there is strength." They think that with a combined effort and a united front they can overthrow the church.

What an imposing array they present! (Rev. 20:9a). "They went up on the breadth of the earth." They "marched up" (RSV) and covered the whole expanse of the earth to the horizon in all directions from "the camp of the saints." The faithful were completely surrounded and outnumbered. "The beloved city," the city which God loved, was left without a single apparent avenue of retreat or escape.

But sudden death and complete destruction struck, consumed, and wiped out the enemy of God's people. "Fire came down from God out of heaven and devoured them." [34] Special mention is made of the fate of the devil. He "was cast into the lake of fire and brimstone" (Rev. 20:10), the infinite and eternal punishment of the lost and damned according to body and soul (Rev. 20:12-15). Brimstone is sulfur. It ignites easily and burns in air with a blue flame and suffocating odor. God used it to destroy Sodom and Gomorrah (Gen. 19:24), a type of the end of the world.[35] The beast and the false prophet are in the lake of fire and brimstone (Rev. 19:19, 20). And they — the devil, the beast, and the false prophet — "shall be tormented day and night forever and ever" (Rev. 20:10). This is God's final answer to all who say that there is no infinitely fearful, painful, and eternal hell. "Devour" (Rev. 20:9) does not mean annihilate. Those in hell are like the bush in Ex. 3:2, being burned without being consumed. (Jude 6, 7; Mark 9:43-48)

2. The Last Judgment of Mankind, Rev. 20:11-15

Rev. 20:11-15 does not give us a complete picture of the last Judgment, but speaks only of "the dead" [36] and of the fate of those who die in unbelief.

---

[34] Rev. 20:9b; see Ezek. 38:17-22; Ps. 46.

[35] Luke 17:29, 30; Jude 7; also see Ps. 11:6; Rev. 14:10; 21:8.

[36] Some will be alive at the end of the world (1 Thess. 4:15-17; 1 Cor. 15:51).

Verse 11   As the scene opens, the eyes of the divine seer are
                caught by the transcendent heavenly splendor of its
magnificent centerpiece, the focus of attention not only of the
apostle but also of those in the scene itself — "a great white throne
and Him that sat on it."

The throne is a symbol of power, rule, dominion, and judgment. It is a "great" throne: there is none greater. It is the seat
of supreme justice and final authority. There is no appeal from
the judgment and verdict handed down from it. And it is a "white"
throne.[37] White is a symbol of holiness, righteousness, and justice.[38]

On the throne sat the Son of God and Son of man, Jesus
Christ, "the Lord, the righteous Judge" (2 Tim. 4:8), to whom
all judgment was committed by the Father.[39]

"The earth and the heaven fled away from the face" of Him
who sat on the throne, "and there was found no place for them"
(Rev. 20:11). Most Lutheran theologians teach a total destruction of the world. But many others, including Luther, say that
only the form of this world as it appears now will pass away.
The point in question cannot be fully decided on the basis of clear
Scripture passages. Rev. 20:11 does not necessarily speak of creation in reverse, as it were, but may be regarded as simply another
way of saying that the first form of heaven and earth passed away
to give place to a new form of heaven and earth (Rev. 21:1).
It may be understood as speaking of the beginning of a marvelous
transformation, rejuvenation, or renewing, in which the present
form of creation ceases to exist. This is the moment toward which
all creation has been moving (Rom. 8:22). Nothing as it is now
is able to stand before the flaming eyes of the Judge.[40]

[37] Cf. the white horse (Rev. 6:2; 19:11) and the white cloud (Rev. 14:14).

[38] Is. 1:18; Rev. 1:14; 2:17; 3:4; 19:11; etc.

[39] John 5:22, 27; also see Matt. 24:30; 25:31; Rev. 19:1, 2, 11.

[40] Rev. 1:14; 2:18; 19:12. Also see Rev. 21:4; Mark 13:31; Matt. 24:35;
2 Peter 3:10-12; Heb. 1:11, 12.

Verse 12   Death does not end all. Some say they believe that
            at least the wicked pass out of existence after death,
but this is usually only whistling in the dark. There is a natural
horror in the idea of eternal punishment. In an attempt to escape
this fear, some try to lead themselves and others to believe that
there is no final Judgment. But John says, "I saw the dead . . .
stand before God," and he describes those whom he saw as being
"small and great." [41] Not a single one is missing, overlooked, or
forgotten.[42] There will not be two or more resurrections. All the
dead will stand before God at the same time.

   "The books were opened." They symbolize the complete and
accurate knowledge of the omniscient and infallible Judge.[43] They
contained the record of the sins of the lost (Matt. 25:41-43), but
did not contain the record of the sins of the saved. The names of
the latter are written in "the book of life," [44] mentioned in distinction from the other books, and their sins have been "blotted
out" of the book of God's remembrance.[45] They have been "nailed
to the cross and taken out of the way" (Col. 2:14), and washed
away by the blood of Christ (1 John 1:7; Rev. 7:14). The books
also contained the record of the good works of the believers. These
works prove that they have saving faith (Matt. 25:34-40). It is
therefore correct to say that both believers and unbelievers are
"judged out of those things which were written in the books,
according to their works." [46]

Verse 13   "The sea gave up the dead which were in it." This
            refers to bodies, not souls. Bodies lost or buried at
sea might seem to be beyond all recovery. They usually are so

[41] Cf. Ps. 115:13; Rev. 13:16; 19:5.

[42] Matt. 25:32; John 5:28, 29; Rom. 14:10; 2 Cor. 5:10.

[43] Dan. 7:10; Ex. 32:32, 33; Ps. 69:28.

[44] See the notes on Rev. 3:5.

[45] Ps. 51:1, 9; Is. 43:25; 44:22; Acts 3:19.

[46] Also see John 5:28,29; 2 Cor. 5:10; 1 Peter 1:17.

far as man is concerned. They lie in unmarked graves in the great uncharted wastes of the deep. If they will live again, so will also the rest of the dead.

"Death and hell delivered up the dead which were in them." "Death" is the separation of the soul from the body. It strikes believers as well as unbelievers. At the moment of death the soul of a believer does not die, but goes immediately to heaven (Rev. 20:4; Luke 16:22). In the case of an unbeliever his soul does not die either at the moment of death, but goes immediately to "hell." [47] In both cases temporal death claims only the body, not the soul. At the final Judgment, "death" delivers up all the bodies it has claimed, and "hell" (Hades) delivers up all the souls it has claimed. The souls and bodies are then joined together again to be "judged every man according to their works." [48] The last Judgment does not reopen the case of anyone who has died, as if there were a second chance for heaven after death in a possible reversal of the first judgment, which took place at the moment of death. It simply confirms the first judgment in a final and public pronouncement of sentence on body and soul.

Verse 14   In Rev. 20:14, 15 the sentence of condemnation is carried out. First, "death and hell were cast into the lake of fire." As for death, here is the fulfillment of 1 Cor. 15: 26, 54ff.[49] With the incomparable beauty of his simple eloquence John puts it this way: "There shall be no more death" (Rev. 21:4). As for "hell" (Hades), this place, as such, will have served its purpose; having delivered up its dead (Rev. 20:13). It will never receive another soul. Both "death" and "hell" are "cast into the lake of fire." [50] The wicked whom they held captive do not

[47] Lit., "Hades." See the notes on Rev. 1:18; 6:8.

[48] See the notes on Rev. 20:12.

[49] Also see Heb. 2:14; Is. 25:8; Hos. 13:14.

[50] See the notes on Rev. 19:20; 20:10.

have a moment's respite. "This is the second death," everlasting torment and damnation. From its infinite suffering there is no return or relief.[51]

Verse 15   "Whosoever was not found written in the book of life [52] was cast into the lake of fire" (cf. Mark 16:16). On the Last Day hell [53] will receive to hold forever, in body and soul, all who died without saving faith in the one and only sin-atoning Savior, Jesus Christ.[54]

[51] Luke 16:24-26; Is. 66:24; Mark 9:44-48; Rev. 21:8.

[52] See the notes on Rev. 3:5; 20:12.

[53] In the sense of Matt. 10:28. Lit., "Gehenna," not "Hades."

[54] The souls of the saved are not further dealt with in this verse, because their eternal reward is set forth in Rev. 21—22.

As the Book of Revelation draws to its climax and close, the divine seer directs the eyes of our faith to that which God has prepared and reserved in heaven for those who love Him.[1] Rev. 21:1, 2 is an introduction to the last main section of the book (Rev. 21:1 to Rev. 22:5). Rev. 21:1, 3-8 speaks of the new heaven and the new earth. Rev. 21:2, 9-27; 22:1-5 sets the New Jerusalem before us.

Rev. 21:1, 3-8: The New World

The old heaven and earth had "fled away, and there was found no place for them" (Rev. 20:11). This repeats in visual form the prophecy of Matt. 24:35.[2] Now "a new heaven and a new earth" (Rev. 21:1) unfolded before the eyes of John under the creative hand of God (Is. 65:17). This does not necessarily mean that the old order is to be annihilated, reversing the action of Gen. 1:1, and is then to be replaced with a new world made out of nothing. It may be taken to mean a basic and complete change, a transformation. God "makes all things new" (Rev. 21:5). When a person becomes a child of God, he is not annihilated and then re-created out of nothing. Yet he is "a new crea-

---

[1] 1 Cor. 2:9, 10; James 1:12; 2:5; 1 Peter 1:4.

[2] Also see Ps. 102:26; Is. 51:6; 34:4; Mark 13:31; Luke 21:33; 2 Peter 3:10.

ture." [3] In a sense every conversion from unbelief to saving faith [4] is a type of the final transformation that will take place at the end of the world. The body, in which our soul lives on earth, is not annihilated in death, but will be ours again in the resurrection, changed, transformed, glorified.[5] The "fervent heat" of 2 Peter 3:10 is no more destructive than the decay of the grave, but prepares the way for the emergence of the new world. "The new heavens and the new earth, which I shall make," says God, "shall remain before Me" (Is. 66:22), not subject to change and decay, as the old was. In this sense "we, according to His promise, look for new heavens and a new world, wherein dwelleth righteousness." (2 Peter 3:13)

In the new world that John saw "there was no more sea" (Rev. 21:1) and therefore no more danger of another beast such as arose out of the sea. (Rev. 13:1)

> To understand this figure of speech we must think of the sea as the Hebrews did. . . . To the people of Bible times the sea played a role which caused them to look upon it with eyes of dread. St. John, therefore, could picture nothing more pleasing in the heavenly future than that it would be without sea. . . . The sea also meant separation. Exiled on the lonely island of Patmos in the Mediterranean, he was separated from friends of other years, from comrades in Christ, and from the work to which he had devoted his life. In the picture of the vanished sea John saw the waters which forbade his feet from reaching Ephesus disappear. He sees the dawning of a day when there will be no more separations. For the believing child of Christ, separations will end; we shall meet nevermore to part.[6]

As John saw the new world, he heard "a great voice out of heaven" [7] speak to him about the new heaven and the new earth.

[3] 2 Cor. 5:17. Cf. Mal. 2:10, which does not refer to physical creation, but to the "creative act whereby God accepts human beings, born in sin and by nature His enemies, as His children and declares Himself their Father." Th. Laetsch, *Minor Prophets* (St. Louis, 1956), p. 525.

[4] The "transformation" of Rom. 12:2.

[5] 1 Cor. 15:51, 52; cf. 2 Cor. 3:18; 1 John 3:2.

[6] L. F. Frerking, in *Portals of Prayer* for Friday, April 27, 1956.

[7] Rather, "out of the throne" (Rev. 21:3).

Because God is not specifically introduced until Rev. 21:5-7, and in view of the parallel thought expressed from two different points of view, "They shall be *His* people" (Rev. 21:3), and "he shall be *My* son" (Rev. 21:7), we regard the voice in Rev. 21:3 not as the voice of God but as such a voice as spoke in Rev. 19:5. The "throne" is the throne of God. (Rev. 4; 20:11)

The voice said, "Behold, the tabernacle of God is with men" (Rev. 21:3). This does not contradict Rev. 21:22, which uses a different word — "temple." For the Jews the tabernacle was God's dwelling place, a special symbol of His presence. We also speak of a church as "God's house." [8] And David's words "I will dwell in the house of the Lord forever" (Ps. 23:6) are underscored by Rev. 21:3. Every child of God can make them his own, "for heaven, where God dwells, will be his eternal home." [9]

In heaven God will dwell with men (Rev. 21:3), that is, with the saved (Rev. 21:7). Notice the repetition "with men . . . with them . . . with them" (Rev. 21:3). He is our great "Immanuel," which means "God with us" (Matt. 1:23). He is with His own, not only here in time (John 1:14; Matt. 28:20), but also hereafter to all eternity.

"They shall be His people" (Rev 21:3). This is not something new for them. Long ago the psalmist said, "We are His people." [10] In 1 Peter 2:9 the words "a peculiar people" (KJV) are beautifully and appropriately rendered "God's own people" in the RSV. No man is able to pluck them out of His hand (John 10:29). They are His — forever! No others are so blessed as God's people. He "Himself shall be with them." [11] As hell is "eternal destruction and exclusion from the presence of the

[8] Ps. 26:8; 27:4; 84:1-4, 10.

[9] Barnes, on Ps. 23:6.

[10] Ps. 100:3; also see Ps. 79:13; Ezek. 34:30; Hos. 1:10; John 1:12; 17:6-10.

[11] Rev. 21:3. The words "and be their God" are not in the best MSS; in fact, the words "and be" are not in any MSS, but were supplied by Wm. Tyndale in 1525. If the words "their God" should be retained, they might well be included as follows: "And God Himself — their God! — shall be with them."

Lord," [12] so heaven is eternal, intimate, and blessed communion with Him. [13]

"God shall wipe away all tears from their eyes; and there shall be no more . . . crying," [14] and "there shall be no more death" (Rev. 21:4). Our last enemy shall be destroyed (1 Cor. 15:26). Death is cast into the lake of fire (Rev. 20:14). All of man's fears are basically a fear of death and of what lies beyond. But Christ, through His death and resurrection, abolished death, brought life and immortality to light, and so delivered them who through fear of death were all their lifetime subject to bondage. [15]

What a flood of thoughts and emotions must have surged through the heart of the aged seer! In his own life and in the experiences of his fellow Christians he had seen and felt more than enough of this world's trials and ills (Rev. 1:9; 1 Peter 5:9b). Some of his close friends (Acts 12:2) had sealed their faith with their blood. The end of his own life could not be far off. For many others the road of affliction still lay ahead. [16] But now, before his eyes, and falling on his ears in a voice from the throne of God: no more tears! no more death! neither sorrow, nor crying, nor any more pain! "The former things are passed away." [17] We take "pain" (Rev. 21:4) to mean any and every kind of pain. The perfect bliss of heaven is well described for us here on earth in negative terms, partly because we cannot conceive or appreciate perfection in positive terms by reason of the limitations of our mind and understanding (1 Cor. 2:9) and partly because we can appreciate the thought and hope of being relieved of such distress as presses upon us. The "former things"

---

12 2 Thess. 1:9 RSV. "Eternal destruction" is not annihilation. "Presence," gracious presence.

13 Rev. 22:4; also see Ps. 16:11; 1 Cor. 13:12.

14 Rev. 21:4. Cf. Luke 7:13; 8:52; John 20:11-13; Rev. 5:5; 7:17.

15 2 Tim. 1:10; Heb. 2:14, 15. Also see Is. 25:8; Rom. 6:23; 1 Cor. 15:54-57.

16 Rev. 2:9, 10; 6:11; 7:14; Acts 14:22.

17 Rev. 21:4; cf. Is. 35:10; 61:3; 65:19.

(Rev. 21:4) are still very much with us now, but then they will have passed away.

This is God's own promise. "He that sat upon the throne [18] said, Behold, I make all things new." It is He who makes the new heaven and the new earth. It is He who makes us new creatures in Christ Jesus (2 Cor. 5:17, 18; Eph. 2:10). This process of renewing is already in progress. In believers a beginning of the renewal of the image of God is made here on earth (Col. 3:10; Eph. 4:24). Only in heaven, however, will this image be fully restored.[19]

That John wrote the Book of Revelation when he saw its visions is indicated by the repeated directions to write.[20] Once he was about to write, but was immediately forbidden to record that particular thing (Rev. 10:4). We have a faithful record from his pen. He did not write on his own initiative, but like all the other holy men of God he wrote only as he was moved by the Holy Ghost (2 Peter 1:21). In fact, one gets the impression that at times he hesitated to write until he heard the specific command "Write!" Besides, there is God's own seal of truth: "These words are true and faithful," [21] or trustworthy. Pilate's question: "What is truth?" (John 18:38) has an answer here.

As God is true, His promises are Yea and Amen in Christ Jesus (2 Cor. 1:18-20). Like His threats (Rev. 16:17), they are already as good as fulfilled. "It is done!" (Rev. 21:6). He said — and heaven is ours! "He that believeth on the Son *hath* everlasting life!" (John 3:36; cf. Rom. 8:30)

Then "Christ, as it were, signs His name to it all." [22] "I am Alpha and Omega, the Beginning and the End" (Rev. 21:6).

[18] Rev. 21:5; see the notes on Rev. 20:11, 12; 4:2, 3, 9-11.

[19] Ps. 17:15; also see Ps. 16:11; 1 John 3:2.

[20] Rev. 1:11, 19; 2: 1, 8, 12, 18; 3:1, 7, 14; 14:13; 19:9; 21:5.

[21] Rev. 21:5; see Rev. 19:9; 22:6; cf. John 17:17; Rev. 19:11.

[22] Lenski, p. 622

No history, no revelation of God, no salvation without Him! He is our perfect Savior! [23]

Those who have come to faith thirst for the eternal glory (Phil. 1:23). Our Savior will personally satisfy their desire. "I will give unto him that is athirst of the fountain of the water of life freely" (Rev. 21:6; 7:16, 17). This passage speaks of heaven. It does not refer to streams of life-giving grace which God pours out for us here on earth during our lifetime. It refers to the "pure river of water of life" in the New Jerusalem. (Rev. 22:1, 17)

"He that overcometh [24] shall inherit all things" (Rev. 21:7), rather, "these things," that is, the new things in the new world, described in Rev. 21:3-6. This is "an inheritance incorruptible and undefiled and that fadeth not away, reserved in heaven for you who are kept by the power of God through faith unto salvation ready to be revealed in the last time." [25] It is the heritage of believers, sons of God by adoption.[26]

God used the future tense in Rev. 21:7: "He shall be My son" — not as though the believer is not a child of God until he gets to heaven but rather in the sense that there he will be in the final, full, complete, and highest sense a son of God, in everlasting possession of the glory of heaven, which is his as an heir of God (Rom. 8:16, 17). Similarly must we understand the words "I will be his God" (Rev. 21:7), not as though He were not our God until we get to heaven, but in the sense that when we are there nothing ever can or will come between us and our God. Once you are in heaven, there is no possibility of ever falling away from God or losing heaven. (Rev. 3:12; 21:3)

Rev. 21:8 contains a warning which gives the lie to the be-

23 See the notes on Rev. 1:8; 22:13; also see Phil. 1:6; Heb. 12:2.

24 See the notes on Rev. 2:7.

25 1 Peter 1:4, 5; cf. Acts 26:18; Eph. 1:11; Col. 1:12.

26 Cf. Rom. 8:14, 15. The thought "I will be his Father" (2 Sam. 7:14) is included in the thought "He shall be My son" (Rev. 21:7).

lief that everyone will finally be saved. There will be many (Matt. 7:13) who "shall have their part in the lake which burneth with fire and brimstone, which is the second death." [27]

"The fearful" (Rev. 21:8) are those who give up the good fight of faith because they are afraid of what they may suffer in it. "The unbelieving" (v. 8) are those who die without saving faith in their heart (Mark 16:16b). The reference here seems to be especially to those who fall away from the saving faith. The words "the abominable" (Rev. 21:8) may refer specifically to the abominable emperor worship, or in a more general way to all heathen profanity and immorality, all of which is an abomination in the sight of God.[28] "Murderers and whoremongers and sorcerers" (Rev. 21:8). Besides their general meaning in common descriptions of the heathen,[29] these terms have a special frame of reference in the Book of Revelation as they come into play in connection with the great whore. The saints and martyrs were murdered by her (Rev. 17:6), whoredom is written into her name (Rev. 17:5) and characterizes her life and activity (Rev. 17:1, 2; 18:9), and by her sorceries all nations were deceived.[30] "Idolaters" (Rev. 21:8), all who worship false gods. Besides this general meaning, the word may have special reference to emperor worship, which was rampant in Asia Minor when the Book of Revelation was written. "And all liars" (Rev. 21:8). The church at Ephesus would take special note of that, because it had the problem of dealing with such as said they were apostles, but were not. They were revealed as liars.[31] The word also refers to the second beast (also called the false prophet) and its lying deception.[32]

[27] See the notes on Rev. 19:20; 20:10, 14, 15.

[28] See such passages as Matt. 24:15; Rom. 2:22; Titus 1:16; Rev. 17:4, 5; 21:27.

[29] E. g., Rom. 1:29; Eph. 5:5; Gal. 5:19, 20.

[30] Rev. 18:23; also see Rev. 9:21; 22:15.

[31] Rev. 2:2. Also the church at Smyrna; cf. Rev. 2:9. Also see Rev. 14:5.

[32] Rev. 13:13, 14; 16:13; 19:20; 20:10; also see Rev. 22:15.

Rev. 21:2, 9-27: The New Jerusalem

The new world and the new Jerusalem were combined in one vision. As John saw the new heaven and the new earth unfold, he also saw "the holy city, New Jerusalem, coming down from God out of heaven" (Rev. 21:2; 3:12). The Old Jerusalem of the Jews was also called the Holy City [33] because of the Holy Place, which was there and around which the entire religious life of the chosen race revolved. That temple had been made a den of thieves (Matt. 21:13), and the spiritual leaders of the people plotted the murder of the Son of God in it (Luke 19:47—20:20). So the Lord "destroyed those murderers and burned up their city" (Matt. 22:7) at the hand of the Romans under Titus A. D. 70. But what the Old Jerusalem had properly stood for as a type was not lost. It is embodied in the New Jerusalem, which is above, which is free, and which "is the mother of us all" (Gal. 4:26). Though the city which John saw in this vision was very different from the Old Jerusalem in appearance (shape, construction, and materials), he was enabled to recognize it for what it was.

John saw the Holy City "coming down from God out of heaven" (Rev. 21:2). The words "from God" tell us who made it (Heb. 11:10). The words "out of heaven" point to the place where it was made. (Heb. 13:14)

The Holy City was "prepared as a bride adorned for her husband" (Rev. 21:2). The meaning of these words is to be found in such passages as 2 Cor. 11:2 and Eph. 5:23-32. The bride is the church.[34]

"There came unto me," writes John, "one of the seven angels which had the seven vials full of the seven last plagues" (Rev. 21:9). Perhaps it was the same angel who appeared in Rev. 17:1. In both cases the angel says, "Come hither; I will show thee. . . ." In Rev. 17 the angel showed John the great whore in all her scarlet sin and shame, vice and wickedness; in Rev. 21 the angel shows

[33] Neh. 11:1; Is. 48:2; 52:1; Matt. 4:5.

[34] Rev. 19:7-9. The picture of the church as bride occurs again in Rev. 22:17.

John the bride of Christ in all her purity and loveliness. In both cases a city is involved in the symbolism of the visions; in Rev. 17 it is Babylon; in Rev. 21 it is the New Jerusalem. Each of them was a "golden" city,[35] but in an entirely different sense. We may also regard this angel as being the angel of Rev. 1:1. (Rev. 22: 6, 16)

"Come hither," said the angel to John, inviting him to draw near and go with him to a better vantage point (Rev. 21:10) to see the final and most magnificent panorama in all of the visions. All the kingdoms of the world, and the glory of them, which the devil showed Jesus from an exceeding high mountain (Matt. 4:8), could not begin to compare with what John was to see from "a great and high mountain." (Rev. 21:10)

"I will show thee the bride, the Lamb's wife," said the angel (Rev. 21:9). The use of both terms, "bride" and "wife," indicates the very moment of the nuptials when the church on earth becomes completely and forever the church in heaven.[36]

Rev. 21:10: "He carried me away in the spirit[37] to a great and high mountain[38] and showed me that great city, the Holy [City] Jerusalem, descending out of heaven from God.[39] As the angel guide "showed" John the Holy City, he not only set it before his eyes but also spoke with him about it.[40] When God condescends to human language to give us, in His own inspired words, a description of heaven, words fail us for restating it in better or clearer terms. We must learn patiently to await a fuller and complete revelation when God takes us to Himself in heaven. Meanwhile let us be content to draw what instruction we can from these verses.

[35] Compare Is. 14:4 with Rev. 21:18, 21.

[36] Rev. 19:7, 9; 22:17. On "the Lamb" see the notes on Rev. 5:6.

[37] See the notes on Rev. 1:10.

[38] Cf. Ezek. 40:2. In Rev. 21:10 to 22:3 there are a number of similarities to Ezekiel 40—48.

[39] See the notes on Rev. 21:2.

[40] See the notes on Rev. 22:2 with regard to "every month."

John mentions first what must have come to his attention first. He saw the Holy City descend, "having the glory of God." [41] Perhaps the best-known Bible passage that speaks of human eyes seeing the glory of the Lord is the story of the shepherds of Bethlehem (Luke 2:9). How appropriate it is that the glory of God should be seen both when the Lord of glory came down from heaven to earth and when He takes His church from earth to heaven and the kingdom of grace becomes the kingdom of glory!

"Her light was like unto a stone (Rev. 4:3) most precious, even like a jasper stone, clear as crystal" (Rev. 21:11). "Her light" is that which gave it light. In the light of Rev. 21:23 we may take this to be God Himself, specifically the Lamb, Jesus Christ, in further description of "the glory of God." The "stone . . . like a jasper stone" was scarcely what we call jasper today, opaque and uncrystalline. "The whole subject of the relation of the precious stones named in the N. T. to those of the O. T., to those both of classical antiquity and of modern mineralogy, is one of greatest obscurity. . . . Fortunately the interpretation here is not affected by our ignorance of these details." [42] It is easiest, and perhaps best, to think of the scintillating sparkle and brilliance of a diamond. In heaven everything is bright and clear and glorious. [43]

The city "had a wall great and high" (Rev. 21:12). This was not for protection, because heaven stands in no threat of danger or attack. We regard the wall as a "symbol of inclusion," [44] which clearly separates and distinguishes between those who are within and those who are outside. [45]

There were 12 gates, [46] distributed evenly around the four-square city for equal opportunity of entrance by all, wherever they

41 Rev. 21:11. Cf. Rev. 21:23; Ezek. 43:2-5.

42 I. T. Beckwith, p. 497.

43 Also see the notes on Rev. 21:19-21.

44 Lenski, p. 631.

45 Cf. Rev. 22:15. On the dimensions of the wall and their significance see Rev. 21:17.

46 Rev. 21:12, with a further description in Rev. 21:21.

might be (Rev. 21:12, 13, 16, 26; 22:14). No one ever goes out
of them (Rev. 3:12). There were 12 gates, because there were
12 tribes of the Children of Israel. Their names were written on
the gates, one name, we take it, on each gate. These 12 tribes
represented not the entire Jewish nation, many of whom are not
among the saved in heaven, but God's chosen people in the sense
of the spiritual Israel, the total number of all who are saved.[47]

"The wall of the city had 12 foundations." [48] The apostles
lend their names to be inscribed on the 12 foundations, one name,
we take it, on each foundation. Because the Holy City is dis-
tinctively the city of the Lamb (Rev. 21:9, 22, 23, 27; 22:1, 3),
the apostles are called the 12 apostles of the Lamb. (Rev. 21:14)

The angel who was John's companion and guide (Rev. 21:9)
spoke with him (Rev. 21:15), but apparently John did not record
what he said. Rev. 21:10-14 reads rather as an account of what
John saw. We may imagine the angel discussing the scene with
John in an interchange of remarks. The services of the angel
guide included this, that he measured the three dimensions of the
New Jerusalem and its gates and wall with a reed, or measuring
rod, which he had and which, quite appropriately, was golden.[49]

The city lay "foursquare," that is, in a square form, with the
length as large as the breadth (Rev. 21:16), "12,000 furlongs,"
literally, 12,000 stadia. This is equal to about 1,200 or 1,500
miles. We are not told whether this was the length along one
side or whether it was the entire circumference. In these figures
we are confronted with symbols, not with space relationships.
Space and time as we know them pass away with the old heaven
and the old earth. With regard to time, for example, how long,
humanly speaking, it must have taken to measure such tremendous

[47] Rom. 11:26. See the notes on Rev. 7:4-8; also notice the parallel thoughts
between Rev. 7:16, 17 and 21:4, 6b; also see Rev. 22:14.

[48] Rev. 21:14. Cf. Heb. 11:10; Eph. 2:20. The only further reference to the
foundations is in Rev. 21:19, 20.

[49] Rev. 21:15, 18. In Rev. 11:1, 2 John was given a reed, not described as
golden, to measure the church on earth.

distances, if we take them literally, with the measuring rod! Yet John writes almost as though it was done in a moment.

As to the symbolism of the figures, 12 and 1,000 come into play, as in Rev. 7.[50] There were 12 tribes in God's chosen race. In Rev. 21:16 we take the figure 12 to stand for the spiritual Israel (Rom. 11:26; cf. 2:28, 29), and 1,000 as emphasizing completeness and perfection beyond all question or doubt. The square and the cube have also been long regarded as symbols of perfection. Perhaps this is why a cube is introduced in describing the Holy City.[51]

When the angel measured the wall of the city, it was found to be 144 cubits. Because the angel measured it, it is literally "angel's measure." Because the dimension is given in terms of standards in common use among men, it is literally man's measure (Rev. 21:17; cf. 13:18). Direction, distance, and space are not the considerations here, but rather the symbolism in "144." This figure is 12 multiplied by itself to express totality.[52] We take it to mean that the walls of the city, symbols of inclusion,[53] completely enclose the final and eternal union and communion of God with all who are His own.

Perhaps the gates are mentioned in Rev. 21:15 only in allusion to Ezek. 40. Their dimensions are not given. That we hear nothing more of them as to their size "seems to be due to the fact that the portals in the wall are a part of the city, and in the measurement from one corner to the next the portals were included." [54]

"The building of the wall" [55] of the city was of jasper.[56]

50 See the notes on that chapter and on Rev. 21:12.

51 Rev. 21:16. Cf. Ps. 50:2. The Holy of Holies (a type of heaven, Heb. 9:24) was also a perfect cube (1 Kings 6:20).

52 As in Rev. 7:4.

53 See the notes on Rev. 21:12.

54 Lenski, p. 635.

55 Rev. 21:18. Cf. the notes on Rev. 3:18.

56 See the notes on Rev. 21:11.

This, we believe, refers to the material of which the wall was built or to an inlay the wall was adorned with. "And the city was pure gold, like unto clear glass" (Rev. 21:18; cf. n. 55). The description of the material the city was built of, like its dimensions, must be understood symbolically. "Pure gold," without any dross. "Clear as glass" expresses purity rather than transparency. Even the city street,[57] where one might expect to find impurities, or at least construction of baser materials, is "pure gold, as it were transparent glass" (Rev. 21:21). The transparency, or clarity, of the glass is evidence of its purity, which is its point of comparison with gold. All of this combines to convey, as far as it is possible for the human mind to grasp and human language to express, the infinite and inexpressible beauty and perfection of heaven.

Even the foundations of the wall of the city were not left unadorned or sunk in dirt and soiled with grime; they were "garnished with all manner of precious stones: jasper . . . sapphire . . . chalcedony . . . emerald . . . sardonyx . . . sardius . . . chrysolyte . . . beryl . . . topaz . . . chrysoprasus . . . jacinth . . . amethyst" (Rev. 21:19, 20). There is no special mystical sense attached to these jewels individually, nor can they be definitely identified in terms of modern nomenclature. They are connected with the foundation of the apostles,[58] which is in the Bible. Gems are among the most durable substances known to man, fit symbols of the Word of the Lord, which lives and abides and endures forever (1 Peter 1:23, 25; Matt. 24:35). And as the stones in the foundations of the Holy City are beautiful and precious, so also is the Word of God precious and beautiful beyond compare! [59] Christian hymn writers have taught the church to sing of heaven's "gates of pearl," drawing the expression from Rev. 21:21.[60]

[57] A collective noun; in view of the 12 gates there must have been more than one street.

[58] See the notes on Rev. 21:14.

[59] Also see the notes on Rev. 21:11.

[60] On the last half of Rev. 21:21 see the notes on Rev. 21:18.

Very likely the life of John, as that of a pious and devout man, had revolved for many years around the temple in old Jerusalem. If the Book of Revelation was written toward the end of the first century after Christ, he had lived to see that city and its temple destroyed. Now the New Jerusalem was before his eyes. Small wonder if his eyes searched it here and there for a new temple. "I saw no temple therein," he says, and immediately adds the reason for its absence: "For the Lord God Almighty and the Lamb are the Temple of it." [61] The tabernacle in the wilderness, and later the temple at Jerusalem, with its sacrificial lambs, had been the focal point of the presence of God on earth (Ex. 23:17). But heaven is so filled with the glorious presence of God that everyone there will at all times be with Him face to face.[62] No more lambs — instead the Lamb! Nor is the New Testament church on earth bound to the old temple (John 4:21, 23, 24), though it is bound to observe special assemblies (Heb. 10:25 a). With this in mind, some have aptly said that in heaven we shall observe an everlasting Lord's Day.[63]

Similarly, "the city had no need of the sun, neither of the moon, to shine in it" (Rev. 21:23). The Sun of righteousness, which rose on our sin-sick world with healing in His wings (Mal. 4:2) when Christ was born (Luke 1:78), shines perpetually and in transcendent glory in the New Jerusalem. "The glory of God is its light, and its lamp is the Lamb." [64] Christ is the light not only of this world (John 8:12) but also of that which is to come.

In Rev. 21:23 we must not take "God" as the counterpart of "the sun," and "the Lamb" as the counterpart of "the moon."

[61] Rev. 21:22. The temple of Rev. 11:19; 14:15, 17; 15:5 ff. has no part in this vision.

[62] Ps. 16:11; Matt. 18:10; Phil. 1:23; Ps. 17:15.

[63] Rev. 1:10. On the phrase "Lord God Almighty" see the notes on Rev. 1:8; 4:8.

[64] Rev. 21:23 RSV; also see Is. 60:19, 20; Matt. 17:2; and the notes on Rev. 21:11.

In the poetic rhythm and balance of Rev. 21:22-26, to which our English translations can scarcely do full justice, a reason why there is no need for the moon in heaven is found at the end of Rev. 21:25: "There shall be no night there" (Rev. 22:5; cf. Gen. 1:16). The sun, as a type of the heavenly glory of God, finds its fulfillment in God and the Lamb in an endless, eternal day, and for lack of night in heaven the moon is forever out of the picture.

"The nations of them which are saved shall walk in the light of it." [65] This does not contradict 1 Tim. 6:16, which speaks of men in this world, not in the world to come. "The nations of them which are saved" are the total number of those who have been redeemed to God "out of every kindred, and tongue, and people, and nation" (Rev. 5:9; 7:9). As these nations are not entire nations according to the flesh, so the kings of the earth, who bring their glory and honor into the Holy City, are not all of those who rule over physical realms here on earth. Their presence in heaven is not the result of the fact that they were kings "of the earth" but rather of the fact that they were kings to God and as such were to reign "on the earth." [66] Would that more kings and rulers, men with power, influence, and authority, would give their hearts and lives to the Lord, and so advance from being mere kings of the earth to be rulers with Christ!

All of the saved, kings and nations together, bring their glory and honor, their most precious possessions, into the New Jerusalem (Rev. 21:24, 26). Here is the final consummation of Is. 60, which finds the beginning of its fulfillment in the New Testament church on earth. "The glory and the honor of the nations are all that they wrought for the Lamb while they were here on the old earth, for which they receive reward in the Eternal City, namely the varying degrees of glory." [67]

[65] Rather, "by its light" (Rev. 21:24).

[66] Rev. 5:10. Also see the notes on Rev. 1:6.

[67] Lenski, p. 645. Also see 1 Cor. 1:31; 10:31; Rev. 4:9-11; 5:12, 13; 7:12; 19:1, 7; on degrees of glory see Dan. 12:3; Luke 19:16-19; 2 Cor. 9:6. — Or "The glory of the nations," the elect out of all nations, not only in the Church Trium-

"There shall be no night there" (Rev. 21:25 b) explains why night is not mentioned in the first part of the verse and why there was no need of the moon (Rev. 21:23). The gates of the city shall not be shut at all — quite a different picture from that in Matt. 25:10. Each has its own lesson to teach. Matt. 25:10 warns us not to wait until it is too late (2 Cor. 6:2). Rev. 21:25 tells us that the gates are open to all who may enter in (Rev. 22:14) and indicates that heaven stands in no danger of invasion by hostile or evil forces.[68]

"There shall in no wise enter into it anything that defileth [anything unclean], neither whatsoever [whosoever] worketh abomination or maketh a lie" (Rev. 21:27). Whoever or whatever is unholy or unclean in a moral, ceremonial, or religious sense is defiling in its contacts.[69] But there will be none of that in heaven — only the holy and the pure! Only "they which are written in the Lamb's book of life" (Rev. 21:27) will enter into the Holy City, the New Jerusalem.[70]

NOTE: The description of the New Jerusalem is concluded in the first five verses of Rev. 22.

phant but also in the Church Militant, who are already glorious in the eyes of God, Rom. 8:30. (A. M. Loth, in the *Concordia Theological Monthly,* II [Dec. 1931], 923, 924.)

[68] On Rev. 21:25 also see Rev. 21:12 and 22:14; also 21:23 and 22:5.

[69] See Acts 10:14, 28; 11:8; Mark 7:20. The reference to abomination and a lie repeats the similar thought in Rev. 21:8.

[70] See the notes on Rev. 3:5. Cf. 1 Cor. 1:26.

Rev. 22:1-5 concludes the description of the Holy City, the
   New Jerusalem
Rev. 22:6-21 brings the book to a close
Rev. 22:6-20a: Divine attestation
Rev. 22:20b: John's reply
Rev. 22:21: John's farewell benediction

Rev. 22:1-5: The New Jerusalem (concluded)

The angel guide to the Holy City, who had come to John to
show him the New Jerusalem (Rev. 21:9, 10), is still with him.
He now points out to John a river which flowed out from the
throne of God and of the Lamb, the Son of God (Rev. 5:6; etc.).
The river was as clear or transparent as crystal and therefore also
"pure." [1] Its water is the "water of life" (Rev. 22:1). Since this
vision carries us beyond the end of time, we may add that it is the
water of eternal life (cf. John 4:14). In the Garden of Eden (Gen.
2:10), in the city of God which is the church on earth (Ps. 46:4),
and in heaven, as John saw the Holy City, a river plays a significant part as a source of pleasure and refreshment. In the New
Jerusalem it reaches into every part of the city, because "river"
(like "street," Rev. 21:21) may be taken as a collective noun,
or in the sense of Ps. 46:4: a river with a number of streams, or

---

[1] Rev. 22:1 KJV; the best MSS, however, do not include this word.

branches. It is a symbol of life, because there is no death in heaven (Rev. 21:4), but only life — perfect life, unpolluted and uncorrupted by any sin or impurity, or touch of death — life flowing from the throne of God, the Author of all life, and from the throne of the Lamb, the Prince of life. (Acts 3:15)

The first part of Rev. 22:2 is a little hard to understand in the KJV: "In the midst of the street, and on either side of the river, was there the tree of life." [2] A similar thought is in the RSV, which takes the first part of Rev. 22:2 [3] with Rev. 22:1. We take it that each street was divided by a little park, formed by the river and the trees.[4] Some modern cities have been beautified with similar parks or parkways.

As to the fruits of the tree, the KJV adds the words "manner of" and translates: "twelve manner of fruits." Similarly, the RSV adds "kinds of" and translates: "twelve kinds of fruit." Actually, the text simply speaks of the tree as "making [bearing, yielding] twelve fruits." In such a connection the word "fruit" can mean "crop." [5] So we understand it here, not as 12 different kinds of fruit but as 12 separate crops, or harvests, one in every month of the year.[6] Since this was the fruit of the tree of life in heaven, it was perfect and completely satisfying. (Cf. Rev. 7:16)

As to the question how there could be "months" without a moon (Rev. 21:23), on earth we have only the language of time with which to speak of eternity. The monthly harvest of the fruit may have been only mentioned by the angel rather than actually observed by John.

"The leaves of the tree were for the healing of the nations" (Rev. 22:2; cf. Ezek. 47:12), not the lost, for whom there is no

---

[2] On "the tree of life" see the notes on Rev. 2:7.

[3] "Through the middle of the street of the city."

[4] "Tree" in Rev. 22:2 being a collective noun, like "river" and "street" in Rev. 22:1, 2; cf. Ezek. 47:7.

[5] Cf. Mark 4:29; Luke 12:17; John 4:36; etc.; "twelve crops of fruit," NEB.

[6] The year of the Hebrews consisted of 12 months. 1 Kings 4:7; 1 Chron. 27:1-15.

healing after the end of their temporal life, but "the nations of them which are saved" (Rev. 21:24, 26), the saints in heaven, who are forever free from sin and sickness. There is no hunger or thirst in heaven (Rev. 7:16), yet food and drink are provided in the fruit of the tree of life (Rev. 22:2, cf. v. 14) and in the water of life (Rev. 22:17). So though there is no sickness for the saints, yet healing, or health, is provided by the leaves of the tree of life. All of this emphasizes the perfection of heaven.

"There shall be no more curse" (Rev. 22:3), that is, someone or something accursed. In the Bible the word occurs only here. It echoes 1 Cor. 16:22: "If any man love not the Lord Jesus, let him be anathema," that is, accursed; none such will be in heaven, but only those who do love the Lord Jesus. It also points to the fact that Christ was made a curse for us and nailed to the tree of the cross to redeem us from the curse of the Law; therefore, for the redeemed in heaven, where there is neither sin nor sinner, there is no accursed tree, only the tree of life! no throne of the cross, only the throne of glory! "And ["but," KJV, RSV] the throne of God and of the Lamb shall be in" the Holy City.[7] God rules supreme, unchallenged, and forever in heaven.

"His servants shall serve Him" (Rev. 22:3), not as slaves but in sincere worship.[8] "Him" refers to "God" (Rev. 7:15) that is, the Father,[9] but not to the exclusion of "the Lamb," Jesus Christ, who is also God.[10]

In heaven the saints shall see God.[11] The servants of God "shall see His face" (Rev. 22:4). Such passages as Ex. 33:17-23 and 1 Tim. 6:16 refer to this world, not to that which is to come. In the latter we shall see God face to face, not simply with the eyes of our mind, or spirit, or faith, but also with the eyes of our

---

[7] Rev. 22:3. See the notes on Rev. 3:21; also see John 10:30.

[8] Phillips, the NEB, and the RSV translate: "His servants shall worship Him."

[9] See the notes on Rev. 4:2, 3.

[10] See John 5:23; Heb. 1:6; Rev. 5:12, 13; and the notes on Rev. 22:6, 16.

[11] Job 19:26, 27; Matt. 5:8. Also see Ps. 17:15; 1 Cor. 13:12; 1 John 3:2.

flesh. To be safely with God face to face is the highest bliss of heaven, the complete opposite of being forever separated from God in everlasting damnation (2 Thess. 1:9). The name of God the Father will be on the foreheads of the saints in heaven (Rev. 22:4) and indicate to whom they belong.[12]

The final lines and touches in the description of the Holy City are briefly added and quickly drawn (Rev. 22:5); some of them repeat or emphasize features which had previously been sketched into the beautiful picture. "There shall be no night there" (Rev. 21:25). Release from night in heaven is set over against the provision of night in this present life (Ps. 104:19, 20). "And they [the saved in heaven] need no candle"[13] because there will be no night, "neither light of the sun, for the Lord God giveth them light. And they shall reign forever and ever."[14]

There is a wonderful harmony of content in the Bible. In the opening chapters of Genesis — Paradise, and man in his state of innocence. In the closing chapters of Revelation — Paradise regained, and man once more in a state of perfect holiness. As in the first Paradise a stream went out to water the garden, so the new Paradise will have a river of unfading joys. The tree of life, lost by man's sin in the first Paradise, will be restored in the assurance that death and sickness have no place in the everlasting Paradise, but man will live to all eternity, because the curse of sin no longer touches the saints. God walked and talked with our first parents in the Garden of Eden; in the Holy City God will dwell with His saints, and they will be His people to live and reign with Him forever and ever!

Rev. 22:6-20a: Divine Attestation

The visions of John are ended. Their final glory fades away before the eyes of the divine seer. But not once does he himself

---

12 Cf. the mark of the beast (Rev. 13:16), and also see the notes on Rev. 14:1.

13 Phillips: "lamplight"; RSV and NEB: "light of lamp."

14 Rev. 22:5, cf. Rev. 21:23; 5:10; Dan. 7:18,27; 2 Tim. 2:12.

speak of this. Instead, he draws his book to a close with the heavenly Jerusalem still very much before us in our heart and mind. So it should always be. What John had seen was not an idle, empty dream but the eternal truth of God, revealed to the eye of faith.

Before we return with him from the mount (Rev. 21:10) to the plain of this world — for such days and years as may still be ours in the providence of God — John shares with us also the final stamp and seal of approval and assurance which he received from God through the angel (Rev. 1:1; 21:9) and from our Savior; this supports and strengthens saving faith. In this faith we soar as on wings through the gates of the Holy City and to the throne of grace. The message of the angel was not only for John; it was for all the servants of God. (Cf. Rev. 1:1 with 22:6)

"He said unto me, These sayings are faithful and true" (Rev. 22:6). The "sayings" are the entire Book of Revelation, "the sayings of the prophecy of this book" (Rev. 22:7; cf. 1:3). They are "faithful and true," the words of "the Lord God of the holy prophets,"[15] whose Word is truth (John 17:17), who cannot lie (Titus 1:2; Heb. 6:18), and the words of His Son, who is Himself the Truth (John 14:6), faithful and true.[16] Since the God of the prophets so highly honored John as to send His angel to show through John to His servants the things which must shortly be done (Rev. 22:6; cf. Rev. 1:1), no one can deny John's claim to be a prophet.

The two statements *"God* sent His angel" and *"I, Jesus,* have sent Mine angel" (Rev. 22:6, 16) combine into one of the strongest statements in the Bible on the deity of Christ.

The angel spoke also the words "Behold, I come quickly" (Rev. 22:7; cf. 22:8). He did not speak for himself, however, but merely repeated the words of Christ,[17] who is constantly, at

---

[15] Or "the Lord, the God of the spirits of the prophets," RSV.

[16] Rev. 19:11. Also see John 18:37 and the notes on Rev. 21:5.

[17] See the notes on Rev. 3:11, and cf. Rev. 22:12, 20.

every moment, the "Coming One." "Quickly" emphasizes the flight of time, without reference to its total extent. No matter how long the world may continue to stand, we are approaching the end at a rapid rate. Jesus does not merely say, "I will come quickly" sometime in the future, but "I am ever coming quickly."

Bible students, commentators, and translators differ among themselves as to whether or not the angel also spoke the last part of Rev. 22:7, which is the sixth beatitude [18] in the Book of Revelation. Some hold that this is an expression of John, as in Rev. 1:3. Be that as it may, the emphasis is not on merely knowing what is in the Book of Revelation but on making it a part of faith and life in a God-pleasing way. Whoever does that is supremely blessed both now and forever.[19]

As a faithful witness, John adds his own specific statement that he saw and heard these things (Rev. 22:8). It is not his nature and style to mention his own name unnecessarily. Here it serves the purpose of attestation. His readers were not to be left in doubt as to who wrote any part of the Book of Revelation (Rev. 1:1, 4, 9; 21:2 KJV), and they were to know that he wrote on the basis of personal knowledge. (John 21:24)

John was overwhelmed by what he had seen and heard (Rev. 22:8). Perhaps the words "Behold, I come quickly" (Rev. 22:7) led him to believe that the "angel" was really God (Rev. 1:4, 8; 3:11; 4:8). For the second time (Rev. 19:10) he "fell down to worship before the feet of the angel which showed me these things" (Rev. 22:8). It is easy for us to say that he should not have caused the angel to repeat the admonition: "See thou do it not! For I am thy fellow servant, and of thy brethren. . . . Worship God!" [20] But let him who has never twice committed any sin cast the first stone of criticism at John as he lies prostrate in his

[18] Cf. Rev. 1:3; 14:13; 16:15; 19:9; 20:6; 22:14.

[19] As to the blessing in store for him who keeps the sayings of the prophecy of this book see the notes on Rev. 1:3.

[20] Rev. 22:9; see the notes on Rev. 19:10.

misdirected piety. Let men develop a proper attitude of worship over against God and respect over against His angel messengers.

The angel in Rev. 22:9 was "of . . . the prophets," that is, a servant of the God of the prophets (Rev. 22:6), and he himself was a prophet in his function of bringing a message from God to man. The prophets were the "brethren" of John; he was one of them, and in that respect the angel stood no higher than he. Also, the angel was "of them which keep the sayings of this book" (Rev. 22:7). He was not above the Word of God but under it, obligated to "keep" it (Rev. 1:3; 14:12) as it applied to him, and in that respect also no higher than John.

We may suppose that at this point John arose and stood with the angel, who then continued speaking: "Seal not the sayings of the prophecy of this book" (Rev. 22:10). As a sealed book it would serve no purpose, since its contents were designed for the servants of God on earth, to strengthen their faith and to help them evaluate the times and chart the course of their lives accordingly.

"The time is at hand" (Rev. 22:10). This does not refer to the end of the world, but to the time in which the various events described in the Book of Revelation take place — the entire span of the ages from the very moment of writing to the end of time. We are living in times spoken of in the Book of Revelation and should draw from it what we can to sustain and strengthen our Christian faith and hope and give direction to our life.

The first half of Rev. 22:11 has left many at a loss. We would expect to read: He that is unjust, let him forsake his evil ways; and he which is filthy (with sin, moral defilement), let him seek cleansing by the blood of Christ (Is. 55:7; 1 John 1:7). Instead we read: "He that is unjust, let him be unjust still; and he which is filthy, let him be filthy still." This may be understood in the light and in the sense of Matt. 13:24-30: let the tares be tares, and let them grow together with the wheat until the harvest. Those who refuse to hear the Word of God and will not keep "the sayings of the prophecy of this book" (Rev. 22:10),

far from being blessed (Rev. 22:7), are forever accursed in their
self-destruction (Hos. 13:9). It is not the business of the church
on earth to exterminate them with fire and sword. They have
their reward, receiving what they have deserved at the hands of
the righteous Judge.

"He that is righteous," that is, justified by faith (Rom. 5:1),
"let him still do what is right;[21] and he that is holy," that is,
sanctified, "let him be holy [22] still." (Rev. 22:11 b)

"Many, however, prefer to understand the verse as announcing
the unchangeable condition of men's character after the Day of
Judgment." [23]

Rev. 22:12-21 lends itself well as a passage to read at dawn
(because of the reference to "the bright morning star," Rev.
22:16), at the close of day (reminding us, as it does, of the
advancing hours in the world's day), and especially at the end
of the year (with its echoes of Christmas, of which there are
a number also in these verses).

Though time has been flying ever since creation, no man can
say how much of it still remains to fly out of the future into the
past. "Quickly" [24] may be taken with reference to speed, without
reference to proximity. We can safely say only: (1) The final
end may come at any time; (2) We are closer to it now than
ever before; (3) We are moving towards it at a rapid rate.
Children of God are "looking for and hasting unto the coming
of the Day of God." [25] Say He is coming "soon," if you will,[26]

---

[21] This is a better reading than "let him be righteous still" (KJV). Cf.
1 John 2:29; 3:7, 10.

[22] Or "keep himself sanctified, holy" (cf. Arndt-Gingrich, *Lexicon*). Or "let
him be made righteous (or let him let himself be made righteous)" (Lenski,
p. 665). The word does not lend itself easily to correct and idiomatic translation. —
Cf. 2 Cor. 7:1; Eph. 2:10; Heb. 12:14.

[23] *Concordia New Testament with Notes.*

[24] Rev. 3:11; 22:12, 20; also see the notes on Rev. 22:7.

[25] 2 Peter 3:12. Cf. Job 7:6; 8:9; 9:25, 26; 14:1, 2; Ps. 39:4, 5; 90; 102:11;
James 4:14.

[26] With the RSV in Rev. 3:11; 22:7, 12, 20.

but do not go beyond the Bible and attempt to say how soon is "soon." Human definitions and standards of time do not apply here. "One day is with the Lord as a thousand years, and a thousand years as one day." [27]

Faith alone saves, and only unbelief damns.[28] In the final Judgment everyone will be rewarded not because of but according to his works. "My reward is with Me," says Jesus, "to give every man according as his work shall be." [29]

The Coming One identifies Himself by name and description in Rev. 22:13, 16. "I am Alpha and Omega, the Beginning and the End, the First and the Last." [30] There is an echo of Christmas here, caught and reflected in the German hymn "Nun singet und seid froh!" An old English translation of its first verse reads:

> Now raise your happy voice, Sing all and loud rejoice!
> Lowly there reclineth Our heart's Delight so blest,
> As the sun He shineth Upon His mother's breast.
> Thou Art A and O! Thou art A and O!

The seventh, and last, beatitude [31] in the Book of Revelation is Rev. 22:14: "Blessed are they that wash their robes,[32] that they may have right to the tree of life, and may enter in through the gates into the city" (Rev. 21:1—22:5). The only effective "washing of the robes" is done in the blood of Jesus Christ.[33] The circle of our salvation comes full round when He, who shed His blood to save us, comes to take us through the gates into the eternal Holy City of God. There, by the grace of God, we

[27] 2 Peter 3:8. — "The last days" are the entire New Testament age. Cf. Acts 2:16, 17.

[28] Rom. 3:28; Eph. 2:8, 9; Mark 16:16.

[29] Rev. 22:12. See also Heb. 11:6; Matt. 25:31-46; Rev. 20:12; Dan. 12:3; Luke 19:16-19; 2 Cor. 9:6; Ps. 62:12; Rev. 2:23.

[30] Rev. 22:13. Also see Rev. 1:8, 17; 2:8; 21:6.

[31] Rev. 1:3; 14:13; 16:15; 19:9; 20:6; 22:7.

[32] As in the RSV, rather than "do His commandments," as in the KJV.

[33] John 1:29; Is. 1:18; Zech. 3:3-5; Heb. 9:14; 1 John 1:7; and the notes on Rev. 7:14.

shall have the "right to the tree of life" and live forever in Paradise regained. "For where there is forgiveness of sins, there is also life and salvation." [34]

Whoever does not enter in through the gates into the city remains outside of it, in the company of his fellows: "dogs,[35] and sorcerers, and whoremongers, and murderers, and idolaters, and whosoever loveth and maketh a lie" (John 8:44; Rev. 22:15). That is the eternal reward of the unbelievers, the lost, the damned, whose life betrayed their lack of saving faith.[36] The word "dogs" expresses complete contempt and rejection and implies that those to whom it is applied are "shameless, impudent, malignant, snarling, dissatisfied, and contentious." [37] Unbelief, the sin which damns (Mark 16:16), is the greatest "lie" of all, because it denies the truth of God's Word.

There are three echoes of Christmas in Rev. 22:16: (1) In the name "Jesus"; (2) In "the root and the offspring of David"; and (3) in "the bright Morning Star."

1. "I, Jesus." He is called Jesus because He is the only Savior of all mankind.[38] Jesus, who was born a true human being at Bethlehem, is also true God. Cf. Rev. 22:6 and 16, and let no one say that Jesus never claimed to be God!

Jesus sent his angel "to testify unto you [plural] these things" (Rev. 22:16). In Rev. 22:6 the angel spoke to John and referred to the servants of God. But in Rev. 22:16 Jesus speaks to the servants of God. The "things" are "the things which must shortly be done" (Rev. 22:6), "which must shortly come to pass" (Rev. 1:1). These things are "in regard to the churches," in the translation of Rev. 22:16 suggested by Lenski, rather than "in the

34 Luther, Small Catechism, "Sacrament of the Altar."

35 Cf. "he which is filthy" (Rev. 22:11) and also Deut. 23:18; Phil. 3:2; 2 Peter 2:22; Matt. 7:6.

36 John 8:44; Rev. 20:15; 21:8; 1 Cor. 6:9; Gal. 5:19-21; on Rev. 22:14, 15 cf. Gal. 3.

37 Barnes, on Phil. 3:2.

38 Acts 4:12. Also see Matt. 1:21; Luke 1:31-33; John 14:6.

churches" (KJV) or "for the churches" (RSV). "All the things of all the visions are revealed in so far as they pertain to the churches, as these things affect them, as thus 'you,' the members of the churches, must know them." [39]

2. "I am the Root and the Offspring of David" (Rev. 22:16). Here Jesus identifies Himself as the Promised One of Old Testament prophecy. The "root" is the "shoot" which springs from the root.[40] "Root" (or "shoot") and "offspring" refer to Jesus according to His human nature.[41] There is in this name also a reference to royalty (Luke 1:32, 33). He is not merely the descendant of a king but is Himself King of kings and Lord of lords, "not the kings of the earth, but the Lamb's loyal followers, who as believers have been made kings and priests to God and the Lamb." [42]

3. "I am . . . the bright [and] Morning Star" (Rev. 22:16). The Christmas Star is not the one which the Wise Men followed, who came to Bethlehem some time after the first Christmas night. It is the star spoken of in Num. 24:17. In Rev. 2:28 "the morning star" is a reward which Jesus says He will give to him "that overcometh and keepeth My works unto the end." But while we, by the grace of God, will receive the Morning Star and "they that turn many to righteousness shall shine as the stars forever and ever" (Dan. 12:3), yet Jesus Himself alone and in His own right is the one and only unsurpassed bright Morning Star.

The New Testament church on earth longs and prays with the psalmist (Ps. 130:6) for the coming of the Lord at the dawn of eternity. "The Spirit and the bride say, Come! And let him that heareth say, Come!" (Rev. 22:17). Here the church on earth, the "bride," addresses Christ in prayer.[43] "The Spirit" is the Holy

[39] Lenski, p. 668.

[40] Is. 11:1: "A shoot from the stump of Jesse," RSV.

[41] Matt. 1:1-16; Luke 3:23-31; cf. "the root of David" (Rev. 5:5).

[42] Little, p. 198, on Rev. 19:16. See 1 Tim. 6:15; 1 Peter 2:9; Rev. 1:6; 17:14; 19:16.

[43] Some understand this verse as speaking of the church at work, bringing the Gospel invitation to the Christless. However, in the light of its larger setting (Rev. 22:12-21) we prefer to regard this as a prayer addressed to Christ.

Spirit, who dwells in the church and in the hearts of its members
(1 Cor. 3:16; 6:19; Gal. 4:6), and by whom the church recognizes and confesses Jesus Christ as Lord (1 Cor. 12:3). It is
He who teaches and moves the church to pray (Rom. 8:15; Gal.
4:6; Jude 20). Everyone who hears this prayer of the church
is to join in it and make it his own, as does John. (Rev. 22:20)

Worldwide Christian mission work is included in this prayer
of the church. "Come!" refers not only to the final coming of
Christ at the end of the world, but it also means come constantly,
day by day; come in the Word and Sacraments into the hearts
of all. No one can truly pray, "Come," who is not willing to use
the means of grace, the Word and the Sacraments, or help support
the preaching of the Gospel at home and abroad. First and fore-
most, however, in the prayer of Rev. 22:17a is the thought of
Christ's coming in His kingdom of glory, for which His current,
daily coming to us and others by Word and Sacrament is a preparation. (Matt. 24:14)

As the Gospel is preached in all the world (Matt. 11:28; John
6:37), "let him that is athirst come. And whosoever will, let
him take the water of life freely" (Rev. 22:17b; 7:16,17; 21:6).
Since the water of life and salvation is free (Is. 55:1), the approach to our Savior and His coming must be the approach of
faith in Him and His Word.[44] The Word is essential to faith
(Rom. 10:14). Without it the soul dies.

"I testify unto every man that heareth the words of the prophecy of this book, If any man shall add unto these things, God shall
add unto him the plagues that are written in this book. And if any
man shall take away from the words of the book of this prophecy,
God shall take away his part out of the book [tree] of life and
out of the Holy City (and from the things)[45] which are written
[described] in this book."[46]

44 Mark 16:16; Rom. 3:28; Eph. 2:8, 9; Rom. 1:17; Hab. 2:4; John 3:16, 36;
Gal. 3:11.

45 The words "and from the things" (KJV) are not in the best MSS.

46 Rev. 22:18, 19: cf. chs. 15 and 16; 21:1—22:5.

These are the words of Jesus, not merely the opinion of John (Rev. 22:16, 18, 20). The reference to "the tree of life" (Rev. 22:19) is the counterpart of the corresponding phrase in Rev. 22:14: "that they may have right to the tree of life." We may take "the plagues that are written in this book" (Rev. 22:18) as referring in the strict and narrow sense to Rev. 15—16, even as the "book" at the end of Rev. 22:18 and 19 is the Book of Revelation, strictly speaking. But by analogy these words apply to the entire Bible (Deut. 4:2; 12:32; Prov. 30:5, 6). The warning in Rev. 22:19 is not only for the ungodly and unbelieving but also for those who have come to faith. They alone can be spoken of as having at any time a part, or share, in the tree of life and in the holy city — a part which he loses who falls away from God's Word and faith.

"He which testifieth these things saith, Surely I come quickly." [47] In a sense this is the last revealed word of God to man. Rev. 22:20 b, 21 is also verbally inspired, but it contains the response of John to his Lord and his parting benediction to his readers. God leaves His church on earth with His own seal of assurance at the end of His Word. (Cf. John 14:3)

Rev. 22:20b: John's Reply to His Lord

We can be sure that it was a very fervent "Amen!" with which John responded to our Lord's final word, as though to say: "Yes! Surely! By all means!" We join the aged seer and the entire church on earth in this "Amen!" and in the simple prayer of timeless sweep and scope: "Come, Lord Jesus!" [48]

It is no mere coincidence that both Testaments end on the note of Christ's coming (Mal. 4:6). We are not created primarily for time but for eternity. Our God will indeed come (Ps. 50:3)! Prepare to meet thy God! (Amos 4:12; cf. 2 Peter 3:11-14)

[47] Rev. 22:20; see the notes on Rev. 3:11; 22:7, 12.
[48] The words "Even so" are not in the best MSS.

Rev. 22:21: John's Farewell Benediction

"The grace [49] of our Lord Jesus Christ be with you all. Amen." [50]

We close the book with the prayer:

Blessed Lord, who hast caused all Holy Scriptures to be written for our learning, that we might have hope, speak through Thy Word to the hearts of all, we beseech Thee, that by Thy grace sinners be converted unto Thee and saints grow together into a holy temple, to the honor and glory of Thy name and the coming of Thy kingdom! Amen.

[49] See the notes on "grace" in Rev. 1:4.

[50] KJV. The reading of the better MSS varies in this verse. Perhaps the best is simply: "The grace of the Lord Jesus be with all."

Readings from Revelation

The Abiding Word. An Anthology of Doctrinal Essays for the Years 1945—46. Edited by Th. Laetsch. 2 vols. St. Louis: Concordia Publishing House. c. 1946—47.

The Americana Annual. An Encyclopedia of the Events of 1952. New York and Chicago: Americana Corporation. c. 1953.

Arndt, Wm. *Does the Bible Contradict Iself?* St. Louis: Concordia Publishing House. c. 1930.

———. *The Gospel According to St. Luke.* St. Louis: Concordia Publishing House. c. 1956.

———. *The Life of St. Paul.* A textbook in the Concordia Teacher Training Series. St. Louis: Concordia Publishing House. c. 1944.

Arndt, Wm., and Gingrich, F. W., *A Greek-English Lexicon of the New Testament.* Published by the University of Chicago Press and the Syndics of the Cambridge University Press. c. 1957.

Barclay, Wm. *Letters to the Seven Churches.* Nashville: Abingdon Press. c. 1957.

———. *The Revelation of John.* 2 vols. Philadelphia: The Westminster Press. 1960.

Barnes, A. *Notes, Explanatory and Practical, on the Book of Revelation.* New York: Harper & Brothers. 1854.

Beckwith, I. T. *The Apocalypse of John.* New York: The Macmillan Co. 1922.

Behm, J. *Die Offenbarung des Johannes übersetzt und erklärt.* Goettingen: Vandenhoeck & Ruprecht. 1949.

Bengel, J. A. *Gnomon Novi Testamenti.* Stuttgart: J. F. Steinkopf. 1915.

———. *Gnomon.* German translation and edition by C. F. Werner. Third ed. Basel: Ferd. Riehm. No date.

Bowman, J. W. *The Dream of the Book of Revelation.* Philadelphia: The Westminster Press. 1955.

Bruce, F. F. *The Books and the Parchments.* London: Pickering & Inglis Ltd. 1950.

Chemnitz, Martin. *Examen Concilii Tridentini.* Berlin: Ed. Preuss, 1861. Leipzig, 1915.

Concordia Bible with Notes. St. Louis: Concordia Publishing House. 1946.

Concordia New Testament with Notes. St. Louis: Concordia Publishing House. 1942.

Concordia Pulpit for 1945. St. Louis: Concordia Publishing House.

Concordia Theological Monthly. St. Louis: Concordia Publishing House.

Cox, Clyde C. *Apocalyptic Commentary.* Cleveland: The Pathway Press. 1959.

Dallmann, Wm. *John.* St. Louis: Concordia Publishing House. 1932.

———. *Paul.* St. Louis: Concordia Publishing House. 1929.

Davis, John D. *A Dictionary of the Bible.* Philadelphia: The Westminster Press. 1936.

Duncan, Malcolm C. *Masonic Ritual and Monitor.* Chicago: Ezra A. Cook. 1947.

Engelder, Th. *Scripture Cannot Be Broken.* St. Louis: Concordia Publishing House. 1944.

Eusebius. *Ecclesiastical History.* Translated by C. F. Cruse. Philadelphia: The Rev. R. Davis & Brother. 1834.

Expositor's Greek Testament. W. Robertson Nicoll, ed. Grand Rapids: Wm. B. Eerdmans. No date.

Finegan, Jack. *Light from the Ancient Past.* Princeton: Princeton University Press. Second edition, 1959.

Foxe, John. *Book of Martyrs.* Wm. Byron Forbush, ed. Philadelphia and Chicago: The John C. Winston Co. c. 1926.

Fuerbringer, L. Mimeographed Classroom Lectures on the Book of Revelation. No date.

Göszwein, G. *Schriftgmäsze und erbauliche Erklärung der Offenbarung St. Johannis.* St. Louis: Concordia Publishing House. 1900.

Graebner, Th. *War in the Light of Prophecy.* St. Louis: Concordia Publishing House. 1941.

Hammond, C. E. *Outlines of Textual Criticism Applied to the New Testament.* Oxford: The Clarendon Press. 1890.

Heerboth, L. A. *The Millennium and the Bible.* St. Louis: Concordia Publishing House. 1933.

Hirschberger Bibel, with foreword by L. Fuerbringer. Constance: Carl Hirsch Verlag. 1926 reprint.

Jamieson, R., A. R. Fausset, and D. Brown. *Commentary, Critical and Explanatory, on the Old and New Testaments.*

Kenyon, F. *Our Bible and the Ancient Manuscripts.* New York: Harper & Brothers. 1951 reprint.

Kepler, T. S. *The Book of Revelation.* New York: Oxford University Press. c. 1957.

Knief, L. E. *Geschichtliche Anmerkungen zu der Offenbarung St. Johannis.* Milwaukee: Northwestern Publishing House, 1909.

Koehler, E. W. A. *A Short Explanation of Dr. Martin Luther's Small Catechism . . . with Additional Notes for Students, Teachers, and Pastors.* River Forest, Ill.: Koehler Publishing Co. c. 1946.

Kretzmann, P. E. *Popular Commentary of the Bible.* 4 vols. St. Louis: Concordia Publishing House. 1922 and various dates.

Laetsch, Th. *The Minor Prophets.* St. Louis: Concordia Publishing House. c. 1956.

Laymon, Charles M. *The Book of Revelation.* Nashville: The Abingdon Press. 1960.

Lenski, R. C. H. *The Interpretation of St. John's Revelation.* Columbus, Ohio: The Wartburg Press. c. 1943.

Lilje, Hanns. *The Last Book of the Bible.* Trans. Olive Wyon. Philadelphia: Muhlenberg Press. c. 1957.

Little, C. H. *Explanation of the Book of Revelation.* St. Louis: Concordia Publishing House. c. 1950.

Luther, M. *Sämmtliche Schriften.* St. Louis Edition.

Lutheran Cyclopedia. E. L. Lueker, ed. St. Louis: Concordia Publishing House. c. 1954.

Mackey, A. G. *Encyclopedia of Freemasonry.* Philadelphia: McClure Publishing Co. c. 1917.

Mayer, F. E. *American Churches.* A textbook in the Concordia Teacher Training Series. St. Louis: Concordia Publishing House. c. 1946.

————. *The Religious Bodies of America.* St. Louis: Concordia Publishing House. c. 1954.

McDowell, E. A. *The Meaning and Message of the Book of Revelation.* Nashville: Broadman Press. c. 1951.

Milligan, Wm. *The Book of Revelation.* New York: A. C. Armstrong and Son. 1899.

Mueller, J. T. *Christian Dogmatics.* St. Louis: Concordia Publishing House. c. 1934.

Myers, Robert Manson. *Handel's Messiah: A Touchstone of Taste.* New York: Macmillan Co. 1948.

National Geographic Magazine. Washington, D. C.: The National Geographic Society. Issue of Dec. 1956.

Newell, W. R. *The Book of Revelation.* Chicago: Moody Press. 1957.

Norden, R. F. *Letters to the Seven Churches.* A series of Bible study outlines. Chicago: The Lutheran Church — Missouri Synod Commission on College and University Work. No date.

Novum Testamentum Graece. 21st Nestle ed. Stuttgart: Privilegierte Württembergische Bibelanstalt. 1952.

Pieper, F. *Christian Dogmatics.* Trans. Th. Engelder et al. 3 vols. St. Louis: Concordia Publishing House. 1950—53.

Portals of Prayer. St. Louis: Concordia Publishing House. April 1956.

Preston, Ronald H., and Anthony T. Hanson. *The Revelation of St. John the Divine.* London: SCM Press. 1955 reprint.

Ramsay, W. M. *The Letters to the Seven Churches of Asia.* London: Hodder and Stoughton. 1904.

Robertson, A. T. *A Grammar of the Greek New Testament in the Light of Historical Research.* Nashville: Broadman Press. c. 1934.

————. *Introduction to the Textual Criticism of the New Testament.* Nashville: Broadman Press. c. 1925.

Sadler, M. F. *The Revelation of St. John the Divine.* London: George Bell and Sons. 1906.

Schumm, F. C. G. *Essay on Revelation Chapter 20.* St. Louis: Concordia Publishing House. No date.

Stonehouse, N. B. *The Apocalypse in the Ancient Church.* Grand Rapids, Mich. 1930.

Tenney, Merrill C. *Interpreting Revelation.* Grand Rapids: Wm. B. Eerdmans Publ. Co. 1957.

Thayer, J. H. *A Greek-English Lexicon of the New Testament.* New York: American Book Company, n. d.; c. 1889 by Harper & Brothers.

Thomson, W. M. *The Land and the Book.* 2 vols. New York: Harper & Brothers. 1880—82.

Triglot Concordia. The Symbolical Books of the Ev. Lutheran Church. St. Louis: Concordia Publishing House. 1921.

Warfield, B. B. *An Introduction to the Textual Criticism of the New Testament.* London: Hodder and Stoughton. 1893.

Webber, F. R. *A History of Preaching in Britain and America.* 3 vols. Milwaukee: Northwestern Publishing House. 1952—57.

Weidenschilling, J. M. "The Book of Revelation," in *The Bible Student.* St. Louis: Concordia Publishing House. Double issue for April and July 1955.

Wernecke, H. H. *The Book of Revelation Speaks to Us.* Philadelphia: The Westminster Press. c. 1954, by W. L. Jenkins.

Translations Used

Vulgate (Latin), according to the edition of Pope Clement VIII (1592)
Wyclif (the first English translation), 1382
Luther (German), 1522
Tyndale, 1525—34
Douay (Roman Catholic), 1582
King James Version, 1611
Young's Literal Translation. First issued, 1862. Third edition, 1898
American Standard Version, 1901
Moffatt. First issued, 1922. Revised edition, c. 1935
Confraternity of Christian Doctrine (Roman Catholic), 1941
Revised Standard Version. First issued, 1946. Revised, 1952
Phillips, 1957
Schonfield, 1958
The New English Bible, 1961

Also translations in various commentaries, such as that of
    Lenski (1943), Barnes (1854), etc.

INDEXES

Both indexes are supplemented by references and cross references
in the text and in the footnotes

SUBJECTS

Abaddon 128

Alpha and omega 14f, 18, 277, 297

Altar, golden, of incense 115ff, 129, 196, 208; souls under 97—100; in the temple of God 141

Amen 12, 14, 66, 91f, 110, 243, 301f

Angel, and little book 134ff; standing in sun 251

Angels, four 105—108, 129f; seven 114f, 151, 155, 198—217, 280; of seven churches 23ff, 28; three 155, 185ff

Annihilation 154, 227, 253, 268, 273f

Antichrist 146, 175, 179, 217

Antipas, martyr 42

Apocalypse 1, 3, 5

Apollyon 128, 174

Apostles 238, 283; false 30

Ark of the testament (covenant) 154

Armageddon 213f

Assurance of salvation 63, 196

Babylon 187ff, 214f, 217—239 (esp. 220, 228, 229ff)

Balaam 42

Bear, feet as feet of 167

Beasts (or "living ones"), four 76—79, 85ff, 89f, 92, 94, 96, 110, 182, 202, 242f

Beasts, two (of sea and of earth) 155, 165—179, 188ff, 199, 206, 209f, 212, 219, 221—228

Beatitudes, seven 7, 192, 213, 246, 264, 294, 297

Beginning and end 14, 277, 297

Behold 12

Black as sackcloth 101

Black horse 95

Book, of life 57, 171f, 222, 270, 272, 288, 300; little (scroll) 134f, 139f

Books, first 82

Bride (wife) of Christ (the Lamb) 217, 244ff, 280f, 299

Brimstone 130f, 190, 253, 258, 268, 279

Calf (ox), beast like 77f

Candlesticks (candelabra, lampstands), seven 18f, 23, 28; two 144

Censer, golden 115ff

Chain 257

Child, woman, and dragon 155—164

Chiliasm; see also Millennialism; 255

Christmas 110, 296ff

Church 26, 36, 82f, 105—113

Church discipline 30

Churches, seven 8, 18, 23, 25ff

Cloud, angel clothed with 135; white 194

Coming One 13, 62, 294, 297

Court of the Gentiles 142

Creation 66, 80, 90, 137

Cross and crown 16, 38

Crown, cross and 16, 38; of life 37f; of rider of white horse 94; taking of 63; woman's, of twelve stars 156

Crowns, casting of 79; golden 75, 194; like gold 127; many crowns 249; seven 157; ten 166

Cube 284

SCRIPTURE PASSAGES

OLD TESTAMENT